Empire's Wake

Empire's Wake

POSTCOLONIAL IRISH WRITING AND THE
POLITICS OF MODERN LITERARY FORM

Mark Quigley

FORDHAM UNIVERSITY PRESS *New York* 2013

THIS BOOK IS MADE POSSIBLE BY A COLLABORATIVE GRANT
FROM THE ANDREW W. MELLON FOUNDATION.

Fordham University Press has no responsibility for the
persistence or accuracy of URLs for external or third-
party Internet websites referred to in this publication
and does not guarantee that any content on such
websites is, or will remain, accurate or appropriate.

Fordham University Press also publishes its books
in a variety of electronic formats. Some content that
appears in print may not be available in electronic
books.

Library of Congress Cataloging-in-Publication Data

Quigley, Mark.
    Empire's wake : postcolonial Irish writing and the
politics of modern literary form / Mark Quigley. —
1st ed.
        p. cm.
    Includes bibliographical references and index.
    ISBN 978-0-8232-4544-4 (cloth : alk. paper)
        1. English literature—Irish authors—History and
criticism. 2. Postcolonialism in literature.
3. Modernism (Literature) I. Title.
PR8755.Q54 2013
820.9'9415—dc23

                                        2012026633

Printed in the United States of America

15 14 13   5 4 3 2 1

First edition

For Elsa,
who waited for me to tell her

CONTENTS

ACKNOWLEDGMENTS

Despite heroic visions of the author working alone in a musty garret or the distilled silence of a library, all books are the products of a communal labor. My keen awareness of how many acts of generosity, faith, hospitality, and labor of all sorts have gone into the making of this book has sustained and driven me as I have worked on it over the years. A sense of this communal investment has brightened many a lonely hour of work while also creating some anxiety that any book could ever prove worthy of all the kindness and sacrifice that helped bring it to fruition. I am fortunate that there is no accounting method that can reveal how extensive my debt is to so many.

The earliest ideas for this project took root in the rather disparate spaces of Tipperary, Los Angeles, and Dublin and came to fruition in the equally disparate climes of Nevada, Oregon, Galway, and California. In Tipperary, my uncle Rodge's warm "Welcome Home" always made me feel like I had never left, and as we sat and talked by the fire I learned more than he may have ever realized. His insightful analysis of Irish and world affairs delivered with a masterstroke of wit in the brief moment he stopped to relight his pipe provided early examples of critical acuity and linguistic compression that were a continuing inspiration and challenge as I strove to find a language for my own ideas. His only rival was our cousin John Joe Quigley, whose gentle teasing and virtuosic turns of phrase always kept me on my toes and who, with his wife, Mary, extended a rich hospitality to me more times than I can count as I worked on this book. My cousins Maura and Tony and my oldest friend, Michael Gleeson, and his wife, Marion, have likewise made me welcome on many nights and helped me realize how the deepest connections endure amid all of the dislocations of contemporary life.

At UCLA and many late nights across the City of Angels, Tracy Curtis, Dave Martinez, Danise Kimball, Mike Miller, Genaro Sandoval, Theresa Delgadillo, Dave Kamper, Tarik Abdul-Wahid, Jim Lee, Edwin Hill, Joanna Brooks, and Mo Lee supported me through good times and bad and kept me thinking and laughing all the way. Val Smith was an especially important source of inspiration and guidance while Joseph Nagy, Cal Bedient, and Joel Aberbach were continually generous in sharing their expertise and time. William Prescott provided me the benefit of his clarifying wisdom, and Saul Friedlander provided generous advice and timely encouragement, the significance of which I'm sure he never knew. Wendy Belcher has been a faithful friend whose consistently perceptive comments played a key role in helping me to focus the argument of this book. Carole Fabricant likewise sustained me with her unstinting support and sharp wit and taught me much by her example of a rigorous and committed scholarship.

I was extremely fortunate to be a part of the Notre Dame Irish Seminar over three summers in Dublin, where I was the beneficiary of the kindness of Chris Fox and the immense intellectual hospitality of Kevin Whelan, Luke Gibbons, and Seamus Deane. It is hard to overstate the richness and vitality of the intellectual community they created during those summers or to credit adequately the influence it has had on my thinking about modernism and postcolonial Irish writing as a result of the conversations in and around the seminar and those that have continued over the years since. I am especially grateful to Luke Gibbons and Kevin Whelan for the ways they shaped some of my initial thoughts about the Blasket texts. I am equally thankful to Joe Cleary for the ongoing exchanges we have had about Sean O'Faoláin's intellectual politics and to Conor McCarthy, Heather Laird, and Kariann Yokota for sharing their warm fellowship and thoughtful insights as we have sustained the conversation across the years and miles.

One of the greatest pleasures of regularly visiting Dublin was the opportunity it afforded to spend time with my aunt Constance. She was the person who first stoked my love of literature, and her encyclopedic knowledge of Dublin and of the succession of its twentieth-century cultural and social "scenes" has been an invaluable resource. Her willingness to throw open her house to me and to offer her support in every conceivable way whether I was in Dublin or the United States enabled a number of research trips that would otherwise not have been possible. My time in Dublin has likewise been brightened by the warm hospitality and stimulating company of Melisa Halpin, Peadar O'Grady, Mary Kate Halpin, and Terry and John Fitzpatrick.

In Galway, I have gained much from the rich intellectual community of the USAC Irish studies summer school and the wide-ranging expertise of Méabh Ní Fhuartháin, Anne Ní Choirbín, Alison Harvey, and Deaglán Ó Donghaile, who was especially generous with his insights about republicanism and the nineteenth-century novel. I am grateful to Angus Mitchell for sharing his deep knowledge of twentieth-century Irish history and for the unfailing sense of humor and solidarity he has maintained over more than a decade of friendship even in the face of more than one ill-fated trek down the back roads of the Burren. Caoilfhionn Ní Bheacháin has likewise been a treasured friend whose keen critical sensibility and thoughtful commentary on Ireland's early postcolonial period have continually challenged and inspired me. My summers in Galway have also been richly illuminated by the immense learning, laconic wit, and warm hospitality of Tadhg Foley and Lillis Ó Laoire.

At the University of Nevada, Stacy Burton, Michelle Cobb, Nancy Beach, and Carmelo Urza were consistently supportive while Jen Hill's discerning eye helped me render my ideas with greater precision. At the University of Oregon, I have been fortunate to be surrounded by a wealth of stimulating colleagues who have likewise been generous with their ideas and support, especially Lara Bovilsky, Karen Ford, Sangita Gopal, David Li, Enrique Lima, Alex Neel, Priscilla Ovalle, Bill Rossi, George Rowe, Lee Rumbarger, Deborah Shapple, Dick Stein, Cynthia Tolentino, David Vázquez, Melissa Walter, Molly Westling, Mark Whalan, and George Wickes.

Sustaining the dynamic intellectual atmosphere of the Oregon English department in both big and small ways has been the hard work of Harry Wonham, and it is difficult to imagine how I would have been able to complete this book were it not for his thoughtfulness and support. I am equally grateful to Tres Pyle for reading earlier drafts of chapters and offering illuminating comments about my approach to literary form. A stalwart friend, Paul Peppis has also been remarkably generous as a reader of my work and as a frequent lunchtime companion eager to help me develop incipient ideas and willing to share his vast knowledge of modernist art and literature. My ideas about modernism have been transformed by participating in the ongoing discussions of the Oregon English department's Modernism Group and by working with a number of talented graduate students. I am particularly grateful to Jenny Noyce and Bill Fogarty for all that I have learned from their engaging work.

As this book unfolded, I have been fortunate to be able to discuss its ongoing development with David Lloyd. His generosity with his ideas in conversation and in comments on drafts contributed immeasurably to my thinking and helped to clarify the stakes of my argument. His friendship and encouragement have sustained me through the project's long gestation. Jed Esty was also an exceedingly generous reader whose thoughtful suggestions and probing questions helped me to situate Irish modernism more fully within a wider array of modernist studies initiatives.

My most long-standing intellectual debt, however, is to Michael North, who helped shape these ideas in their earliest form and who has been unfailingly generous with his time and support. His remarkably unassuming and good-humored dedication to both scholarship and teaching continue to inspire.

I count myself very lucky to have been able to work with Helen Tartar and Fordham University Press. Tom Lay has been a particular pleasure to work with at Fordham, and his kindness, patience, and incredible efficiency have kept the project moving and saved me much trouble and anxiety along the way. I am also grateful to the Oregon Humanities Center and the College of Arts and Sciences at the University of Oregon for their support and particularly their help in underwriting the costs associated with preparing the index for this book.

Sustaining me over the long haul has been the faith and humor of dear friends and family. Matthew Fraleigh has seen me through more challenges than either of us can remember, and David Sarabia has been an unshakable comrade. Brian Quinn, John O'Brien, Steve Martinez, William Ruller, and Sr. Fabian Quigley have likewise been a constant source of encouragement while not letting me take things too seriously. Roberta Gillerman and Joe Gillerman zt"l welcomed me into their family and taught me much about the meaning of faith, especially in the past year.

Amid much wandering on two western coasts, my home and my hopes have been with Sharon and Maya. Though they have endured many absences, the bright beacon of their love and support has never dimmed. Their presence permeates these pages.

Infusing these pages, too, is the faith and the labor of my parents, Sean and Elsa, who sacrificed much to enable my education and have been unwavering in their support and love. I am humbled by their devotion to family and their care for others and have been equally humbled by my brother, John's, and sister-in-law, Julie's, quiet selflessness and loving attention to my parents during my mother's long illness. My mother was so involved in bringing this book to life and eagerly following its progress that it is quite bittersweet to see it published after she has gone. I hope it may be a worthy testament to her fierce love.

| | |

An earlier version of a portion of chapter 1 previously appeared as an essay in *Interventions* and is reprinted by permission from Taylor & Francis; an earlier version of chapter 3 appeared as an essay in *Samuel Beckett Today/Aujourd'hui*, and grateful acknowledgment is also given to Rodopi for permission to reprint material here.

Introduction

*Rerouting Irish Modernism: Postcolonial Aesthetics
and the Imperative of Cosmopolitanism*

As we consider the complex energies animating Irish literature in the
wake of empire, some initial insight into the challenges faced by the
generation of Irish writers emerging in the 1920s and 1930s and the
unique value of the body of literature they produced may be gleaned
from a rather unlikely source. In the "Introductory Note" to the English translation of Muiris Ó Súillebháin's Blasket Island autobiography, *Twenty Years A-Growing*, published in 1933, E. M. Forster
remarks admiringly on the "odd document" (v) the book constitutes
as a text at once framed by the legacy of the Irish Literary Revival and
one representing a radical new departure from the terms of the Revival's overarching aesthetic. Grasping for a language capable of conveying this somewhat contradictory position, Forster says of the book:
"[I]t is worth saying 'This book is unique.' . . . [The reader] is about
to read an account of neolithic civilization from the inside. Synge and
others have described it from the outside, and very sympathetically,
but I know of no other instance where it has itself become vocal, and
addressed modernity" (v). Gregory Castle has suggested this description by Forster indicates that the "anthropological modernism" he
so insightfully elucidates in *Modernism and the Celtic Revival* "has
become available, by 1933, to mainstream European intellectuals"
(256). I want to propose, however, as part of a larger argument about
modernism and postcoloniality very much indebted to Castle's analyses, that Forster's portrayal of *Twenty Years A-Growing* points us
instead toward the emergence of a distinct variety of *late*-modernist
practice which the more long-standing accounts of modernism and

its place within Irish literary history have tended to obscure. Indeed, this late modernism can be seen to arise from the internal rupture of the anthropological object that Castle sees taking different forms in Synge, Yeats, and Joyce and that recurs in the primitivism and ethnographic privilege anchoring the syncretic ambitions of high-modernist aesthetics more generally.

As we shall explore, much of the value of Ó Súillebháin's "odd document" lies precisely in its oddness and the ways it unsettles modernism's ontological and aesthetic categories. For, as Forster's note recognizes, *Twenty Years A-Growing* does not merely offer a more informed ethnography of the Gaelic periphery "from the inside" that simply reiterates or improves upon the earlier versions offered by famous "outsiders" like Synge. Ó Súillebháin's text instead shatters the division between anthropological object and observing subject that organizes the artistic consciousness of the earlier generation of modernists shaped by a late-imperial age. As Forster continues, his mention of Ó Súillebháin's love for the movies and his acknowledgment that key portions of the book recount Ó Súillebháin's experiences away from his Blasket Island "stronghold" as he travels to Dublin and Galway stand at odds with Forster's initial emphasis on a pristine "neolithic civilization" (v–vi). Rather than a lapse on Forster's part, however, the contradictory impulses marking his preface might be best understood as registering a transition within modernist thought wherein an anthropological language of the "neolithic" continues to resonate even as it proves increasingly inadequate to address an emergent postcoloniality.

The Blasket Islands have now been mostly forgotten by the wider body of modernist studies scholars. They once loomed large, however, in the imagination of John Millington Synge, who referred to them in a letter to Lady Gregory as being "probably even more primitive than Aran" and described himself as "wild with joy at the prospect" of visiting them (*Letters*, 1: 120).[1] As E. M. Forster's preface underscores, the Blasket Islanders themselves produced a literary sensation in the late 1920s and early 1930s that became an important touchstone for an era of Irish literary and intellectual culture in addition to drawing such notable attention from a member of the Bloomsbury circle. But their importance to modernist studies ultimately lies less in their associations with famous figures from London or Dublin than in the ways that the texts written by the Blasket Islanders reveal how as early as the late 1920s, modernist practice and thought had already begun to be reframed by the emergence of a postcolonial modernity. These shifts, which remain relatively unremarked within modernist studies, prefigure in significant ways the more well-known versions of late modernism such as we see from Beckett by midcentury.

Most immediately, the Blasket texts provide a means for examining and reevaluating the primitivism of a more classic high modernism, a topic that has generated much illuminating scholarship over the past two decades and promises to take on a new importance as the "new modernist studies" directs increasing attention to so-called "global" or "transnational" modernism.[2] In addition to interrogating the positions and politics underlying modernist primitivism, however, the Blasket texts—along with other early Irish postcolonial texts—reveal deceptively simple late-modernist narrative forms whose very plainness ironically intensifies their antimimetic character. We thus encounter new forms of modernism less reliant on pyrotechnic effects and the notion of a visionary artist capable of transmuting the quotidian into the symbolic so as to orchestrate the symphony of a wider order from the disparate fragments of a shattered modernity. The eclipse of a heroic artist figure and of a sense of an underlying or incipient order connects, in turn, with a critique of subjectivity that becomes increasingly pronounced with a new generation of modernist writers that begins to emerge by the 1930s. In addition to filling in the picture of modernism's historical development—especially in relation to the passing of empire—the late-modernist features of postcolonial Irish writing help to clarify the political investments and limitations of the different varieties of "high" and "late" modernism that unfold over the first half of the twentieth century. What these texts begin to reveal in both stark and subtle ways is the loss of a privileged artistic consciousness and a turning of modernist scrutiny upon itself.

The far-reaching implications of this shift become increasingly clear as we look at the work of other Irish writers from this generation such as Sean O'Faoláin and Samuel Beckett, whose greater critical sophistication and prominence within Irish and European intellectual networks enable a more explicit account of the shift under way in modernist aesthetics. Beckett's role as a late-modernist writer and thinker obviously looms large in any discussion of the development and decline of modernist literary modes. O'Faoláin also makes a significant contribution to the elaboration of a late-modernist aesthetic, however, with extensive essays during the 1930s and 1940s that complement and occasionally overlap with Beckett's insights. Indeed,

Beckett's own acknowledgment of O'Faoláin's importance in shaking off what he perceives as the dead hand of the Revival underscores the value of considering their work in relation to each other and, perhaps more broadly, impels us to consider anew the ways that Beckett's work connects with a strain of late modernism emerging from a distinctly postcolonial problematic. At the same time, O'Faoláin's deployment of an anachronistic realism as an alternative to the insufficient aesthetic radicalism and excessively naturalistic tendencies he diagnoses in the previous generation of Irish modernist writers alerts us to the potential for a late-modernist practice to express itself in forms other than the pyrotechnic stylistic displays and inscrutable fragmentary arrays that typically characterize a high-modernist mode.

In this regard, we might understand the late-modernist aesthetic being articulated by early postcolonial writers such as the Blasket writers, O'Faoláin, and Beckett as one positioned between the anthropological modernism Castle identifies in Joyce and the Revivalists and a different sort of anthropological modernism that Jed Esty traces in the later writings of English modernists such as Woolf and Eliot. Describing how an anthropological method shapes the modernist aesthetics of the earlier generation of Irish modernists in divergent ways, Castle writes: "While Yeats chose to revive an autochthonous folk tradition by evoking it using methods borrowed from anthropology and ethnography, Joyce chose to create a national literature by engaging in an immanent critique of revivalism in which colonial and anthropological discourses are appropriated and criticized. . . . In both cases, an ethnographic imagination comes into play, either as a method of cultural preservation and authentication (as with Yeats) or as a strategy of cultural critique (as with Joyce)" (175). This culminates, according to Castle, with Joyce's "anti-mimetic" modernist aesthetic that draws on the minutely detailed accounts of anthropological observation to revel in "*in*authenticity" rather than the premodern "authenticity" that the Revival might propose as part of a project to disrupt the elaboration of a singular imperial modernity (179, 176). Saikat Majumdar has recently offered a parallel account of Joyce's treatment of the banal object as a vehicle for undermining imperialist epistemology and what he refers to as "the dominant consciousness of the subject" (221, 230). Perhaps even more helpfully, Rebecca Walkowitz proposes in *Cosmopolitan Style* a concept of "triviality" as a conscious *stylistic* feature that allows Joyce to maintain the tension between what she calls "two, somewhat different models of national culture: a fixed culture that can be described through the collection of minor details; and a transient culture for which minor details mark the principle of inexhaustible, proliferating characteristics" (30).

The postcolonial writers I examine effectively build on that underlying antimimetic tendency while developing a more thoroughgoing critique of the modern subject that we can see early on in the texts from the Blasket Islands and that significantly accelerates by the time we encounter Beckett's novel "trilogy" at midcentury. We can apprehend this work as helping to elaborate a distinctly "late" modernist aesthetic in two primary ways.

Firstly, these writers emerge in the midst of the historically later moment of postcoloniality, which in the Irish case begins in the very same year as modernism's *annus mirabilis* of 1922 and largely coincides in its first major phase with literary modernism's own major phase as it comes to a close by the late 1940s. Even as Yeats and Joyce continue to write and produce some of their most important work during this period, and, indeed, even though each, respectively, forms a significant association with O'Faoláin or Beckett, they nonetheless occupy a very different historical plane as writers who came to artistic maturity in a late-imperial context and who in very different ways had contributed significantly to modernism's emergence. The later generation, by contrast, labors in empire's wake and in the shadow of a modernist aesthetic phenomenon already well under way. As a result, as James McNaughton has illustrated through his discussion of Beckett's letters and fiction from the 1930s, high modernism was a significant presence within the intellectual and cultural discourses of early postcolonial Ireland and had, indeed, already begun to get a bit stale (63).

This strange combination of contemporaneity and historical disjuncture obtaining between these two generations of Irish writers thus produces a late modernism that is in many ways temporally and stylistically out of phase with the more established modernist practices with which it coincides. In particular, we encounter work from a variety of early postcolonial writers that is decidedly *not* "avantgarde" or evidently "difficult" and instead appears quite archaic and accessible in its forms and structures. Indeed, the extent and complexity of the modernist dimensions of much of this work only becomes fully apparent as we have begun to reexamine the bases of what constitutes modernist thought and aesthetics under the auspices of "the new modernist studies." The result, as Douglas Mao and Rebecca

Walkowitz note in their introduction to *Bad Modernisms*, is that many writers "hitherto seen as neglecting or resisting modernist innovation" are shown to be quite significantly engaged with developing or refining a modernist project in ways that at turns parallel, challenge, or build upon the more familiar expressions of modernism (1).

The extent to which these early postcolonial writers actually *make use* of their significant formal or stylistic departures from conventional modernism in order to pursue a critique of its shortcomings and find a means of extending the impact of its antimimetic approach through more prosaic forms thus marks the second way that we can understand these texts as part of a "late" modernist project. In other words, these writers not only compel us to attend to postcoloniality as a distinct historical framework within modernism but alert us to the variety of forms that a "second-generation" modernist thought can take as it turns inward to critique both the heroic artistic consciousness of high modernism and the stability of the anthropological objects against which that consciousness would seek to define itself.

Jed Esty's astute account of a parallel "late modernism" unfolding in English literature during roughly the same period helps set in relief the late-modernist features I am tracing in postcolonial Irish writing. Charting the effects of imperial contraction and "demetropolitanization" on English modernism, Esty argues in *A Shrinking Island* that the later works of modernist writers such as Eliot and Woolf tend to elaborate a new sense of cohesion and groundedness within a more localized "English culture" that differs markedly from a previous emphasis on a British and imperial "metropolitan perception" that "registered an attenuated or absent totality *at the core*" (7). Eloquently capturing the shift within English modernism in this era, Esty observes: "If the metaphor of lost totality is one of the central deep structures of imperialism and modernism, it follows that the end of empire might be taken to augur a basic repair or reintegration of English culture itself. Such a turn of geopolitical events would therefore reinflect those aspects of modernist style that were based on lost social totality with a new—or newly imagined—sense of spatial and cultural consolidation" (7). This sense of consolidation and a turn toward more precisely defining "the core" starkly contrast with the late-modernist practices that we see marking the emergence of the postcolonial in Irish writing at the same moment. Rather than consolidation and definition of a stable, localized core, we find an effort to push against such confident assertions and get beneath the surfaces of a defined national object.

Most immediately, we might understand this opposite tendency in early Irish postcolonial writing as a complementary response arising from being on the other side of this epochal process of imperial contraction. Having been the object of imperial knowledge and what Esty describes as the "synthesizing universalism" (7) of an imperial modernist consciousness, Irish writers can experience postcoloniality and imperial contraction as phenomena affording considerable relief from a quite relentless round of definition. We thus see the concept of a more defined or fixed core being undermined by an Irish late modernism expressed at different moments through adaptations of archaic realist modes or through the more dramatically antirepresentational mode for which Beckett is famous.

Fundamental to Irish late modernism are the ways it extends an earlier modernist critique of the colonial state to the postcolonial state so as to address the newly invigorated discourses of "tradition" and modern subjectivity. If we understand such overwhelming insistence on "tradition" in terms of the "sterile formalism" (204) and "outworn contrivances" (224) that Frantz Fanon links with a bourgeois official nationalism sustaining an atmosphere of historical arrest and counterrevolution in the early postcolonial era, we can more easily see why Irish late modernism might be driven to unsettle at once the ethnographic object of high-modernist aesthetics and the reified object of an official nationalist hegemony that is its rather drab doppelganger.[3] Indeed, the extent to which the essentialism and primitivism of Revivalist modernism has increasingly been overtaken by the rank commodification of "tradition" in the postcolonial era serves as an important impetus for late modernism's critique. At the same time, the postcolonial context of Irish late modernism also impels its challenge of modern subjectivity as a key political, ontological and artistic framework whose seeming indispensability and "naturalness" is ironically reinforced by the shared primitivism of high modernism and populist "tradition." Both rely on the perceiving consciousness of a normative modern subjectivity in order for the nonsubjective "primitive" to become visible and, perversely, to be mourned for its inevitably imminent demise.

While calling into question the notion of a consolidated modern subjectivity as the inexorable consequence of Irish postcoloniality's integration into a broader global modernity, Irish late modernism simultaneously rejects the mimetic impulses driving both official nationalism's Revivalist inheritance and a disillusioned postcolonial naturalism that would seek to repudiate it. Indeed, the failure to discern the difference between the modified realist modes of Irish late modernism and a more straightforwardly mimetic naturalism has been the primary reason that critics have tended to frame the bulk of early postcolonial Irish writing as aesthetically retrograde or naïve. Lost in this standard critical account of a dour "Counter-Revivalist" skepticism is the rich texture and complexity of Irish intellectual life in the decades immediately following 1922. Lost, too, in the shadows of this stark critical contrast are the contours of a distinctly postcolonial late modernism that is the aesthetic complement of the English late modernism Esty discerns at empire's erstwhile core. Rather than turning the anthropological gaze homeward via "demetropolitanization" to fill in and "repair" the void at the imperial center, a postcolonial late modernism implodes the ethnographic project structuring the ambitious effort of aesthetic integration common to both high modernism and the iteration of late modernism charted by Esty.

This understanding of the late modernism produced by early postcolonial Irish writers usefully complements and complicates the critical accounts of "alternative," "peripheral," and "postcolonial" modernisms that have become a growing focus within modernist studies in recent years. We can see in Irish literature some of the earliest examples of a postcolonial modernism "made," as Laura Doyle and Laura Winkiel put it in their groundbreaking collection *Geomodernisms*, "from the *outside in*" (3). Indeed, as Doyle and Winkiel show, the value of understanding how modernism constellates itself on the geopolitical or aesthetic peripheries extends beyond the light it may shed on specific postcolonial texts or literatures. Such analyses also yield crucial insights into fundamental assumptions about modernist aesthetics that a more limited focus on canonical modernist writers obscures.

Postcolonial modernisms provide particular opportunity for reflecting on the tendency to conceive of modernist aesthetics primarily in universal and transcendent terms and to consider anew the benefits of grounding modernist thought and practices more fully within specific local and material contexts. Indeed, the failure to consider writing that eschews grander gestures of aesthetic transcendence to engage with more immediate and local horizons may be a significant part of the reason why many alternative modernist practices—especially those from the former imperial periphery—have been overlooked. Attending to the details of more "localized" modernisms does not mean simplifying analyses of modernist form or producing accounts of modernist aesthetics that have only narrow critical relevance, however. It enables us, rather, to consider what we might see as the negative dialectics of modernism that can draw from the insights of postcolonial studies so as to reevaluate the fixity of "local" categories such as "the nation" and "tradition" while at the same time challenging the inevitability and desirability of a refurbished "global" orientation.

For their parts, postcolonial studies and the study of particular national or regional literatures can benefit from reconsidering how modernist thought and practice have impacted bodies of writing and thought in their purview in ways that have not been apparent when modernism has been conceptualized solely in reference to standard notions of high modernism. For example, the first generation of postcolonial Irish writers—with Beckett as one of the few exceptions—tend to be misapprehended by critics as being aesthetically naïve or backward in ways that suggest a complete disengagement from modernism. An exploration of the late-modernist writing produced by this generation thus not only allows us to reevaluate the standard critical view of early postcolonial Ireland as hopelessly provincial but to consider, as James McNaughton so intriguingly proposes, how discourses of provincialism may actually *buttress* a self-congratulatory high modernism that has not yet pursued its more revolutionary insights to their truly radical ends. As McNaughton writes: "Such critique turns on modernism itself by exposing the allegory of a revolutionary modernism whose form of revolt repeats regardless of its actual capacity to critique. By the 1930s works of modernism . . . open the movement to this criticism that the new is not so new. But the backward province provides a good way to displace this conclusion" (64–65).

The value of McNaughton's point about "the backward province" lies as much in what it helps to reveal about the internal critique of modernism offered by Irish late modernism as in what it reveals about the limiting effects of some persistent assumptions within the prevailing current of modernist studies. An understanding of modernism as an ironically provincial aesthetic response has deep roots within modernist studies going back to the work of Richard Ellmann and Hugh Kenner.[4] Developing the concept of provincialism as a key feature of British modernism in his 1970 study *Exiles and Émigrés*, Terry Eagleton argues that "access to alternative cultures and traditions" provides the means for writers such as Eliot, Yeats, Pound, Joyce, and Lawrence to make sense of "the erosion of contemporary order" (15) by way of a perspective unavailable to those more fully ensconced within that order.

Though Eagleton's study offers much illuminating commentary on the crucial role played by exiles and émigrés in the elaboration of a British modernism, it also reinforces the perception that modernism be apprehended primarily—perhaps even entirely—in relation to the center. Whatever insight their provincial or exilic status may afford these modernist writers, it would seem that the significance of that insight can only be realized when directed toward the crises of the center and "contemporary order" from which they are able to stand some distance apart. As a result, their relation—at least as modernists—to "provincial" concerns located outside the center can only be as ambivalent skeptics. Despite their "provincial" origins or sensibilities, these modernist writers, according to this long-standing critical view, are effectively cosmopolitans who have transcended the limits of the province to bring their outsider's perspective to bear upon the concerns of the center and, equally importantly, to the end of articulating a newly emergent order. A consequence of this tradition within modernist studies is that Irish modernist writers have historically been framed as necessarily separate from an Irish context such that Irish "provincial" concerns are approached either ironically or via a knowing primitivism. The result is that the Irish elements of Irish modernist writing—and perhaps even Irishness itself—tend to be effectively recapitulated within modernist studies in terms of a sort of "off-kilter Englishness," to the extent that they are taken up at all.

A later version of this account of modernism and provincialism that seeks to attend more fully to decentered concerns and perspectives is offered by Robert Crawford in *Devolving English Literature*, first published in 1992 and then appearing in a revised edition in 2000. Rather than bringing an outsider's perspective to the center so as to interpret its dissolution, Crawford argues that provincials such as Eliot, Pound, and Joyce work to assemble a hodgepodge of cosmopolitan cultural elements in a way that "outflanks the English cultural centre" and purposefully contaminates "modernism's cosmopolitanism" and "the centre of high art" with "provincial improprieties" (262, 270).

Crawford emphasizes an underlying "demotic urge" in a modernism that addresses itself simultaneously to the province and the center

(262). While we might see such an approach that reconciles "provincial" modernist writers with "provincial" concerns and readerships as an advance within modernist studies, Crawford significantly undercuts this advance by routing it through a necessary cosmopolitanism such that the function of "provincial" modernists is at once to adulterate an elite cosmopolitan culture at the center while bringing back the cultural riches of an international cosmopolitan sophistication for the benefit of their introverted and impoverished provinces of origin.

Modernism is, for Crawford, always animated by a "cosmopolitan drive" (262). The implications of this inevitable orientation toward cosmopolitanism for Crawford's emphasis on the demotic can be seen in his remark about Joyce that "the Irish demotic in particular is used to give his voice at once a local, provincial as well as an international, cosmopolitan accent" (263). We might reasonably wonder what is particularly "cosmopolitan" about the accent of the Irish demotic—or the Dublin demotic—and why it need fulfill such an expectation. That the "local" is so readily reprocessed and revalued as an essential aspect of the "international" and "cosmopolitan" suggests that not much has changed within modernist studies in its apprehension of the "provincial" as inevitably in service to the center and an overarching order, even if in a more subversive mode. The main effect of Crawford's contribution to the discourse of provincialism within modernist studies would thus seem to be to articulate a multiply located modernism that might be seen as more hospitable to an interest in "global modernism" increasingly coming to the fore within modernist studies.

Jahan Ramazani's treatment of global modernism has been guided by a similar impulse, and he has developed an influential account of postcolonial modernism that emphasizes hybridity and a "plural" and "polyphonic" "cross-culturalism" aimed at "the continuous remaking of 'traditions'" and a fostering of "mutually transformative relations between the poetics of metropole and margin" (449, 460). Ramazani offers illuminating accounts that trace how a range of postcolonial poets have innovatively borrowed from and reworked a rich archive of high-modernist poetry by way of illustrating modernism's particular utility for undermining "local and imperial monisms" (449) and articulating the collisions, juxtapositions, and potentials accompanying imperial collapse.

While he does much to reveal different aspects of modernism's potential as a postcolonial and even an anti-imperialist aesthetic, Ramazani unfortunately misconstrues the objection to a potential modernist "Eurocentricity" as relying entirely on a false sense of modernism's inherent complicity with empire and an equally false dichotomy of an imperial heterogeneity and "a pristine native culture" (448). In the process of dispelling these false notions of modernism and postcoloniality, Ramazani thus overlooks the ways that modernist studies—rather than modernist poets—might give rise to a sense of Eurocentrism or coercion through an insistence that postcolonial modernism be apprehended only by way of cosmopolitanism and global exchange. Such approaches not only exclude the possibility of sophisticated non-nativist postcolonial modernisms constituting themselves on their own local terms—whether they may want to understand "the local" on provincial, national, regional, or other grounds—but also ignore how the concomitant emphasis on "polyphony" and the "plural" silently privileges certain forms and readings of high-modernist aesthetics that revel in fragmentation and multiplicity. Left out is a more austere or skeptical modernism that pares back its elements and is oriented more toward absence and the abyss than polyphony and plurality. That these features are more characteristic of late-modernist aesthetics that coincide historically with the era of postcoloniality and that—like postcolonial modernism—are significantly marked by their critical reflections on a more advanced capitalist modernity and on modernism itself makes their effective exclusion from prominent critical approaches to postcolonial modernism a potentially profound loss.

As articulated in her deftly executed study *Cosmopolitan Style*, Rebecca Walkowitz's concept of a "critical cosmopolitanism" that involves ongoing critique of what constitutes "the local" and "the distant" or "home" and "exile" goes a long way toward addressing some of the unacknowledged biases attending the conceptualization of cosmopolitanism in modernist studies by those that stress a model of exchange and equivalence as much as for those that emphasize modernist cosmopolitanism as a means of overcoming an inherently atavistic localism. Accentuating the flavor of decadence attaching to a late nineteenth-century notion of cosmopolitanism as "a model of perversity, in the senses of obstinacy, indirection, immorality and attitude," Walkowitz highlights a series of explicit "tactics" that writers from the early and late decades of the twentieth century use to effect a critical cosmopolitanism through marked innovations in literary style (13, 27).

Walkowitz's critical cosmopolitanism thus seems to permit a grounded or "fixed" local specificity that resists being superseded

by a global sophistication or transcendent polyphony while simultaneously insisting on the perversely protean or "transient" nature of
what constitutes the local (30). As she says of Joyce, "Joyce's project
is cosmopolitan in two important ways: it is critical of authenticity as
a measure of belonging and it promotes intellectual vagrancy, what I
call 'triviality,' as a condition of materialist critique and social transformation" (57). Walkowitz does still retain some strains of the more
established notions of cosmopolitan transcendence in her claim that
Joyce's cosmopolitan style is partly in service to a notion of "transnational community" (56). A transnational emphasis is arguably not an
inevitable consequence of her approach, however, and her transposing
of cosmopolitanism into an intrinsic aspect of style that "perverts"
the fundamental concepts of both province and metropole represents
in any case a significant advance over Crawford's account of a modernist cosmopolitanism that "outflanks the English cultural centre"
by revealing the ineradicable presence of "provincial improprieties"
contaminating "the centre of high art" (262, 270).

Resonating in some key ways with Walkowitz's approach, Marc
Manganaro's reflections on the relationship between anthropology
and modernism help to illustrate how an analysis more attuned to
local dimensions can yield nuanced readings of modernist form. His
proposal in *Culture, 1922* for an "ethnographic" reading of Joyce is
thus offered as a conscious alternative to a long-standing critical tradition he roots in T. S. Eliot's 1923 review of *Ulysses* and its famous
account of the "mythical method" (112). Rejecting the broader critical consensus that such an approach is disabled by investments in
a naïve mimeticism, Manganaro argues that an ethnographic reading "entails the recognition that Joyce . . . in some very complex ways
works with words *in the very terms of* the 'things' those words attach,
refer, or at least point toward" (113). Asserting that "the argument for
an ethnographic Joyce . . . is hardly antisymbolic" (114), Manganaro
insists that consideration of Joyce's symbolic aesthetic take account of
the local contexts of the material elements being rendered into symbols and of Joyce's own relationships to those contexts and that process of transformation. Manganaro's approach is especially valuable
for the example it offers of a modernist criticism that does not privilege categories of cosmopolitanism or a presumed universalism and
yet remains highly sensitive to the intricacies of aesthetics and form
in ways that maintain a broad critical and theoretical purchase. That
he does so from a critical orientation outside of Irish studies only

underscores the fact that critical treatments of modernism oriented toward the local rather than the cosmopolitan should not automatically be construed as narrowly nativist or aesthetically naive.[5]

Though there has thankfully been much useful criticism addressing the specificity of Irish modernism's Irish and colonial dimensions, the tendency that we see within modernist studies to apprehend the "provincial" by way of the "cosmopolitan" remains a significant limitation, especially as modernist studies grapples more fully with postcoloniality.[6] As Manganaro hinted some time ago in his introduction to *Modernist Anthropology* (9), the underlying problem within modernist studies remains what Edward Said diagnoses as "the fundamental historical problem" of modernism itself: a failure "to take the Other seriously" (223). In the late-modernist texts of the early decades of Irish postcoloniality, however, we find particularly striking examples of the impetus for modernism that Said describes as "the subaltern and the constitutively different suddenly achiev[ing] disruptive articulation" (223). Rather than being muffled and enclosed by the classic modernist frameworks of "myth," "provincialism," and "primitivism" that underlie what Said decries as modernism's "paralyzed gestures of aestheticized powerlessness" (223), however, these late-modernist works allow us to perceive more easily how such "disruptive articulation" can play a key role in the development of modernist practice and thought on its own distinctive terms.

Since Irish postcolonial modernism chronologically and geographically overlaps or abuts modernist expressions typically framed within a high-modernist or metropolitan perspective in ways that other postcolonial or "peripheral" modernisms do not, it is especially important to be able to consider how the late modernism of Ireland's first generation of postcolonial writers takes up and challenges some of high modernism's key aesthetic and conceptual binaries within the terms of a distinctly postcolonial perspective. Indeed, one reason Irish literature from this late-modernist era is so valuable is the opportunity it affords for considering how modernism is being inflected by a new generation of postcolonial writers emerging in the very midst of high modernism's rise and decline.

Consideration of Ireland's much earlier entry into postcoloniality additionally enables the often overlooked benefit of more precisely historicized accounts of postcolonial structures and aesthetics. As a result, we can more easily distinguish and compare the contexts and features of different postcolonial modernisms. This benefit becomes more evident as we look at the midcentury novels of Beckett and consider how they signal a transition to a new phase of a more globalized Irish postcoloniality. Emblematized by the remarkable "Celtic Tiger" boom which has recently collapsed in such an epic and tragic fashion, this latter phase of a globalized Irish postcoloniality is, in turn, marked by an ironic postmodern reiteration of the earlier Irish postcolonial narrative modes, as I explore in chapter 4.

Another significant way we can understand the modernist practices of the first generation of postcolonial Irish writers as "late," therefore, may lie in their anticipation of aspects of modernist expressions emerging from other postcolonial sites that decolonize in the latter half of the twentieth century. To the extent, in turn, that these more "delayed" postcolonial modernisms share characteristics that notably differ from those exhibited by the first generation of Irish postcolonial writers, that contrast can also prove useful in pointing us toward specific features of a "late" postcoloniality and the effects of late twentieth-century structural contexts that may produce modernist or postmodernist aesthetic responses depending on particular circumstances.

Such efforts to sketch more precisely historicized accounts of postcolonial modernism also help to put studies of postcolonial aesthetics in dialogue with a wider array of analyses of modernist aesthetic development. Thus, we can consider the historical rupture of postcoloniality alongside the "long bout of war neurosis" (42) Tyrus Miller identifies as a key stimulus for late modernism in his excellent study of 1930s aesthetics, *Late Modernism*. Similarly, to Miller's account of a more elite late modernism marked by a sense of aesthetic exhaustion and belatedness (14) and an immersion in a world of objects and consumption (35), we can compare the sense of a new departure for modernist aesthetics from Irish writers who present, at least initially, a less thoroughly modernized social and economic space and rehearse a critique of the fixity of the object from the inside.

The value of focusing on Irish writing lies at once in the opportunities it affords for examining a postcolonial literature that emerges in the shadow of a still vibrant high modernism and the potential it offers for a more sustained longitudinal analysis that can allow us to discern discrete moments and aesthetic impulses arising within postcoloniality over time. This study thus adds to the consideration of form and aesthetic history within postcolonial studies and helps develop our understanding of the ways that different postcolonial phases register in formal shifts.[7] At the same time, an engagement with some lesser-known writers and atypical modernist aesthetic practices helps to fill out the picture of the development of modernism and enables reflection on the ways that modernism generates some quite different "second-generation" or "late" aesthetic responses from within. Functioning both as critique of the more prominent aesthetic practices of modernism's initial phase and as extensions of key aspects of modernism's underlying logic as it is able to be realized more fully within a postcolonial historical context, work such as the Blasket texts and O'Faoláin's novels, essays, and criticism proves particularly useful in helping to bridge the gap between Beckett and the rest of his generation of fellow Irish writers.[8]

As we see how public controversies over the revolutionary shortcomings of early postcolonial culture can be integrated within and, indeed, significantly enhance our analyses of modernist thought and aesthetics, we have further confirmation of the value of what Douglas Mao and Rebecca Walkowitz label the "vertical expansion" of modernist studies in their well-known *PMLA* overview of the new modernist studies (738). Likewise, to the extent that Irish postcolonial writing outside of the immediate high-modernist ambit has for the most part been ignored within modernist studies, this more extended engagement with Irish postcolonial modernism can also be seen in a certain way as part of the "spatial expansion" Mao and Walkowitz identify within the new modernist studies as a means of describing work that examines modernist art and thought generated by artists outside of the standard spaces of the European metropole.

Within Irish studies, my exploration of the early postcolonial era complements the growing scholarly interest in the intellectual and cultural histories of the first decades of postcoloniality. The late-modernist aesthetic I trace through postcolonial narrative forms helps to round out the picture of early postcolonial modernism that critics have more recently begun to sketch through accounts of Irish avant-garde poetry and painting.[9] My analyses provide further evidence that modernist aesthetic practices are a good deal more complex and generically varied than standard Irish literary histories have tended to suggest. Indeed, even as greater attention has begun to be devoted to previously neglected Irish avant-garde poets such as Thomas MacGreevy and Brian Coffey, leading critics have continued to frame emerging understandings of them so as to reinforce the sense of the general character of early Irish postcolonial literature as stylistically primitive and dominated by an aesthetically retrograde prose.[10]

As Clair Wills concisely expresses in her insightful alternative account of 1940s Ireland, however, "grumbles about intellectual stagnation were, paradoxically, evidence of the energy and dynamism which was resisting that stagnation" (14). A dynamic intellectual and cultural scene emerges, in particular, from the pages of the era's little magazines and cultural reviews in ways that can help us appreciate more fully how the unsettled political and social atmospheres of the period help foster an aesthetic radicalism and openness to experiment that belies the sense of artistic naiveté and resignation so frequently attributed to the first generation of Irish postcolonial writers. My discussion of literary magazines from the 1930s and 1940s such as *Ireland To-Day* and the *Bell* thus adds to the revealing recent work on periodicals within Irish studies and—mindful of the growing interest in literary periodicals within the broader field of modernist studies—considers how we might read the postcolonial little magazine as itself constituting a complex modernist form.[11] As Mark Morrisson argues in his groundbreaking study of the little magazines that offer some of the earliest expressions of modernist aesthetics, I find that the little magazine provides a means for Irish postcolonial modernists to vigorously reassert art's public function (6, 12–13).

At the same time, my treatment of the recently concluded Celtic Tiger boom era brings into focus key aspects of the longer historical trajectory of Irish postcolonial culture in ways that shed new light on the early postcolonial era and the contemporary period alike. Analysis of how Irish postcoloniality's gradual synchronization with the rhythms of capitalist modernity registers in narrative form builds on Joe Cleary's illuminating accounts of naturalism and postmodernity in *Outrageous Fortune: Capital and Culture in Modern Ireland* even as I propose a very different reading of the early Sean O'Faoláin as republican realist. Like Cleary, I also take a serious look at popular texts and genres sometimes seen as "less literary" in order to examine how the structural features of late capitalism and late postcoloniality combine to shape narrative form toward the end of the century. My reading of Frank McCourt's *Angela's Ashes* thus addresses itself at once to the text's surprising efficacy in recapitulating and ironizing earlier postcolonial narrative modes and to the wider insight it affords into the ways that the histories of empire and postcoloniality are reimagined or, indeed, dematerialized under the sign of globalization.

I begin with a chapter on the Blasket texts as much to explore their grossly underappreciated formal features as to consider what they might reveal about a late modernism that turns the primitivism of the Revival on its head. Despite a persistent critical tendency to treat their texts as a sort of naïve auto-ethnography, the Blasket writers show themselves to be keenly aware of the ways that they are being figured as fetishes of premodern authenticity and make skillful use of autobiographical form to intervene in that process. Indeed, the Blasket Islanders were quite familiar with the controversies surrounding Synge's portrait of the Gaelic West and expressed significant resentment about his account of Blasket life published after a visit there in 1905 (Mac Conghail 133).

Though the Blasket writers' own texts afford rich opportunities for reevaluating the primitivist discourses of the Revival and the early postcolonial era from a space that is at once within and without the bounds of the modern nation, scholars have tended to frame them as incapable of sustaining a more "literary" reading. My reading of the Blasket writers shows, however, how a careful analysis of formal features illuminates their differing relationships to the binary of "tradition" and "modernity" that plays a key role in the elaboration of both high modernism and an "official" postcolonial nationalism.

Tomás Ó Criomhthain's fascinating autobiography, *An tOileánach* (1923/1929), translated by Robin Flower as *The Islandman* (1937), offers a remarkably sophisticated reflection on Ó Criomhthain's own position and on the broader generic politics of autobiography in a way that calls into question his all-too-frequent framing as a beautifully naïve chronicler of a dying way of life. As we read Ó Criomhthain's text "against the grain," we are immediately confronted by his ingenuity in exposing and resisting the reifying demands of the autobiographical project. In the same instant, we are likewise confronted by the dominance of a reading practice governed by primitivist fantasies inherited from the Revival by an official nationalism that would simply obliterate such deftness of thought and writing as it reduces Ó Criomhthain to the role of fetish for the new state.

Complementing the insights afforded by Ó Criomhthain and his reflection on autobiographical form are those which arise from a careful reading of the autobiography of his much younger neighbor on the Great Blasket, Muiris Ó Súilleabháin. Ó Súilleabháin's autobiography, published virtually simultaneously in Irish as *Fiche Blian ag Fás* and in English as *Twenty Years A-Growing* in 1933, records with a surprising fidelity the processes by which an experience of Gaelic alterity is made to give way to postcolonial subjectivity and "tradition" is rendered a discrete object to be managed and surveilled by the postcolonial state. Taken together, Ó Criomhthain's and Ó Súilleabháin's texts offer invaluable insight into a postcolonial late modernism emerging in response to the consolidation of an integrated modernity by way of official nationalism's mediation of "tradition." The Blasket autobiographies' insistent reminder of an *incomplete* modernity and a realm beyond the regime of subjectivity testifies to the rich vein of material a late modernism might mine amid the fissures and absences that scar the surface beyond modernity's edge.

Turning then to consider Sean O'Faoláin's reflections on the politics of postcolonial narrative form, I trace his efforts to elaborate an aesthetic of postcolonial realism as a consciously anachronistic alternative to the high-modernist narrative forms he sees sustaining an atmosphere of political and aesthetic arrest. O'Faoláin's repeated linkage of Joycean modernism with naturalism underscores the extent to which his effort to develop a realist narrative mode forms part of an innovative late-modernist project to realize modernism's radical antimimetic potential more fully. In this regard, I show how the standard reading of O'Faoláin's writing as a retreat into a more conservative "descriptive" aesthetic stems from a lack of engagement with his early accounts of Irish and European literary history and a more fundamental critical failure to distinguish between realism and naturalism.

A prolific writer of fiction, essays, and literary criticism and the founding editor of the crucially important Irish literary magazine the *Bell*, O'Faoláin plays the primary role in defining the shape of an Irish literature being produced by the generation of writers coming to prominence in the first decades of postcoloniality. His interest in developing a late-modernist aesthetic engaged with the dynamism churning beneath the surfaces of quotidian reality thus helps, in turn, to illuminate the parallel efforts being pursued along different lines by other Irish writers of this generation such as Elizabeth Bowen, Liam O'Flaherty and Flann O'Brien, all of whom O'Faoláin promoted and published in the *Bell*.

Scholars typically portray O'Faoláin as an antinationalist skeptic and a key progenitor of an important strand of cultural criticism within Irish letters and historiography that has come to be known as "revisionism." Such accounts rely primarily on O'Faoláin's writings from 1949 onward, however, and employ a retrospective reading practice that overlooks key features of his large body of work from the 1930s and 1940s. I show how the first two decades of O'Faoláin's writing are marked by an intense focus on questions of narrative form and the prospect that experiments in an anachronistic realism might be developed as a means of advancing a nationalist critique of postcolonial political arrest from a more radical left–republican perspective.

Drawing together his extensive writings on the novel form, his early criticism and essays, and the three novels he writes during the 1930s, I first trace the intricate connections between O'Faoláin's republican critique and his effort to develop a realist aesthetic as an alternative to naturalist and high-modernist forms he sees as politically and aesthetically inert. In this regard, I show how his critical reflections on realism parallel those being developed at the same moment by Georg Lukács. Considering then how O'Faoláin finds it increasingly difficult to sustain a postcolonial realism within the novel genre, I subsequently examine how he turns to the genres of historical biography and the little magazine as alternative means to develop his late-modernist aesthetic. As he ultimately finds it necessary to concede the failure of a postcolonial Irish realism as an aesthetic strategy, I discuss how O'Faoláin signals the end of that initial era in Irish postcoloniality by calling in December 1949 for a completely new form of novel capable of responding to an emergent postwar order defined by relations of multinational capital rather than those of empire.

O'Faoláin's clear-eyed analyses of the ultimate failure of his realist initiative and the implications of the global realignments of space and power he sees taking shape in the wake of World War II help, in turn, to clarify how Samuel Beckett's radical interventions fit into a dynamic history of Irish postcolonial thought. Indeed, Beckett cites O'Faoláin as an early exemplar for an alternative Irish literary sensibility that he would like to see displace the Yeatsian legacy of the Revival.[12] The third chapter thus reads Beckett's seminal 1950s novels in relation to the fundamental shifts in the nature of postcoloniality occurring at midcentury as narratives of postcolonial history and culture are increasingly folded into those of multinational capital and what will come to define itself in terms of a postimperial network of "globalization." In this context, we can more easily discern how Beckett's role as the key transitional figure between modernist and postmodernist narrative overlaps with his role in articulating the emergence of a new iteration of postcoloniality specific to the late twentieth century. As Irish postcoloniality is increasingly imagined in relation to a global capitalist modernity, I argue that Beckett's radical antirepresentational aesthetic provides the means for a writing of "absence" that dramatically accelerates the critique of subjectivity and mimetic fixity I have been tracing in the late-modernist practices of O'Faoláin, Ó Criomhthain, and Ó Súillebháin during the initial phase of Irish postcoloniality.

Contextualizing his treatment of the novel in relation to the broader currents in Irish fiction, I thus explore how Beckett provides a crucial alternative to the naturalist novel that comes to dominate Irish fiction from the midcentury onward and encodes the immersion of postcolonial political agency in the object-world of late capitalism, as Joe Cleary has insightfully shown.[13] At the same time, I consider how this understanding of the postcolonial contexts contributing to Beckett's radical formal innovation helps further explain his departure from an earlier Joycean modernism that would luxuriate in language and a surfeit of narrative possibility. In its austere emphasis on "absence" and "silence," I show how *The Unnamable* resonates with a Blasket text like Ó Criomhthain's *Islandman* and its emphasis on the potential realized by pushing literary form to the point of failure. Rather than conventional readings that frame Beckett's relationship to Irish literature solely in terms of his relationship to Joyce and a response to later expressions of a more established Irish modernist tradition, then, I suggest we can see fascinating new dimensions of the late-modernist character of Beckett's project emerge as we read his work as part of a range of alternate modernist practices being developed by a new generation of Irish writers contending with the possibilities and limitations of different phases within a dynamic postcoloniality.

The formal beginning of Irish postcoloniality's synchronization with an emergent global capitalist order can be dated to the Irish governmental White Paper *Economic Development*, published in 1958, the same year as Beckett's English translation of *The Unnamable*. This becomes the basis of the transformative *Programme for Economic Development* that the reform-minded prime minister Seán Lemass famously launches as he takes the reins of government as the new *Taoiseach* in 1959. Lemass's vision of a globally integrated Ireland forms the basis for profound and rapid changes in the complexion of Irish society from the 1960s onward that carry significant implications for our understanding of postcoloniality and its relationship to capitalist development.

As Lemass's project of modernization and capitalist integration finally comes to fruition under the signs of "globalization" and the "Celtic Tiger' in the 1990s, autobiography emerges as a key genre for articulating the passage from provincial pauper to cosmopolitan consumer. A number of critics have noted that the remarkable proliferation of Irish autobiography and memoir during the Celtic Tiger era can be read in large part as the assertion of a thoroughly modern and individualist cosmopolitanism set in opposition to the perceived demands of a retrograde nationalism associated with an outdated dispensation of Irishness and Irish postcoloniality. Kevin Whelan sums this up most succinctly in his account of "a deliberate privatization of memory" (193).

In its movement from the peripheral to the cosmopolitan perspective, Celtic Tiger autobiography retraces in part the trajectory of the much earlier Blasket autobiography *Twenty Years A-Growing*, but with a crucial difference. For Ó Súilleabháin, the passage through "tradition" constitutes an important part of that narrative and official nationalism serves to manage and maintain that "tradition" while providing the means of access to an ascendant modernity. A key distinction of more recent Irish autobiography, by contrast, is the extent to which "tradition" has become a quaint—and potentially disabling—remnant from an unenlightened past.[14] As such, "tradition" is rendered in terms of an ethereal and subjective "memory" rather than the more materially substantive terms of a "hard" primitivism or beloved archaism that marked its earlier treatment by high modernism and the "official" nationalism of the early postcolonial state.

The Celtic Tiger text that best conveys this obliteration of the material traces of empire and its aftermath is, perhaps not surprisingly, that which has been the most successful in transforming Ireland's postcolonial poverty into a commodity. Frank McCourt's *Angela's Ashes* thus can in many ways be understood as a bookend for a study which begins with Ó Criomhthain and *The Islandman*. The radical potential of Ó Criomhthain's writing of absence contrasts sharply with McCourt's ironic detachment and assured narrative delivery of the youthful Frankie from the self-defeating fictions of a postcolonial Ireland mired in poverty and misfortune seemingly all of its own making. The crucial gaps in Ó Criomhthain's text and the remarkable modesty with which he relates the spare existence of Blasket life are almost perfectly inverted by the surfeit of documentary detail and voyeuristic wallowing in the travails of the McCourts and their Limerick neighbors. The profound differences between Ó Criomhthain's and McCourt's writing underscore substantial issues of form that illuminate how a postmodern emphasis on infinite representability contrasts with a late-modernist practice that ironically grounds versions of a materialist critique within an aesthetic of antimimeticism. In *McCourt's hands,* the "real" dissolves not into absence as it might with Beckett but into the infinite presence of the commodity.

The fourth chapter thus proposes that we read *Angela's Ashes* as an exercise in a mode of postmodern naturalism wherein McCourt's account of the deprivation of 1930s and 1940s Ireland is screened through the Celtic Tiger's gilded narrative of a globalized opulence. The formerly colonized "object" follows its prescribed course under the aegis of late capitalism to become a commodity increasingly unmoored from any material correlate or any sense of a history beyond the frozen temporality of a never-ending present. *Angela's Ashes* thus restages and ironizes the earlier narrative forms of postcolonial Irish writing and turns to representing the formation of markets within which different narratives acquire their exchange value.

McCourt's recombination of postcolonial Irish writing's major narrative modes makes his memoir a remarkably useful text for reflecting on the longer process of Irish postcoloniality's synchronization with the narrative logic of global capitalism. Such reflection prompts a renewed appreciation for the complexity and dynamism of the antimimetic aesthetic approaches developed by the late-modernist writers I initially consider along with a deeper sense of how their irreducible materiality resonates with an earlier phase of postcoloniality preceding the ascendance of globalization. By contrast, the ways *Angela's Ashes* commodifies and, indeed, dematerializes Irish poverty helps to explain why its remarkably grim depictions of Irish penury prove so ironically emblematic of an era of unprecedented Irish wealth and confidence. *Angela's Ashes* normalizes an arrest of history under the auspices of a late twentieth-century *pax Americana* that promises liberation from a historical hangover of empire, provincialism, and want to offer entry into a globalized cosmopolitanism where there is no history—and, equally, no present acknowledgment—of exploitation or underdevelopment.

At the same time, if we take "empire's wake" to refer not simply to the rippling aftereffects of empire but also to standing vigil over a corpse, we can perhaps interpret the current crisis within globalization as a last lingering that marks a moment of profound transition as a hypercapitalism wavers between consolidating its final triumph and plunging headlong into the abyss. In the midst of such uncertainty, the recent changes in Ireland, especially with regard to immigration and the interplay of supranational entities such as the IMF and the EU, carry important opportunities for a critical postcolonialism. These consist at once in clarifying the ways in which imperial ideological and aesthetic structures "live on" and in opening up new lines of critique less liable to being caricatured as atavistic, rigid, or outmoded. As Ireland's—seemingly very brief—emergence as an important node within the circuits of global capital prompts us to reconsider Irish postcoloniality's relationship to broader global developments within capitalism and the aftermath of empire, its shifting position within global migration flows compels us to consider anew how the Irish experience might both inflect and be inflected by anticolonial and postcolonial formations emanating from other former imperial spaces. As we do, we must remain alert to the sometimes unlikely insights to be gleaned from a history of form as we work to realize the interpretive possibilities of "empire's wake" in all their fullness.

CHAPTER ONE

Modernity's Edge

Speaking Silence on the Blaskets

Just off one of the more remote stretches of Ireland's southwestern coast and within close view of the Dingle peninsula lie the Blasket Islands. A diminutive archipelago extending south and west from Slea Head, near the tip of the peninsula, the Blaskets loom tantalizingly close to the mainland even as they stand apart. In that regard, they resemble countless other small islands dotting the waters all along the Irish coastal periphery. In the case of the Blaskets, however, what makes this geographic liminality more significant and, indeed, emblematic is the way in which it becomes intertwined with the political and cultural liminalities being constructed and contested as part of the initial coalescence of Irish postcoloniality. For out of the Blaskets in the late 1920s and early 1930s come a series of remarkable autobiographies that give voice to a Gaelic alterity at once constitutive and critical of a notion of "tradition" upon which an array of the era's competing cultural initiatives will come to rely.

An initial difficulty one encounters with the texts from the Great Blasket is the extent to which they have already been overwritten as fixed cultural artifacts not liable to being actively read. Instead, they tend to be construed as curious anachronistic treasures bared by a receding historical tide. Celebrated for the window they offer onto an older life in the remote Gaelic periphery, the Blasket texts effectively function as emblems of cultural cohesion and continuity standing in stark relief to a broader sense of traumatic division and reinvention permeating Irish life in the 1920s and 1930s. Such an understanding of the texts can prove useful to the extent that it illuminates the historical tensions of the early postcolonial era and exposes the underlying irony of a discourse of "tradition" that is at once celebratory and elegiac. Too often, however, such approaches apprehend the Blasket writers solely in terms of an unmediated collective enunciation rather than attending to them as individual writers or composers of text.[1] As a result, the texts tend to be framed as a single undifferentiated body of work and one best understood in terms of cultural history or naïve auto-ethnography rather than those of literature.[2]

Placing the Blasket texts in a literary framework, however, not only enables us to consider more fully their complex orchestrations of voice, genre, and form but to clarify how the outlines of a distinctly postcolonial literature begin to emerge from the shadows of the Irish Literary Revival.[3] Most obviously, the Blasket writers offer valuable opportunities for reflecting on the function of the Gaelic West in the elaboration of Irish postcolonial literature and culture. As we shall explore, the first works from the Blasket emerge in the context of a formative moment for Ireland's postcolonial politics as the forces that will become the major political parties in post-Independence Ireland struggle to define themselves and their constituencies in the aftermath of civil war. This larger political struggle overlaps significantly with a series of polemics being waged in the literary and cultural spheres over the status of the Irish language, the characteristics and purposes of a "truly" Irish literature, and the prominence accorded rural life and "tradition" in postcolonial culture.

As Gaelic texts from the remote rural periphery focusing on a fading "tradition" and composed by writers from within the community rather than an external literary elite, the books coming from the Blaskets in the late 1920s and early 1930s stand right at the center of such debates. Describing the impact of the Blasket autobiographies and their English translations, Philip O'Leary observes: "No depictions of Gaeltacht life from this period were . . . to have and hold such a fascination. . . . As a result, almost immediately the Gaeltacht autobiography became the keystone of the evolving canon of writing in Irish" (*Gaelic Prose* 133–34). The Blasket texts' most important contribution, however, lies not in the evidence they provide of the importance of "tradition" as a central aspect of postcolonial Irish culture or, conversely, in their demonstration of the deadening effect that such an emphasis has on the era's cultural vitality. Their more lasting contribution lies instead in producing a literature that interrogates the discourse of "tradition" from within. Indeed, as Muiris Mac Conghail notes, the Blasket Islanders were quite engaged with the controversies and enthusiasms surrounding Revivalist portraits of the Gaelic periphery and were particularly incensed by Synge's account of his visit to the Great Blasket in 1905 (132–33). In striking ways, then, the Blasket autobiographies reveal how a Revivalist primitivism is reconfigured to provide the means for a late-modernist practice simultaneously challenging to the elitism of an earlier strand of modernism produced by Yeats and Synge and to its populist reinflection by a bourgeois institutional nationalism that has taken the reins of the postcolonial state.

Reading Blasket writers such as Tomás Ó Criomhthain or Muiris Ó Súillebháin in terms of a late-modernist literary practice may initially seem surprising or counterintuitive. On the one hand, modernism tends to be associated with a sophistication and aesthetic self-awareness arising from experiences of profound alienation or temporal dislocation and typically poised to offer a bitter critique of a modern bourgeoisie's degraded commercial culture. On the other hand, the Blasket writers tend to be associated with a lack of sophistication and awareness of themselves as writers that endows their works and the islanders themselves with a simplicity and gritty integrity completely separate from the concerns and corruptions of the modern world. Ironically, however, this more standard reading may be part of the legacy of an earlier iteration of modernism that the Blasket texts themselves challenge and revise.

Notwithstanding the substantial objections of elitism leveled against Revivalist aesthetics from their own day down to the present, it is important to recall that the primitivist construction of "the folk" and the Gaelic periphery by Yeats and Synge was not simply an exercise in nostalgia. Indeed, their social elitism and aesthetic radicalism coincide unapologetically in their elaboration of premodern "peasant" or Gaelic figures embedded in an antique epic realm that continually disrupts the triumph of modern bourgeois rationality. What marks this primitivist framing as part of a distinctively modernist aesthetic is the alienated consciousness of the artist constantly oscillating between the two realms of modernity and "tradition" and suffused with the tragic awareness that it can never be reconciled to the organic wholeness attributed to the peasant and the Gael. The late-imperial contexts of the Revival reinforce this sense of a division between the artist and the emblematic figure of the Gael even as the larger project of the Revival realizes much of its aesthetic and political force by championing the irreducible complexity of the Gaelic periphery in opposition to the great synthesizing project of empire.

The advent of postcoloniality and the establishment of the Irish Free State in 1922 reinflect the Revivalist vision of rural Ireland and the Gaelic West in important ways, however. With the people and practices of rural life scarcely a generation removed from most of those occupying the defining social, political, and artistic roles in the new postcolonial state, the distance between periphery and modernity has ostensibly been bridged, and the stress falls less naturally on the fractured artistic consciousness sliding between the two. The constructions of rural life offered by the Revival are nonetheless preserved and merged with the less nuanced celebrations of rural simplicity that had been staples of a conservative strand of nationalism for some time.[4] The resulting notion of "tradition" frames a portrait of the western periphery whose features strongly resemble those sketched by the Revival but which lacks the aesthetic and political radicalism of its predecessor. Modernist primitivism is effectively reduced to an inert nostalgia.

The nostalgia of "tradition" can be understood to be at once politically and aesthetically inert. With the periphery rendered more in terms of a poorer relative tending the family hearth, it no longer affords the means for a critique or disruption of the modern bourgeois order. The two realms stand seemingly reconciled even as the stark material realities of rural Irish life in the early postcolonial era would indicate otherwise. This reconciliation encoded in the concept of "tradition" produces a remarkably flat aesthetic virtually devoid of any animating tension and suited to an almost endless reproduction.[5] Even the tinge of elegy running through the concept of "tradition" generally fails to add aesthetic depth or texture as its regret is rendered so passively and formulaically. Instead, the repeated staging of the passing of alternate modes of life and community on the periphery function to produce a sort of ironic cathartic exhaustion in service to a narrative of inevitable accession to a singular bourgeois modernity. Anger over the startling poverty and hemorrhage of emigration from the rural districts that might stir the large sections of population still disaffected in the wake of the Civil War can thus be transmuted into a trite sentimentalism.[6]

Importantly, however, this gap between the pressing material need of the Gaelic periphery and the sentimental portrait of "tradition" provides a key basis for the Blasket texts' iteration of a distinctly postcolonial modernism that might be understood as both a sort of "modernism from below" and a late "meta-modernism." Most immediately, the modernist character of the texts coheres in their account of life on the Blaskets being constituted from the convergence of multiple temporalities and spaces. Rather than the pristine refuge from modernity that the notion of "tradition" might suggest, the Blaskets emerge as an almost quintessential modernist location marked by a constant shuttling of discrepant orders and peoples as the islanders negotiate in different languages with mainland authorities, continental fishermen, returning and departing emigrants, and a series of foreign scholars and Gaelic aficionados.

To the extent that we understand a modernist sensibility as marked by an irresolvable duality or a sense of being forever "in between," we can see that the Blasket writers offer a perspective that in many ways parallels the oscillations of the writers of the Revival. The crucial difference is that the Blasket writers experience instability, unevenness, and the ongoing negotiation of different orders as a constant and constitutive feature of life on the periphery. Rather than relying on the foil of the unalienated primitive consciousness of the Gael as an image of respite and escape as the Revivalists do, the Blasket writers instead reflect on its status as a construct that must itself be subject to the skepticism characteristic of modernist thought. In this way, we can see how the Blasket texts begin to articulate a much more radical modernist vision that analyzes the structures and categories of an earlier and more well-known modernist practice to reveal their complicity with the regime of bourgeois modernity and the processes of commodification they so famously sought to critique.

The fact that the Blasket texts may not "look" modernist in the typical sense and operate in a more modest and accessible literary register than is characteristic of more classically modernist writing should not mislead us into overlooking their modernist features or dismissing them as "naïve." As the new modernist studies makes the full range of modernist practice more visible, the consideration of modernist writing emerging from more marginal class and historical formations such as we see with the Blaskets not only illustrates the wealth of texts still to be explored but, perhaps more importantly, reveals how more narrowly framed understandings of modernism as an elite practice have caused us to misread texts and periods in significant ways. In this regard, we can begin to see how an appreciation of the modernist features of the Blasket texts at once offers important opportunities for developing a more robust understanding of the history of modernism while also providing the means for reevaluating modernism's relationship to postcoloniality and the standard accounts of early twentieth-century Irish literature.

Published in the midst of the initial coalescence of a distinctly postcolonial culture, the first texts emerge from the Great Blasket against a backdrop of volatile change within Irish politics. In the wake of the immediate devastation and confusion following the end of the Civil War in 1923, a significant portion of those who had supported the losing Republican side in the Civil War were drawn back into a more vigorous engagement with electoral politics by Eamon de Valera's new Fianna Fáil party, founded in 1926. Though certainly controversial within republican circles, the formation of Fianna Fáil provided a vehicle for more direct political confrontation with the Cumann na nGaedhael government, formed by the core supporters of the pro-Treaty position during the Civil War. With a platform of opposition that combined the explosive idea of a united islandwide republic with calls for a new commitment to the Irish language and a land policy more oriented toward the smallholder, Fianna Fáil provided a jolt to Irish politics and culture that brought to the fore basic questions of how Irishness could be defined in the postcolonial era.

The same year that marked the founding of Fianna Fáil—1926— saw the creation of the publishing entity *An Gúm* under the auspices of the Cumann na nGaedhael government as part of a state initiative to publish and disseminate Irish-language writing in the Free State. Though not a direct response to the emergence of Fianna Fáil, *An Gúm* significantly complicated the language and cultural politics of the era and blunted Fianna Fáil's effort to define questions of language and cultural authenticity in terms solely favorable to itself.[7] *An Gúm*'s publication of the first two Blasket texts, Tomás Ó Criomhthain's *Allagar na hInise* in 1928 and his more influential work *An tOileánach* in 1929, must thus be understood in relation to a newly invigorated political battle in the late 1920s over the status of the Irish language and the place of the rural periphery in the imagining of postcolonial Irish society. Illustrating how the role of the Gaelic periphery in the Irish cultural and political imagination had shifted in the wake of Independence, Diarmuid Ó Giolláin notes: "Irish-speaking districts were characterized by subsistence farming and were incapable of sustaining a significant population of farm labourers. The idealization of a region with very limited social stratification as a model for the nation helped to elide the social divisions that were very clear elsewhere in the country" (148). With the festering issue of Northern partition joined with popular skepticism about the class interests served by the conservative fiscal policies and modernization program of W. T. Cosgrave's Cumann na nGaedhael government, the Blasket texts thus offered opportunities for demonstrating a dedication to the Irish language and for integrating a peripheral social geography into a broader narrative of modernization.

In that regard, it is worth noting how the publication of *An tOileánach* in 1929 strikingly coincides with the opening of the massive Shannon hydroelectric scheme at Ardnacrusha, the signature project of Cosgrave's modernization initiative.[8] We can read in this conjunction the complex interrelationship of "tradition" and modernization in early Irish postcoloniality and trace the ways that *An tOileánach*'s elegy for a dying Blasket life can be apprehended in relation to a narrative of historical continuity that normalizes modernization as part of a natural process of national consolidation. This narrative arguably comes to completion in Muiris Ó Súillebháin's subsequent Blasket autobiography published both in Irish as *Fiche Blian ag Fás* and in English as *Twenty Years A-Growing* in 1933.[9] In his account of an early twentieth-century Blasket childhood and subsequent recruitment to the newly formed Free State police force, Ó Súillebháin narrates the formation of a representative postcolonial subject who emerges from the realm of "tradition" into that of modernity. Ó Súillebháin's ultimate perspective on the *Gaeltacht* as a space set apart that is in need of both preservation and policing rehearses the integration of the geographic, linguistic, and social periphery of Irish postcoloniality into a new national imaginary presided over by the Free State regime.

Even as we can thus understand the Blasket texts in relation to the elaboration of the larger phenomenon of "tradition" in early postcolonial culture, we can detect in the texts themselves a more nuanced and skeptical reflection on this phenomenon. As we read them, therefore, we must attend simultaneously to the larger historical and political contexts framing their composition and reception and to the ways the texts' late-modernist practice reveals these frameworks as impositions working to foreclose alternative narratives of postcoloniality. Doing so not only restores a sense of the texts' dynamism and complexity often lost in accounts of their role in that era's cultural history but compels us to reckon anew with the rich cultural array that animated this key moment of historical and political transition at the end of the first decade of Irish independence.

One of the most illuminating ways to explore the complexity of the Blasket writers' relationship to the larger discourse of "tradition" that overwhelmingly defines them is through an examination of form. Indeed, a consideration of Ó Criomhthain's and Ó Súillebháin's treatment of autobiographical form reveals significant differences in their reflections on "tradition" and their role in mediating between life on the Blaskets and an emergent Irish postcoloniality. Ó Criomhthain combines savvy analyses of various efforts to fix and commodify life on the Blaskets with a mode of modest self-presentation in *An tOileánach* that highlights the generic pressures of postcolonial autobiography through his ongoing frustration of the genre's demand for disclosure. He thus effectively turns the genre upon itself to produce an autobiography of "tradition" rather than of himself.

For his part, Ó Súillebháin repeatedly points to a tendency within early postcolonial Irish culture to construe the Blaskets and Gaelic in fetishistic terms that he finds at turns amusing and condescending. Nonetheless, in his use of modern autobiographical conventions to convey detailed accounts of his interior reflections, Ó Súillebháin presents himself as a representative modern subject whose narrative relies on the reader's sense of identification rather than the sense of distance activated by Ó Criomhthain's. In this regard, his text narrates the move from Revivalist alienation to the nostalgia of "tradition." As a result, it is not ultimately surprising that Ó Súillebháin increasingly comes to present the people and practices of the Gaelic periphery in abstract and objectifying terms that are entirely distinct from himself and are recalled in terms of fond sentimentalism. A consideration of autobiographical form thus enables us to develop a more precise understanding of the mechanism of "tradition" and its relationship to different sorts of modernist practice within early twentieth-century Irish culture while remaining alert to visions of the periphery that resist such reduction. In this way, we are able to understand works such as *An tOileánach* and *Fiche Blian ag Fás* as simultaneously part of a larger cultural phenomenon and as sophisticated literary texts that interpret that phenomenon from within.

Attendance to autobiographical form clarifies, in particular, the significant continuities and discontinuities between the Blasket writers and the writers of the Revival in their treatment of the Gaelic periphery. Their most important precursor in that regard would be, of course, John Millington Synge and especially his 1907 work *The Aran Islands*, characterized as it is by a mixture of autobiography and ethnography. *An tOileánach* and *Fiche Blian ag Fás* obviously differ most notably from Synge's text in that they are written by islanders themselves rather than by a curious visitor from the capital. As we shall explore, however, this relocation of authorship does not mean we should take Ó Criomhthain's and Ó Súillebháin's orientation to "tradition" as identical nor see either of their texts as entirely outside the discourse of primitivism that permeates Synge's writing.

Gregory Castle's nuanced reading of *The Aran Islands* helps cast the postcolonial context of the Blasket writers in relief so that we can trace the relationship between Revivalist primitivism and Free State "tradition" and begin to discern the initial outlines of a later moment in modernist thought. Castle reads *The Aran Islands* as a text that draws from the narrative energies of fin de siècle anthropological treatments of the Gaelic periphery and simultaneously critiques that perspective as part of a particular modernist literary response that "posits a native Other as the salvation of a dissociated subjectivity" (131). He notes how Synge's text shares with the anthropological accounts "a common investment in primitivism and a common desire for a 'total picture' of the peasant society" (108). Nonetheless, Castle argues, Synge's use of the autobiographical genre allows him to deconstruct the fiction of the ethnographer's authority and distance so as to enact a fantasy narrative of submerging his alienated and fractured consciousness within the ostensibly unbroken realm of the Arans' premodern life and culture. The ambivalence of Synge's narrative orientation and his ongoing concern that the islanders' "primitive simplicity was inaccessible to him" (113) mark *The Aran Islands* for Castle as a distinctively modernist text and one produced from the confluence of late-imperial discourse and a Revivalist critique sharing many of the same notions of inherent colonial differences of race and class.

We can perhaps most easily understand the relationship of Ó Criomhthain's and Ó Súillebháin's texts to these ideas in terms of their different renderings of what we might call "modernity's edge." For Synge, the Arans provide a balm to his alienated consciousness by virtue of their separation from modernity and his sense of a cultural vitality and coherence that persists because of its remote location beyond the edge of modernity's penetration. At the same time, Synge's awareness of the modernity of his own consciousness and his

movement back and forth across modernity's edge in both his travels
and his writing necessarily provokes an even greater sense of alienation and loss as he repeatedly confronts the impossibility of his complete immersion in his vision of Aran life. Indeed, the *frisson* attending this contradiction energizes some of the key underlying tensions
of the Revival's aesthetic politics.

Ó Súillebháin's text can be understood to provide a vision of modernity's edge and of "tradition" that builds on Synge's account and
effectively works to resolve the tension and alienation of the Revivalist consciousness under the auspices of a new postcolonial dispensation. Presented from the perspective of an "authentic Gael" whose
narrative rehearses the formation of a new national subject coming
to see life in the *Gaeltacht* as a quaint preserve of "the old ways," Ó
Súillebháin's text maintains the notion of modernity's edge demarcat-
ing a peripheral space of primitive life while integrating it more easily into postcolonial modernity by way of the concept of "tradition."
Ó Súillebháin thus ironically overcomes Synge's alienation by reinforcing a sense of the reality of modernity's edge within postcolonial
Ireland's cultural geography and simultaneously reducing a sense of
its significance as an impermeable barrier for a modern postcolonial
consciousness. *Fiche Blian ag Fás* suggests, in other words, that the
primitive and the modern can be perceived in the postcolonial context as reconciled and interpenetrating. Rather than Synge's tortured
experience of a cultural and temporal limbo, modern alienation can
be effectively salved by the postcolonial subject's sense of an untrou-
bled intimacy with "tradition." For a Free State regime engaged in a
program of modernization, this understanding of the rural periphery has the added benefits of tempering the sense of an abandonment
of nationalist pieties by an acquisitive bourgeois elite and deflecting
alternative postcolonial discourses not fully reconciled to the state
into the realm of quaint anachronism.[10]

Even with its emphasis on postcolonial integration, however, Ó
Súillebháin's text also points to the unacknowledged sense of separation and distance that the discourse of "tradition" inevitably enacts
between the modern national subject and the peripheral figure of "the
Gael." Though he does not worry over it as Synge does, the separation is all the more striking for Ó Súillebháin because his narrative ultimately frames members of his own family and community as
primitive others and embodiments of an older order that he has left
behind. In this regard, Ó Súillebháin simply makes more explicit the

inherent bias toward a bourgeois modernity in the concept of "tradition" that its champions in the new postcolonial regime would prefer to disavow. Thus, even as *Fiche Blian ag Fás* illuminates the connections between an earlier modernism of the Revival and the nostalgia of postcolonial "tradition," Ó Súillebháin's own modernist practice coheres ironically by showing how a more subtle exoticization of "the Gael" and the periphery undercuts the discourse of postcolonial integration from within.

For his part, Ó Criomhthain presents a more complicated account of modernity's edge that foregrounds the reductive character of the Revivalist approach and its fantasy of a pristine premodernity while also providing for a position of separateness that can facilitate the critique of a single all-encompassing modernity. Like Ó Súillebháin, Ó Criomhthain shows the Blaskets to be a space where the realms of modernity and nonmodernity continually interpenetrate. Rather than providing for the resolution of Revivalist anxiety and alienation by way of "tradition" and the reconciling figure of the postcolonial subject as Ó Súillebháin does, however, Ó Criomhthain effectively uses the notion of modernity's edge to articulate the potential of an *incomplete* modernity. This experience of incompleteness produces a more radical modernist vision at once denied the consolation of an unalienated primitivism and electrified by the challenge of an ongoing negotiation of self outside the bounds of modern subjectivity.

Indeed, a key aspect of Ó Criomhthain's modernism lies in his ongoing critique of postcolonial subjectivity. He refuses to provide access to an interior consciousness in his text. Instead, through his ongoing accounts of visitors from outside the Blaskets prevailing upon him to produce taxonomies of Blasket life and, ultimately, himself, Ó Criomhthain disrupts the possibility of the postcolonial subject's seamless elaboration of an integrated consciousness across modernity's edge. By contrast, *An tOileánach* reveals the subject to be a means of imposing a false singularity on an experience of historical, cultural, and linguistic unevenness. Rather than a realm of blissful premodern isolation and simplicity, Ó Criomhthain shows life on the Blaskets to be constituted by the experience of constant negotiation between the local and the foreign, the primitive and the modern, the enduring and the transitory. In this way, he reverses the standard trajectory of thought and shows the alienated metropolitan's aspiration toward a single unified culture to be the naïve perspective rather than that of the supposedly simple islanders. Engaging more directly with the experience of dwelling amid an array of discrepant orders, *An tOileánach* instead offers glimpses of a very different version of modernist thought than that which prevailed for the Revivalists. As his ongoing challenge to the disciplinary function of the subject makes more apparent, Ó Criomhthain's writing surprisingly anticipates Samuel Beckett and his emphases on "absence" and "silence."

In order to appreciate the significance of Ó Criomhthain's approach to autobiographical form, it is useful to consider the modalities that typically govern the narrative operations of modern autobiography. Autobiography is commonly thought to "represent" in two primary ways. It re-presents the self and life history of the writer, and in so doing it rehearses the formation of a subjectivity common to writer and reader. Conceived in this way, autobiography serves a heuristic purpose, offering the stories of exemplary individuals to prompt "self-reflection" and facilitate "self-realization."[11] In the context of the shift from Gaelic subaltern to postcolonial citizen, this process can be understood to realize itself by means of a series of relays. At the most basic level, the autobiographer must constitute her-/himself as a discrete identity separate from the subaltern mass or other more local communal identities and most fully comprehensible in terms of individual origins, desires, and perspectives.

The Blasket texts are particularly valuable in this regard as they simultaneously draw the far-flung *Gaeltacht* regions into the purview of the state and create the illusion of a common cultural substratum uniting all Irish postcolonial subjects. In Ó Criomhthain's case, of course, it is important to note that the manuscript of *An tOileánach* is initially purchased from Ó Criomhthain for publication by the government-affiliated publisher *An Gúm*.[12] Even as *An tOileánach* is pressed into service for the state, though, Ó Criomhthain's text can be seen to frustrate its agenda by limning the edges of representation itself and revealing the ways in which the Gael is commodified by a discourse of "tradition." In so doing, Ó Criomhthain not only points to the coerciveness of the regime of postcolonial subjectivity but alludes to a rich presence beyond its horizon. Viewed in this context, his famous claim that "the like of us will never be again" (244) becomes a lament not for the Blasket Islanders alone but for any who might seek the fullness of life that lies beyond the bounds of subjectivity.

Conventional autobiography and autobiography theory tend to militate against such resistance with their consistent privileging of a

speaking subject. A modernist critique of autobiography must therefore operate simultaneously as meta-critique—drawing out the political function of the autobiographical form as a means of exposing the
vulnerability constituted by the dominant regime's excessive reliance
on subjectivity—and incomplete critique. Only by gesturing toward
the unrepresentable that cannot be conveyed in the terms of the autobiographical subject does the inadequacy of the autobiographical representation become fully apparent.

Ó Criomhthain's autobiography illuminates both the necessity and
legitimacy of such a modernist critique of autobiography in the postcolonial context. Though Ó Criomhthain's text obviously has a particular relevance for Irish writing, its mediation of "tradition" and a subaltern consciousness previously excluded from representation lend it a
broader significance for modernism and its relationship to postcoloniality. What is most fascinating about An tOileánach is its transitional
character. As a record of the emergence of autobiographical subjectivity, Ó Criomhthain's text discloses a realm outside of subjectivity and
sheds light on the processes and politics attending the installation of
the autobiographical subject in the geographic and politically liminal
zone of the Blaskets. One simultaneously reads a giving way to subjectivity and its regime of representation and a refusal to succumb fully
to a postcolonial subjectivity that would frame the Gaelic periphery
in terms of a reified "tradition." Indeed, Ó Criomhthain's self-por-
trait may emerge most "authentically" in this refusal.

The role envisioned for the Blasket writer and the importance of
the autobiographical genre in that process emerge quite clearly in the
translator's foreword that Robin Flower includes in his English translation of An tOileánach, which he publishes as The Islandman. A
former language pupil and close associate of Ó Criomhthain's, Flower
casts Ó Criomhthain as an earnest chronicler who straightforwardly
represents himself and the life he has known on the island. Though
Flower credits Ó Criomhthain with being an insightful observer with
a remarkable facility for language that is at once lively and precise, he
dramatically circumscribes Ó Criomhthain's agency as a writer. He
does not allow Ó Criomhthain a capacity for irony or restraint, or
indeed much complexity at all. Rather, Flower would have the readers
of his translation encounter Ó Criomhthain as little more than a perceptive recorder of events and traditions.[13] Indeed, the apparent lack
of mediation in Ó Criomhthain's account is what makes it so valuable in Flower's eyes. Flower suggests that this direct and unadorned

account provides a rare insider's perspective untainted by modernity. *The Islandman* can thus evoke the essence of life on the islands and, by extension, of "tradition" more completely.

In addition to a concern about the condescension inevitably—if perhaps unintentionally—bound up with his emphasis on the unmediated character of Ó Criomhthain's text, we might reasonably add the objection that Flower's characterization does not sufficiently account for the circumstances of the text's production. One must be mindful of the more basic constraints of audience and editors with which Ó Criomhthain must contend. Following the intervention of Brian Ó Ceallaigh, who assembled the manuscript from fragments sent by Ó Criomhthain in the form of letters, the manuscript was handed over for editing to Pádraig Ó Siochfhrada, who, following the convention used by many Gaelic writers of the era, chose to write under a pen name, "*An Seabhac*," or "The Hawk." The editing process, according to James Stewart (234–46), involved significant redaction of text as Ó Siochfhrada cut parts of the text he found unsavory. In addition to a general intolerance for almost anything vaguely sexual, Stewart notes that Ó Siochfhrada's editing minimizes the Islanders' "command . . . and *need* of English" (240, emphasis mine). Ó Siochfhrada also requested a number of additions by Ó Criomhthain including a new conclusion that is known to have greatly annoyed Ó Criomhthain.[14] Flower's translation then follows on the heels of this editing and is itself submitted to Ó Siochfhrada for review.

Although Flower's translation and publication do not occur under the auspices of the Free State government as the original publication of *An tOileánach* does, his framing of Ó Criomhthain as an unsophisticated recorder advances the larger project of enclosing the Gaelic periphery within a concept of "tradition." Indeed, Flower's publication arguably serves these ends even more effectively by virtue of being outside of direct state sponsorship. As an unmediated chronicle of a dying life on the Blaskets, *The Islandman*—at least as framed by Flower—at once operates as eulogy for Gaelic alterity and harbinger of a newly invigorated regime of "tradition." The transitional aspect of Ó Criomhthain's text enables these complementary operations even as it also inhibits the perfect execution of both.

This tension between representation and self-abnegation that is to some extent characteristic of the autobiographical genre is immediately apparent in the translator's foreword to *The Islandman*. Flower emphasizes the sense of imminent doom hanging over Blasket life as something that endows Ó Criomhthain's writing with greater truth. Thus, to establish the particular importance of Ó Criomhthain's text, Flower writes, "The great value of this book is that it is a description of this vanishing mode of life by one who has known no other, and tells his tale with perfect frankness, serving no theory and aiming at no literary effect, but solely concerned to preserve some image of the world that he has known" (vii). Flower here links the urgency of Ó Criomhthain's project to document "this vanishing mode of life" to his mode of "perfect frankness." He extends this still further through his emphasis on the limits of Ó Criomhthain's theoretical sophistication and experience of life as features that make the account more transparent and truly representative.

In this framing, we can trace a parallel with Revivalist primitivism and see how profoundly it shapes a practice of reading that is unable to account for the agency and awareness of the Blasket writers and their potential for sophisticated interventions in the figuration of "the Gael." The claim that Ó Criomhthain "aim[ed] at no literary effect" serves to authenticate Ó Criomhthain's account according to this perspective. To be "literary" would seem to be too modern and affected and would diminish the importance of *The Islandman*, the value of which would seem to have already been established as relying entirely on the Gael's simplicity and unified consciousness.[15] Flower thus stresses the fact that Ó Criomhthain has "known no other" life and says of the islanders that their experience "is necessarily narrow in its range, but within that range it is absolute and complete" (viii).

This sense of absolute completeness and continuity comports with the Revivalist fantasy of the Gaelic periphery and the broader category of "the peasant" as entirely outside of modern complexity and multiplicity. The Revivalist parallel seems particularly valid in light of Flower's subsequent comments about the strong literary tradition to which Ó Criomhthain stands heir: "There has always been a strong literary tradition among the Munster peasantry. They have preserved orally a considerable corpus both of folk-song and of the more elaborate poetry of the eighteenth century. And their folk-tales are related by the best exponents in a fascinating idiom which has a natural quality of literature. All this tradition Tomás inherits from the poets and taletellers with whom he consorted eagerly in his young days" (viii–ix).[16] The important distinction for Flower seems to lie in a difference between "literary effect" and "literary tradition." The latter involves "preservation" and "inheritance" and renders cultural expression a reified heirloom rather than a creative act on the part of the writer.

Despite his clear affection and regard for Ó Criomhthain, Flower seems intent on confining him within that closed metaphysical circle both as a means of eliminating any significant authorial agency within the text and a way of establishing a link between autobiography and an older folk culture. This likely reflects Flower's own scholarly training and orientation as a collector of folklore and keeper of medieval manuscripts. In doing so, however, Flower not only neglects the fluidity of folk culture and the generic emphases of autobiography but also directly contradicts Ó Criomhthain's own expression of a vexed relationship with the exponents of that culture on the Great Blasket. Repeatedly in *The Islandman*, Ó Criomhthain expresses his antipathy for Dunlevy, the island's poet (86–87, 140, 152), and clearly resents being pressed into service as the bearer of tradition.

Indeed, Ó Criomhthain's relationship to various aspects of what might typically be grouped under the rubric of "folk culture" or "folklore" sheds important light on his late-modernist sensibility and how it tends to be misapprehended. Ó Criomhthain was quite expert in folklore and wrote extensively on a variety of related topics of folktales, *dinnseanchas* (place-name lore), and traditional song. O'Leary notes that Ó Criomhthain was "especially prolific" in that regard, publishing articles and stories in an array of journals and newspapers before he began writing the books that would win him fame (*Gaelic Prose* 112). Despite this, as Irene Lucchitti points out, Ó Criomhthain's extensive experience as a writer tends to be effaced in most accounts of his life and authorship of *An tOileánach*, a fact that is all the more remarkable given the amount and breadth of his published writings (193). Lucchitti suggests that this effacement arises from the dominant construction of Ó Criomhthain as "a literary naïf" and argues persuasively that "while the usual version of the story [of the writing of *An tOileánach*] is that visitors were drawn to Tomás because of his speech, and that the process that turned him into a writer emerged from this, it seems quite likely that the opposite is true," and visitors were originally drawn to the Blaskets because of the reputation Ó Criomhthain had developed through his writings (193). Awareness of Ó Criomhthain's longer publication history not only demonstrates his lack of naiveté as a writer, as Lucchitti notes, but underscores his sophistication and experience with the construction and commodification of folk culture and "tradition." We can thus see how Ó Criomhthain could at once be engaged with and even genuinely appreciative of "folk" culture while still being capable of critical reflection on the ways it is being framed as "tradition," especially by those standing in a more external relationship to the sources, practices, and spaces being presented. Consideration of Ó Criomhthain's experience and growth as a writer also allows us to appreciate more fully how eager he might be to distinguish between his folkloric writings and his own construal as a folk figure in his autobiography.

Despite the construction of a closed world on the Blaskets by Flower and others, Ó Criomhthain's extensive intellectual engagement with the outside world—including, ironically, through his ongoing contact with Flower himself—provides a key context for the emergence of his late-modernist sensibility and the refinement of his critical reflections on the primitivist constructions of the Gaelic periphery. As Mac Conghaill observes of Ó Criomhthain's ongoing exchanges with Flower: "Tomás drew on much of Robin Flower's knowledge of Irish and other literatures to enrich his own mind. Their correspondence enabled Tomás to write on topics other than folklore" (139). Extending this point further to account for Ó Criomhthain's broad traffic with a panoply of modern ideas, Lucchitti asserts that it stands strikingly at odds with the ways that Ó Criomhthain and his autobiography tend to be framed:

> The volume of reading material that made its way into Tomás' hands, and its diversity, has long been understated. . . . He received a multitude of books from friends in the Gaelic League as well as newspapers and journals of the League itself, newspaper clippings from Brian Ó Ceallaigh, usually exotic in nature, as well as newspapers from the mainland. He also received some English newspapers, especially *The Daily Sketch* which was a favourite on the Island. Tomás also received more books and newspapers from relatives in America and more still from the fishermen on the big lobster boats that visited the Island. (120)

Considered from this perspective, it becomes increasingly difficult to maintain the idea of Ó Criomhthain's world as "narrow" and entirely removed from modernity. As Lucchitti proposes: "It is unlikely that the minimalist account of the reading material Tomás encountered, which originates with An Seabhac's introduction to the autobiography, was a matter of oversight. It reflects An Seabhac's assertion of a pure, uncontaminated Irish culture, both past and present" (120).[17]

Such a view reflects the "nativist" view that O'Leary identifies as one of the primary positions in the central polemical battle of the Gaelic revival between "nativism" and "progressivism" from the late nineteenth century onward (*Prose Literature* 102). The apprehension of folklore as a fixed repository constituting the central means of Gaelic cultural expression and continuity is a recurrent issue in this larger battle, as O'Leary explains (*Prose Literature* 102, 161–62). In this regard, we can see how the primitivism of the Literary Revival of Yeats and Synge overlaps with the constructions of certain strands of the Gaelic revival even as they may be directed toward different political and aesthetic ends. Understood in terms of his broader intellectual and cultural milieu, Ó Criomhthain's approach arguably brings to crisis the central categories of both discourses as he is at once immersed in the ongoing reinvention of a distinct folk culture and acutely aware of the contradictions of modernity that would seek to fix his experience as "naïve" and "pure." As Ó Giolláin observes, "The Blasket Island literature was motivated by the 'external discoverers of folklore,' but there the discourse was not monopolized by them, allowing individuals such as Tomás Ó Criomhthain to find a modern voice which would outlive the imminent death of his community" (174).

Indeed, the richness of Ó Criomhthain's text as reflected in Flower's translation stands at odds with Flower's own foreword and shows how desperately restrictive is his framing of *The Islandman* as unmediated representation. In particular, an attentive reading of Ó Criomhthain's autobiographical form reveals a series of remarkably complicated and insightful reflections on the ways he is simultaneously constrained by a notion of folkloric "tradition" and a postcolonial subjectivity that would seek to encompass and supersede such divisions. Even as the writing of autobiography does to some degree mark a capitulation on Ó Criomhthain's part, his form consistently calls into question the regime of subjectivity upon which it rests.

At the most basic level, Ó Criomhthain frustrates the project of autobiographical representation throughout the book by generally refraining from giving voice to deep emotion or any sort of extended romantic meditation. Thus, for example, he describes the deaths of his children dispassionately and fatalistically: "Ten children were born to us, but they had no good fortune, God help us! The very first of them that we christened was only seven or eight years old when he fell over the cliff and was killed. From that time on they went as quickly as they came. Two died of measles, and every epidemic that came carried off one or other of them" (147). Ó Criomhthain's dispassionate account need not indicate a general lack of feeling on his part. He hints at deeper feeling at a number of points (198, 218, 239) but seems reluctant to give voice to it in his writing beyond simply describing that he had been troubled. The sense that there is much that Ó Criomhthain is simply not saying is underscored by his comments toward the end of the book: "I have made no secret of our good traits or of our little failings either, but I haven't told all the hardships and the agonies that befell us from time to time when our only resource was to go right on" (242). While one can read such lines as an attempt to increase the pathos of the book and the islanders' situation, one can simultaneously read them as a refusal to engage fully with a project of autobiographical representation.[18] Rather than autobiographical representation providing the most authentic or illuminating expression, Ó Criomhthain's suggestion that the only resource is "to go right on" underlines the limits of the genre and points instead toward the power of the realms of starkly unrepresentable silence.

Ó Criomhthain's reflections on the circumstances of the text's creation can be seen as further meta-autobiographical elements that militate against the elaboration of an authentic representation of the autobiographical subject. Autobiography typically exerts a reifying effect in terms of the formation of the autobiographical subject and the sense that the narrative lays the inner self of the writer before the reader. In Ó Criomhthain's case, however, the reifying effect of the book is not simply a matter of the autobiographical genre but rather its relationship to the wider reifying discourse of "tradition."

For Ó Criomhthain, the first significant figure in the process of his reification is the linguist Carl Marstrander. According to Ó Criomhthain, Marstrander attributed his interest in the Blaskets to the fact that "he had observed that the best Irish was [there]" (224). Learning from the islanders that Ó Criomhthain is the most literate and has the best Irish and English on the island, he engaged Ó Criomhthain as his teacher for first one and then two lessons a day. Ó Criomhthain obliged Marstrander at no small cost to himself and his energies:

> It was after the day's work was done that I used to go to him, for
> the nights were long at that time of year. We were fishing and I had
> a boat with another man, and that wouldn't permit me to spend
> any time in [Marstrander's] company that would interfere with the

fishing. I could only have the second sitting with him in the day-time;
but, all the same, how could I give the gentleman a refusal? I told
him I'd do my best for him. So we went at it together, and, whenever
I came in for my dinner I would go to him, and that wouldn't set me
back in my fishing for long. (224–25)

Ó Criomhthain's account makes it quite clear how much he extended
himself for Marstrander. That he is so explicit in that regard and
includes the line, "how could I give the gentleman a refusal," reveals
an abiding impression about the sacrifices he made and subtly hints
at a resentment that such heavy demands would be made upon him
when the customs of hospitality would require him to accede. The
reference to the fishing-boat arrangement marks a delicate but determined emphasis on the material conditions and social and economic
relationships that constrain Ó Criomhthain and necessarily precede
the more luxurious activity of language study with "the Norseman."[19]

Indeed, the mention of his fishing partner and the importance of
his obligation to him subtly contrasts Ó Criomhthain's regard for
others with his portrait of a more self-regarding Marstrander. Ó
Criomhthain discloses his awareness of the beginnings of his own
commodification and his distaste for the breach of manners and fel-
low-feeling this involves in typically pithy fashion: "It was just Christ-
mas Eve when he got home after leaving us. He sent yellow gold to me
when he had got home. I haven't heard anything from him for many
a long day" (225). With his brilliant talent for understatement, Ó Criomhthain comments insightfully on the ways that he and his experience are being transformed into commodities. Marstrander's relationship to him is expressible in "yellow gold." He does not "hear" from
Marstrander in any real sense.

Ó Criomhthain underscores the significance of the last line of the
passage a paragraph later when he notes that shortly afterward a letter arrives from Marstrander, "full of paper, so that I could send to
him in Norway the name of every animal on the land, of every bird
in the sky, of every fish in the sea, and of every herb that grows; with
orders that I was not to have recourse to any book, but to spell them
after my own fashion" (225). Although he receives a letter from Marstrander, it cannot be thought of as "hearing from" him as it is but
another transaction, another withdrawal from the bank of authentic Gaelic knowledge. Indeed, most of the missive consists of blank
pages. The reifying process is pushed still further by virtue of the vast
project Marstrander presents. He seeks to have Ó Criomhthain quite

literally reify the world of the Blaskets in the guise of some sort of Gaelic Adam.

Largely as a result of this contact with Marstrander, Ó Criomhthain acquires a reputation as a teacher of Irish and finds himself contending with a regular stream of pilgrims seeking Irish from a pure source. His account of the effort he has to expend on those interested in Irish reiterates the ambivalence he expresses about his sessions with Marstrander. More importantly, it calls attention to the labor involved and to its intrusion upon his other work as a fisherman and farmer: "Many people have been coming to the Island for years in quest of Irish. Most of them spent a month here. I had to spend a time in the company of each one of them, and do my own work into the bargain" (238). The frequency and duration of visits from outsiders underscore Ó Criomhthain's degree of contact with the outside world and illustrate the absurdity of construing him and the Blaskets in terms of an almost hermetically sealed zone of premodern "tradition."

Recording that the visitors come "in quest of Irish," Ó Criomhthain also makes quite explicit how he and the islanders are quite conscious of the ways that they are being framed in terms of a repository of "tradition" and how this has begun to be regularized in the form of an incipient cultural tourism. At the same time, Ó Criomhthain's emphasis on labor disrupts his own commodification and insists upon the dynamism and effort underlying the deceptively smooth surface of the reified object of "tradition." Indeed, we can see how the encounters with "tradition" are actively created rather than being mere "natural" encounters with a premodern "essence." Ó Criomhthain's framing of the sessions with the visitors as another task to be fit in alongside his other work of fishing, farming, and, indeed, writing shows how thoroughly "modern" his life is as he inhabits his multiple roles with their different rhythms and expectations. Increasingly, however, as the text itself chronicles and interrogates, Ó Criomhthain's life is overtaken by his transactions with an outside world seeking to construe him in terms of a primitive simplicity. His foregrounding of this process nonetheless separates him from the imagined figure of the Revival and "tradition" and allows the primitive consciousness itself to be subject to a modernist splitting and skepticism.

As Ó Criomhthain's reputation grows, it is not surprising that autobiography is ultimately thrust upon him. Characterizing the decision to take up the autobiography in the context of the larger pressures that had begun to build on Ó Criomhthain as a minor celebrity figure for those pursuing a direct access to "tradition," Cathal Ó Háinle strikingly remarks that "it is utterly unlikely that he would have undertaken the writing of his autobiography had he not been almost driven to it" (134). Indeed, the demand for autobiography effectively functions as an extension of the reifying task of cataloguing that Marstrander puts before him; he is finally asked to "name" himself. Thus, after spending a year in study with him, Brian Ó Ceallaigh prevails upon Ó Criomhthain to begin writing his life story.

Much in the vein of Marstrander, the project begins with a request to catalogue the events of daily life and then extends to urging Ó Criomhthain to encapsulate his entire life in text: "When [Ó Ceallaigh] had gone, I used to send him a journal every day for five years. Then nothing would satisfy him but that I should write of my own life and tell him how I had passed my days. It was never my way to refuse anybody, so I set about the job. What you're reading now, reader, is the fruit of my labours. I was putting the world past me like this for some time more; people coming in ones and twos and threes, and every one of them having his own sitting with me" (239–40). Not only does Ó Criomhthain's account emphasize the external impetus for producing the text, it clearly contextualizes the writing in terms of the "sittings" with language enthusiasts.[20] He thereby reinforces the connections between the autobiography and the burgeoning cultural phenomenon arising under the influence of the various Irish revivals of the early twentieth century that would seek to enlist the people and spaces of the Gaelic periphery in a fantasy of premodern purity that could renew a jaded modernity.

By making his autobiography an extension of his "sittings" with the wave of cultural tourists he must entertain, Ó Criomhthain highlights the ways he and it are already being read even in advance of his writing. At the same time, his inclusion of this material and account of being on the inside of this phenomenon of "tradition" operating around him conveys some measure of his own voice and perspective. We can thus see the strange intricacies of his late-modernist practice as the text and its generic imperatives are set against each other and only fulfilled in their being revealed as false impositions.

In rendering the text a "sitting," however, Ó Criomhthain also undercuts its reifying effect. Through this moment of meta-autobiography, he effectively enacts the self-consciousness of the commodity in the Lukácsian sense.[21] In so doing, Ó Criomhthain not only insists on the substance of his own labors but calls attention to those of

Marstrander, Ó Ceallaigh, and others that work *upon* him to bring forth the commodified product of *The Islandman*.

Ironically, however, by depicting its consummation, Ó Criomhthain inhibits this reifying project's ultimate success. His observations about the state of his life as he completes the autobiography present a fascinating meta-autobiographical reflection on the process of commodification of which the autobiography is a key part:

> I have another young son with me, and he has to stay around the house, for there is little good in me except in my tongue. We have neither cow nor horse, sheep nor lamb, canoe nor boat. We have a handful of potatoes and a fire. I have been twenty-seven years hard at work on this language, and it is seventeen years since the Norseman, Marstrander, came my way. Something or other comes to me now and again, one thing after another, that keeps me from starvation. I hear many an idle fellow saying that there's no use in our native tongue; but that hasn't been my experience. Only for it I should have been begging my bread! (240–41)

Ó Criomhthain's account is obviously quite arresting with his references to the continuing threat of starvation and his negative catalogue of all that he and his son lack. Despite the stark portrait, one may be tempted to read the passage as rehearsing a clichéd version of Irish poverty that is almost too perfect in its reduction of life to potatoes and fire. The vision threatens to lapse into primitivist fantasy—or nightmare—with the Gaelic savage crouched in a crude shelter on a rock in the Atlantic and wolfing down a potato as he huddles into the fire to escape the howling wind. Indeed, Ó Criomhthain approaches a sort of self-parody here in his strange mixture of poignant realism and bitter irony.

This remarkable passage is at once a statement of the very real material deprivation that Ó Criomhthain faces and a complex encoding of its relationship to the commodification of the Gael under the auspices of the primitivism of the Revival and postcolonial "tradition." Framed within the terms of primitivist fantasy, Ó Criomhthain's poverty and hardship increase his value as a literary and cultural commodity and therefore can perversely serve to ease his poverty.[22] As a result, one can detect two voices in the passage: the voice of "tradition" that frames poverty, modesty, and endurance as emblems of primitive virtue; and the voice of modernist skepticism that discloses the sophisticated consciousness of the writer forced to inhabit this figuration. Though these two voices may at first appear to be at odds, they ultimately can be seen to share a common material emphasis. The focus on material contexts that Ó Criomhthain consistently highlights over the course of the book here leads him to chart how materiality comes to transcend itself as the most pressing material realities lose their preeminence over the conventions of figuration and straitened material conditions themselves become commodities.

Ó Criomhthain deftly expresses this complex relationship between representation and a more immediate materiality through his deployment of the tongue. In his account, "tongue" is both language and body part, at once a representational system and the physical means by which signs within that system are articulated. As language and representation become Ó Criomhthain's sole means of material support, he finds himself reduced to the organs of articulation. In a grotesque metonymy, he becomes, almost literally, a disembodied talking head. He finds himself trapped between the corporeal and the representational as "tongue" slides back and forth between the two realms. Entering into the domain of representation affords him the means of staying alive in the material world.

In this regard, Ó Criomhthain's use of the tongue serves as a powerful example of Paul de Man's notion of autobiography as "de-facement."[23] In Ó Criomhthain's case, however, the violence of the defacement stands out much more in that he is compelled to disfigure himself in a desperate attempt to remain physically whole. His dating of his life from the time he started working on the language and from his meeting Marstrander clearly links this disfigurement to his status as a linguistic artifact. In a sense, he is dating the length of his reification, the gradual transmogrification into "the Islandman."

This devolution into "tongue" usefully illustrates Spivak's assertion that the subaltern cannot speak. Considering the complex workings of Ó Criomhthain's late-modernist practice, however, An tOileánach would seem to urge us to take this point further by suggesting that the subaltern is not so sealed off from these deliberations or from modernity more generally. Indeed, Ó Criomhthain's writing reveals a subaltern consciousness remarkably aware of how the subaltern is being framed by its modern contemporaries. In pushing subaltern "speech" to the limits imposed by this narrow frame and pointing to the ways in which the subaltern and her/his looming demise are commodified, Ó Criomhthain actually *does* speak in a silent tongue that pointedly defies representation.

This sense of Ó Criomhthain's relationship to language and writing may at first seem to recall Flower's construction of Ó Criomhthain as artlessly producing a text that "serv[es] no theory and aim[s] at no literary effect" (vii). The problem, however, is not with the shortcomings of Ó Criomhthain's "literary" effort but with the limits of a reading practice unable to grapple with a writing produced by those who have already been *written* as "non-literary" primitives by the literary establishment. Ó Criomhthain's charting of the commodification process that culminates in his reduction to a tongue shows his language to be constrained by his status as the primitive Gael, which makes his writing always already an "authentic" linguistic and cultural artifact of "tradition." As the authentic *source* of language, he ostensibly stands in an intrinsic relationship to language. Indeed, he ultimately becomes a sign himself as "the Islandman." Dissolving this paradigm from within as he does by revealing the limits of both "tradition" and modern subjectivity, however, Ó Criomhthain's effort is quite an important literary contribution that represents a significant advance in modernist practice in the postcolonial era.

In addition to disrupting reification by revealing the constant flurry of activity and work needed to sustain the deceptive stillness of an ostensibly timeless "tradition," Ó Criomhthain's emphasis on materiality also proves disruptive by illuminating autobiographical representation's chronic incompleteness. With the autobiography as an ongoing activity and only one job among many, it stands incapable of providing a complete portrait. Much remains outside its ambit. Thus, even as Ó Criomhthain finds himself in the sad condition of being progressively reduced to a figure of "tradition," his account of this process and the labor involved points to the vast realm that remains outside of autobiographical representation. This reminder of the incomplete and unrepresented crucially complements the portrayal of his commodification and "de-facement."

The encoding of *An tOileánach*'s status as incomplete autobiography clarifies that what Spivak refers to as "the constitution of the Other"—or of the subject—is not simply inevitable (294). More than a lamentable aspect of "progress," the elaboration of postcolonial subjectivity via "tradition" involves a conscious suppression of alternatives in the service of a particular agenda. In this case, the agenda is that of stabilizing the bourgeois regime of the postcolonial state by conveying a sense of the anticolonial revolution's completion, the idea that the periphery has finally transcended the subordination of "otherness" and thus can and should disappear into the misty realm of "tradition."

In what is perhaps the book's most famous passage, Ó Criomhthain reflects on his motivations for writing and on the likely fate of life on the Blaskets: "I have written minutely of much that we did, for it was my wish that somewhere there should be a memorial of it all, and I have done my best to set down the character of the people about me so that some record of us might live after us, for the like of us will never be again" (244). This reads, at one level, as a straightforward account of the project of autobiography with its emphasis on "set[ting] down" a "record" or "memorial" that captures and, indeed, *constitutes* a discernible, fixed self. It is not surprising, therefore, that Flower finds the passage so appealing and quotes it in his foreword (vii) as evidence of the "frankness" of the text and its connection to the imminent demise of Blasket life. In recording that connection, however, the passage also signals the extent to which Ó Criomhthain embarks on the project under significant duress and uses it as a vehicle to point to something beyond the new regime that is in the process of overtaking and effacing a distinct Blasket life.

Absence haunts Ó Criomhthain's text. Over the course of the book, this sense of absence builds from all that Ó Criomhthain does not say and all that he cannot say. As he reflects on the making of his book, that sense of absence combines with an impression of transience and things having already begun to pass away. Thus, even the straightforward account of his attempt to document and preserve Blasket life is shot through with a flickering, spectral quality.

Viewed in the light of what Ó Criomhthain shows to be outside and inassimilable to the text, Flower's celebration of the greater authenticity and artlessness conferred on Ó Criomhthain's writing by a sense of looming demise seems at once naïve and insensitive. For it is "tradition" and the regime of postcolonial subjectivity which it heralds that, in large part, doom the Blaskets. And indeed, one cannot actually construct Ó Criomhthain as being as naïve and artless as Flower does without placing him in the natural, "epic" realm that precedes subjectivity and that autobiography necessarily shatters. That is why one sees this elegiac tone running through the book and becoming increasingly evident in its final pages as Ó Criomhthain mourns something that has not yet passed. It is not simply an anticipation of a loss that is imminent but a sense of the immanence of loss in the autobiographical form itself that infuses its elegiac strains.

Therefore, when Ó Criomhthain writes, "for the like of us will never be again," he alludes at once to the changes he sees unfolding in island life—with greater emigration, different types of farming, and shifts in landholding practices—and to the prospects for alterity and life in the dark, shifting zone outside the bounds of subjectivity. His phrase itself captures the dilemma of autobiographical representation for in sketching "the like of us," Ó Criomhthain brings them within the sphere of reification and ensures they "will never be again." This most famous phrase of modern Gaelic literature thus simultaneously encodes presence and absence. As such, it wonderfully sums up Ó Criomhthain's book and its relationship to autobiography and postcolonial subjectivity. Though he is unable to resist entirely the imposition of autobiography and its accompanying regime of subjectivity, he inscribes absence so deeply that it cuts through to the very grain of the text. By insisting on the ineradicable absence adhering to autobiography and postcolonial subjectivity, Ó Criomhthain thus reveals the potential of a late modernism unable to be fully realized from his marginal position but all the more powerful and courageous for its silent witness.

Ó Criomhthain's achievement in this regard becomes more apparent as one compares his text to the other Blasket autobiographies that follow it, most notably Muiris Ó Súilleabháin's. *Fiche Blian ag Fás* clearly follows in the wake of Ó Criomhthain's work and is obviously driven by the commodification of the Gaelic subaltern already under way in the early postcolonial era. Ó Súilleabháin's autobiographical form more fully encloses the Gaelic subaltern in a simple and dying "tradition" that limits its capacity for presenting an alternative postcolonial vision. His text thus ironically underlines the success of *An tOileánach* as a text that sets out the function of subaltern autobiography within early postcolonial Irish culture and resists fully succumbing to it. In part, this highlights *An tOileánach*'s role as a transitional text. But it also compels acknowledgment of Ó Criomhthain's skill in laying bare the project of "tradition" and frustrating its full completion. With Ó Súilleabháin, the reflexivity of meta-autobiography slides into the intense self-regard of the romantic subject that is more typical of the autobiographical genre. The larger cultural function of the Blasket texts thus intensifies the more it slips beneath the surface.

Not surprisingly, Ó Súilleabháin's text is a far more commercially successful enunciation of "tradition" than Ó Criomhthain's. The fact

that Ó Súilleabháin's text is the first to appear in English translation is certainly also an important factor in this regard. In an October 1933 letter, Ó Criomhthain's son Seán Ó Criomhthain complains
bitterly about *An tOileánach*'s fate as a Gaelic text hopelessly outstripped by the *Twenty Years A-Growing* translation:

> According to our book [, *An tOileánach*], it was not very successful.
> Irish [Gaelic] books do not bring much money for Readers are scarce
> as you ought to know that. . . . There is an English translation in
> two month's time. . . . You know it should be Published long ago by
> Jonathan Cape But it took so Long and He gave it up so now it will
> be published By the Educational Co. of Ireland, Dublin. It was a great
> loss for us for O'Sullivan's book *Twenty Years A-Growing* took the
> market from us and that is the Reason Cape gave it up. Flower should
> have the translation done within nine months but he was sick and
> could not Have the work done in time. So it can't Be Helped and We
> do not Blame any Body. (Ní Shúilleabháin 24–25, nonstandard punc-
> tuation and capitalization in original)

Seán Ó Criomhthain's savvy comments about literary markets and
publishers coincide with his father's account of the commodification
of "tradition" and underscore the extent to which the construction
of the islanders as unsophisticated "primitives" is a fantasy. At the
same time, Ó Súilleabháin's greater success in navigating the shoals
of publishing and marketing his book cannot be attributed solely to
the timeliness of the English translation. Though the translation certainly makes his book more widely accessible to both an Irish and
an international audience, its autobiographical form and consistently
modern orientation play an equally crucial role in making Ó Súilleabháin's text more immediately legible to a wider audience already conditioned by the Revival.

E. M. Forster's intriguing preface to *Twenty Years A-Growing*
helps to illuminate the essentially modern character of Ó Súilleabháin's sensibility in a way that at once links it to the Revival and
shows how the legacy of the latter is being folded into the nostalgia
of "tradition." Forster notes how "Synge and others" have presented
the Gaelic periphery "from the outside" but suggests that the unique
value of *Twenty Years A-Growing* is that Ó Súilleabháin depicts it
"from the inside" (v). Indeed, in an insight that remarkably distills
the transition effected by postcolonial "tradition" and perhaps most
perfectly by Ó Súilleabháin's text, Forster describes the book in terms
of the "neolithic civilization" of the Gael "itself becom[ing] vocal,
and address[ing] modernity" (v). Forster thus reinforces the sense of

the Blaskets' profound difference with his striking construct of "neolithic civilization" even as the account of that civilization "becom[ing]
vocal, and address[ing] modernity" conveys the process of subject
formation we might associate with autobiography and the larger
national project of postcolonial integration.

Forster portrays Ó Súilleabháin as "a lively young man, who likes
dancing and the movies, and was smart at his lessons. But he is able
to keep our own world in its place, and to view it only from his own
place, and his spirit never abandons the stronghold to which, in the
final chapter, his feet will return" (v–vi). This framing of Ó Súilleabháin as one who at once "likes . . . the movies" and yet is grounded
in "the stronghold" of "his own place" marks his consciousness as
one encompassing multiple locations and temporalities in a manner
that has now become quite familiar as a result of the Revival. Even
as Ó Súilleabháin may resemble Synge in that regard, however, his
apparent comfort in integrating the two realms demonstrates how
the radical edge of Revivalist modernism has been blunted by "tradition." Forster's emphasis on the "neolithic" and the "inside" perspective of *Twenty Years A-Growing* nonetheless remind us of the
necessarily incomplete nature of this integration. As a result, Ó Súilleabháin's text ultimately reveals a late-modernist practice of its own
that parallels and affirms Ó Criomhthain's by showing how primitivist accounts of "the Gael" are constructed and commodified even
as Ó Súilleabháin refrains from the damning critique offered by his
neighbor.

Far from the incomplete autobiography of Ó Criomhthain, Ó Súilleabháin embraces autobiography and the typical romantic sensibility of the autobiographical subject. Significantly, much of his text is
taken up with events that take place away from the Blaskets. Leaving
the Blaskets to train for the police in Dublin, Ó Súilleabháin finds
himself returned to the periphery as he is posted to another *gaeltacht*
in Connemara, a quite familiar territory for the writers and readers of
the Revival. Thoroughly absorbed into modernity and the apparatus
of the postcolonial state, he returns to the Great Blasket in the final
chapter on holiday. "Holiday travel" and an allotted holiday period
from work would, of course, be inconceivable to Ó Criomhthain
and the "neolithic" life of the Blaskets. They are clearly features of
a modernity with a more defined relationship between work and leisure and signal, more profoundly, how Ó Súilleabháin would like to
mark himself as a *consumer* of the cultural tourism of the *Gaeltacht*

as much as the producer or purveyor that the book itself necessarily designates him as being.

The form of *Twenty Years A-Growing* likewise differs markedly from Ó Criomhthain's text. Ó Súilleabháin's detailed accounts of conversations and inner monologues contrast sharply with the sparse style of Ó Criomhthain. Where the older writer is reserved to the extreme, Ó Súilleabháin is confessional. Ó Súilleabháin's account of his tortured decision to follow his friend and translator George Thomson to Dublin rather than emigrate to America usefully illustrates this:

> I looked west at the edge of the sky where America should be lying, and I slipped back on the paths of thought. It seemed to me now that the New Island [of America] was before me with its fine streets and great high houses, some of them so tall that they scratched the sky; gold and silver out on the ditches and nothing to do but gather it. I see the boys and girls who were once my companions walking the street, laughing brightly and well-contented. I see my brother Shaun and my sisters Maura and Eileen walking along with them and they talking together of me. The tears were rising in my eyes but I did not shed them. . . . I was too long in silent meditation without giving an answer to my friend. What answer would I give him? Would I tell him that it would be more to my liking to go among my companions beyond than to set out for the capital city of Ireland along with him? I turned to him. He was looking south-east towards Iveragh the way I could only see his cheek. (235–36)

Such a passage would simply be impossible in *The Islandman.* The detailed recounting of his mental processes—from his imaginings to his emotions to his wavering and self-interrogation—discloses the subject in a way that Ó Criomhthain assiduously avoids and, in fact, undercuts. Moreover, the level of detail and pictorial immediacy in the passage such as in his description of Thomson in the last line extends this sense of openness and endows the account with a surprising sensuality.[24] In passages such as this throughout the text, Ó Súilleabháin endeavors to represent himself completely—or at least convey the impression of a complete representation—and sketch his development in a rich narrative style. In tracing his development in this way, he narrates the postcolonial subject into being.

In this regard, it is perhaps useful to think of the Blasket autobiographies in terms of a continuum. At one end of the continuum, Ó Criomhthain foregrounds the commodification of the Gaelic subaltern and actively seeks to undermine that process through a combination of an incomplete and meta-autobiography that highlights the artificiality of "tradition" and points toward the richness of the unrepresentable beyond the bounds of the subject. Ó Súilleabháin, as the most modern, takes his place at the continuum's far end. The passage into subjectivity is one that the narrator himself undergoes to an increasing degree over the course of the book, although the romantic sensibility is one that marks the text from the beginning.

Ó Súilleabháin's journey from the Great Blasket to Dublin rehearses this process most explicitly and clearly ties the territorial integration of the Blaskets to the elaboration of postcolonial subjectivity. Shortly after young Muiris arrives in Dingle, only some twenty miles from where he first lands with the mailboat from the Great Blasket, he is asked who he is. Ó Súilleabháin's playful responses frame his identity and emphasize the importance of language in constituting it:

> "Where did you come from?" said he, "or who are you at all?"
>
> I was surprised when I saw that he did not know me, though indeed it was long since I had been in Dingle. I went up and gave my two heels to the fire.
>
> "Faith," said I, "I am no Irishman anyway."
>
> "You are not?" said Martin in astonishment.
>
> "I am not indeed, though I have Irish blood in me."
>
> Both he and his wife were now looking at me intently.
>
> "When did you come to Ireland, so?"
>
> "Today."
>
> "And how the devil then did you pick up the fine Irish?"
>
> "Arra, my dear sir, isn't it we who have the best Irish?"
>
> "It seems so," said he, looking at me between the eyes, "but if you are not an Irishman, what are you?"
>
> "I am a Blasket man, my boy," said I. (246)

At the most basic level, this exchange functions as a comic scene of dramatic irony and clever wordplay as Ó Súilleabháin teases an old acquaintance from Dingle for failing to recognize him. It is significant, however, that it comes as he is setting out for Dublin and his training as part of the new postcolonial administration. In fact, it is the third time in a matter of hours that he must identify himself or provide some sort of credentials since arriving on the mainland. In each instance, language plays a crucial role. When seeking a certificate of identity from the parish priest in Ballyferriter at the farthest tip of the Dingle peninsula, he finds he must resort to English to make himself understood (243). Similarly, when he stops on the road to ask for directions to Dingle, he is asked if he has any English

(245). Immediately, therefore, the narrator must confront a sense of difference in terms of a rupture with the previously naturalized Gaelic world of the Blaskets. Not only is Gaelic not taken for granted in this new world, but it is indeed graded and, as Ó Súilleabháin will increasingly find on his journey inland, commodified.

At turns an asset and a liability, Ó Súilleabháin's Gaelic-language skills mark him as distinct and strange. He must determine when and how to deploy English or Irish depending on shifting circumstances. As a key element in negotiating this new status of a stranger in a strange land, Gaelic thus plays a crucial role in the development of a distinct subjectivity and Ó Súilleabháin's transformation from "Blasket man" into "Irishman."

It is striking that this process begins in the Dingle *gaeltacht* only a few miles from the Great Blasket and still obviously within the Gaelic linguistic sphere. Though his metamorphosis into postcolonial subject accelerates rapidly as Ó Súilleabháin pushes on toward Dublin and becomes more deeply entangled in the infrastructure of nation, it is important to note that it is not simply the typical modernizing forces of technology and urbanization that carry him into modernity. His encounters on the Dingle peninsula make it clear that this process finds its roots in a much deeper experience of alienation. In this way, we can also see the modernist character of Ó Súilleabháin's text and the ways in which it is bound up with the process of integration and the formation of postcolonial subjectivity.

As Ó Criomhthain shows and resists in *An tOileánach*, it is the alienation attending reification and the birth of "tradition." Already, in the Dingle *gaeltacht*, Ó Súilleabháin begins to perceive language as reified object rather than medium of expression. This perception, in turn, facilitates the emergence of a strong sense of self as individual subject and marks the onset of the new perspective of spectator. As the text continues, we see that this self-regard is crucial for the constitution of subjectivity—and postcolonial subjectivity most of all.

Ó Súilleabháin's account of Dingle shows how these complementary notions of subjectivity and "tradition" extend their hold over the farthest geographic, cultural, and linguistic reaches of the postcolonial national space. That is the essence of the project of postcolonial subjectivity: making spectators and consumers out of all, even those who would seem to perform and preserve the traditions of Irishness for the rest of the country. Indeed, it is they whom the Free State most urgently needs to make into spectators. As much as national spectacle, then, the postcolonial state must transform the Gaelic sub-altern into national *spectator* in order for its project of national integration to take hold.

Ó Súilleabháin's account of his passage through the provincial railway stations of Kerry and Cork strikingly illustrates this process. To his eye—and ear—the bustle and hubbub of Tralee amply signify how distinct modern Ireland is from the Gaelic world of the Blaskets it would venerate. It is, of course, quite telling that Ó Súilleabháin must rely almost entirely on English to make use of the technologies of transportation and communication that bind Ireland together in the "homogenous, empty time" of the modern nation and facilitate his pilgrimage to the capital.[25] As he navigates his way through the various offices, stations, platforms, and cars or tries to send a telegram to Dublin, he finds that practically the only use for his Gaelic is to amuse himself with the quizzical looks that meet his occasional Gaelic remarks and insults (252).

This sardonic deployment of Gaelic coincides with his insightful observations about its ironic status as a tongue at once so sought after and so devalued by the mainlanders. Significantly, it is that more than anything else that would seem to underline the modernity of the people and space of the nation constituted by the crowd in the Tralee station:

> Great God of Virtues, the chatter and gabble of the people! And not a word of Irish to be heard! I don't know in the world what brings strangers into the Blasket to learn Irish, for so far as I can see, when they come back to this place after leaving the Island they have it thrown under foot. Look at myself now? What would I do if there was not a word of English on my lips? Wouldn't I be a public show? Where is the man or woman would give me an answer? Will the day ever come when Irish will be poured out here as English is poured out today? I doubt it.
>
> Those are the thoughts which were passing through my mind; no thought of the train or of Dublin, but yielding to the sight of my eyes, the rush and the roar, the chatter and laughter, the welcoming one with another, big fat bucks of men along with lean and lanky spindle-shanks, and the women likewise. (255)

Ó Súilleabháin thus shows himself acutely aware of the extent to which Gaelic and the Gaelic subaltern register as spectacle within the postcolonial nation. His awareness of that and his deflection of Gaelic from the function of "public show" to secret mockery illustrate how he moves from spectacle to spectator. His observation of the crowd and his own autobiographical observation of himself observing the crowd amplify his status as spectator and serve to embed him more deeply in the complementary regimes of subjectivity and surveillance. Though this is a defensive maneuver on Ó Súilleabháin's part to take account of his situation and seize the power of the gaze, it draws him inexorably into the modern dominion and again reveals some of the ways that his late-modernist practice coincides with Ó Criomhthain's.

Set in motion during his passage through Dingle and Tralee, this embrace of spectatorship intensifies as Ó Súilleabháin continues his journey to the Dublin metropole. Modern spaces and technologies become increasingly relevant aspects of the process of subject formation and postcolonial integration. Treating us to a typically modern account of the experience of train travel, Ó Súilleabháin reveals the important role it plays in the framing of his newly emerging perspective of spectator:

> I was soon deep in thought, looking out through the window at the fields and valleys which were darting by, and looking at the people, wondering who they were, where they had come from, or what business had taken them from home to send them rushing through the middle of Ireland. I sat meditating on the world. Look, it is many a thought comes to the man who goes alone. With the power of his mind he brings the great world before his face, a thing which is not possible for the man who is fond of company. I believe it is in solitude that every machine and work of ingenuity was created. (258)

Ó Súilleabháin, here, becomes the spectator *par excellence* as he surveys the countryside from his locomotive perch and bears witness to the territorial cohesion of the nation in his move from periphery to "middle." More importantly, he sees himself in comparison to the other travelers. Though they occupy the same space and share an experience that is largely the same, they do not in any sense constitute "company." Each remains an entity onto itself. Ó Súilleabháin, likewise, maintains his separateness and finds himself alone in the midst of a crowd. Subjectivity thus takes hold through immersion in the mass; proximity without community or rootedness yields a new sense of self. Most remarkably, Ó Súilleabháin draws a connection between this newfound isolation and creativity, thereby linking subjectivity with representation. Considered in the context of autobiography, this makes particular sense. Ó Súilleabháin is simply narrating how he becomes his own spectacle by means of his constitution as spectator.

The larger implications of this awareness for Gaelic alterity and the fate of the Blaskets become clear as the journey continues. Summoning his newly invigorated creative power, Ó Súilleabháin blends the "duga-ga-dug, duga-ga-dug" sound of the train with his memory of the "glug-glag" of the water rippling on the sides of the curraghs as the Blasket fishermen row out with their nets and hear the "cág-cág-cág" of the gulls wheeling overhead (268–69). Through imaginative onomatopoeia, Ó Súilleabháin merges two kinds of modern travel: mechanized long-distance mass transportation and the modern mind's slide among multiple temporalities and locations. Indeed, when considered in the broader context of subject formation and a voyage into modernity, we can see how the latter sort of travel where one simultaneously occupies multiple sites is an almost inevitable product of advanced transportation technologies such as rail travel.

This moment is similar to the earlier one where Ó Súilleabháin is discussing his options with Thomson and imagining New York's skyscrapers and its gold-laden ditches. A crucial difference here, however, is that Ó Súilleabháin actually has direct experience of all the different places and times that now flow together to fill his mind. Thus, although both passages are similarly modern in their detailed account of his mental processes, this latter passage illustrates how far Ó Súilleabháin has already crossed over into modernity. For now, rather than the fanciful accounts of America, he presents detailed portraits of the different realms he has passed through, most notably that of the Blaskets. Life on the Blaskets has passed into elegiac spectacle that he, as modern subject, can conjure up and manipulate at will. As he writes: "I shut my eyes close and soon the village appeared in perfect likeness before my face, for 'with eager desire I was making my fullest endeavour to see my love,' as the poet said long ago. So great is the power of the solitary man" (269). Proceeding to lay out a vision of the Blaskets and the islanders' activities in the present tense, Ó Súilleabháin shows how fully they have been drawn into the domain of representation.

By the time Ó Súilleabháin arrives in Dublin, then, he has already passed through the terminus of modernity. Though Dublin certainly immerses him more deeply in modern life with its size, technologies, and cosmopolitan air, his experiences in the city do not work any fundamental changes upon him; they only confirm the shift in ideas and perspective effected by his journey. Thus, going to the cinema (276–77) reinforces his status as spectator but cannot ultimately compare with the impact of the visions that have already passed before his mind's eye in the railway carriage. Similarly, when he enters the police force and begins his training, he finds that Gaelic serves a mostly ornamental function consisting primarily of the recruits being expected to respond "Annso!" (sic) or "Here" during roll call (286). This orientation toward Gaelic is significant in that the Guard is an institution of the postcolonial state. It therefore suggests a certain discontinuity between the deployment of "tradition" by the Free State and a true embrace of the Gaelic subaltern. The state is interested in the *performance* of Gaelicness but only as it is mediated through the scrim of spectatorship. This relationship to Gaelic is one that Ó Súilleabháin had already begun to grasp, however, even before leaving Kerry.

When Ó Súilleabháin departs Dublin to take up duty policing the countryside, he has not undergone significant further transformation. The difference between the moment of departure and that of his arrival in the capital is simply that he has become a spectator for the state. In that role, he is both an agent of surveillance and an embodiment of the subaltern alienation required under the regime of "tradition" fostered by the Free State. Not surprisingly, then, Ó Súilleabháin finds himself assigned to the Connemara *gaeltacht* in Galway. For there he can serve the dual purposes of monitoring the Gaelic-speaking population and modeling its assimilation within the postcolonial nation.[26] Placing someone from the Blaskets in Connemara suggests a certain Gaelic interchangeability and furthers the logic of a single shared "tradition." At the same time, the fact that he is an outsider reduces the chances of local interests being put ahead of those of the state; it conveys the sense that the "untamed" *Gaeltacht* is no longer a community unto itself. The Gaelic subaltern must accept the spectator within, and "the Gael" must give way to the modern subject of "Irishman" and "Irishwoman."

Ó Súilleabháin's train journey to his Connemara posting usefully illustrates this process. Changing trains in the west, he finds himself sharing a compartment with two "bauneen men" wearing the cream-colored wools of Connemara and speaking Gaelic (293). Taking note of Ó Súilleabháin's uniform, the bauneens identify him with external state authority and assume he does not know Gaelic. In response to his companion's observation that it is unlikely that "the peeler" has any Gaelic, the second bauneen replies: "How would he? Who has Irish but the wretches of the world?" (293). They thus begin talking about him openly—speculating that he has come in search of illegal *poitín* liquor and complaining more generally about the number of police that plague them. All the while, Ó Súilleabháin pretends to read a book and appear unaware of what is being discussed. When they arrive at the station, however, he speaks to them in Gaelic and observes that they must be from Connemara. Having been caught in their comments about the police, the bauneens curse him mildly and note in what ends up sounding like a strange echo of Synge how "no one can be trusted these days on road or on path" (294). The incident ultimately reads as one of gentle fun, however, with the lack of hard feeling signaled by the bauneen men's saving Ó Súilleabháin from accidentally leaving his bag.

Ó Súilleabháin's trick on the bauneens reverses the trickery of his earlier "inbound" journey to Dublin where he was secretly mocking those who did not know Gaelic. This reversal reveals how definitively and assuredly Ó Súilleabháin now occupies the position of spectator. His comment to the bauneens about their being from Connemara must thus also be read as a mild threat or warning. As the bauneen men learn to their chagrin, there is no more refuge for "the wretches of the world" in the obscurity of their wretchedness. With the rise of an integrative postcolonial subjectivity, they are not only more subject to state scrutiny but have become the agents of their own surveillance. For it is not just that the state has drafted native Gaelic speakers who can more effectively surveil the *Gaeltacht*. The train trips to and from Dublin illustrate that the shift for the Gaelic subaltern is not simply a result of something that happens *in* the metropolis or of state authority that emanates *from* the capital. As Ó Súilleabháin's parallel journeys reveal, the transformation occurs "in the middle" as the subaltern contends with a new surveillance and spectatorship out of which each must negotiate her/his subjectivity.

The benevolent aspect of this process is, of course, key to integrating the postcolonial state's surveillance within its regime of postcolonial subjectivity. It is not simply a matter of being surveilled from the outside or even of being spied upon by an insider in the employ of outside authorities. It is more a question of the alienation that attends the entry into subjectivity. In the case of Ó Súilleabháin and Connemara, we can see how the notion of interchangeability enables the introduction of a "Gael" who is strange in dress and dialect and who clearly stands outside of the community. As a result, the residents of the Connemara *gaeltacht* see a "Gaelicness" that is external to them and is, in fact, watching them. They thereby acquire the new perspective of spectators of "Gaelicness." This experience robs "Gaelicness" of its alterity and redeploys it as a ground of "tradition" for the coalescent postcolonial nation. We can see the early moments of this process with Ó Súilleabháin's first forays into Dingle and the Kerry interior. Its end result can be seen in his perspective on Connemara.

Just as the "gentleness" of his trickery with the bauneens relies on a simultaneous assertion of identification and difference, his reaction to his new Connemara surroundings arises from the same mix. Thus, walking along the road from the train station, he observes, "Faith, . . . I am among the Gaels again. Isn't it well they are keeping up the old ways—the costume, the language and the houses" (295). Ó Súilleabháin has come to speak as an outsider who has much experience of "the Gael" but is not himself one of them. "Ways" that had been normal practice to him just a short time before on the Blasket have now become "old" and consciously "kept up."[27] This distanced vision of "the Gael" and "tradition" marks the final stage in Ó Súilleabháin's development as spectator of the Gaelic subaltern.

As we evaluate Ó Súilleabháin's movement toward modernity and the nostalgia of "tradition," however, we must be careful not to underestimate the richness of his text. He does not simply concede to the sentimentality and condescension of those who would celebrate the quaintness of Blasket life and grow blissfully misty-eyed over its demise. His portrait does more justice to himself and his fellow islanders and offers much deeper insight into this crucial moment of transition for the Blaskets and for the nation. We thus read *Twenty Years A-Growing* most honestly as an account of the subaltern's succumbing to postcolonial subjectivity. It is not ultimately a celebration of modernity's triumph, not even in that most insidious and conniving guise of elegy and regret.

Ó Súilleabháin's achievement in striking such a delicate balance becomes particularly apparent as we consider what was made of his work by the hand of another. Some years after *Twenty Years A-Growing* was published as a book, Dylan Thomas rewrote it as a film script. Though he draws heavily on material from Ó Súilleabháin's text, Thomas offers a dramatically different vision of the Blaskets. The narrating voice of Ó Súilleabháin that Thomas inserts as voice-over throughout the script *is* the voice of modern sentimentalizing elegy that remains so notably absent in Ó Súilleabháin's writing. With his theatrical use of Gaelic (15, 16, 27, 33) and his presentation of "cloudy, immemorial peasant figures" (35), Thomas proffers a representation of the Blaskets that is the epitome of an elite modern conceit. The Great Blasket takes on the aspect of a quasi-mythical "land of the young" inhabited by naïve and happy peasants tragically doomed to imminent obliteration by modern "progress."

Thomas displays his tendency toward condescension and caricature most clearly in the synopsis he provides at the end of his script. Here, he casts Ó Súilleabháin's friend George Thomson as the one who "announces the beginning of doubt [and] introduces into the idyllic timelessness of the island the first sound of the time-bound outer world and the first suggestion of adult responsibility" (90). Thomas insists, however, that Thomson must be portrayed sympathetically: "[H]e is not the serpent in the garden but the voice of the world beyond the Blasket horizon. He is the voice that is heard in all man's growing up. 'There is a world beyond your own,' that voice has always said" (90). Against this, Thomas suggests, Muiris's character will put forth "the ageless argument for the dignity and beauty of life in the small peasant community" even as he begins to realize "that the life of small peasant communities is noble and suffering, dignified and poor, beautiful and bitter" (90, 90–91). Faced with this, Thomas asks in his synopsis, "[S]hall he go into the wide, unknown world, forsaking his tradition?" (91).

In the world of Thomas's script, Muiris's innocence remains intact, however, and he decides not to leave the island, hearkening instead to his grandfather, "the enduring figure, the eternal peasant" (91). As a result, according to Thomas, "He faces poverty, privation, labour and loneliness; he faces a life without Mauraid [his emigrating love-interest] and without help; but he is sure" (91). Thomas's rapturous fetishizing of the "eternal peasant" presents an exaggeration of the Revivalist fantasy of the Gaelic periphery dilated for the Hollywood screen. Though the troubling characteristics of Thomas's portrayal are quite evident, it is nonetheless worth noting both for the light its exaggerations shed on the more delicate and complex figurations of the Gaelic periphery offered by the Revival and for its contrast with the postcolonial elaboration of "tradition" by Ó Súilleabháin, which depends on the figure of Muiris leaving the island.

By means of his heavy-handed paean to peasantry, Thomas inadvertently illuminates the late-modernist aspect of Ó Súilleabháin's rendering and clarifies how its sensitive and thoughtful account of crossing modernity's threshold makes Ó Súilleabháin's text a worthy complement of An tOileánach. Ó Súilleabháin offers the itinerary of a passage that Tomás Ó Criomhthain had long anticipated and long resisted. Though the more thoroughgoing modernness of Ó Súilleabháin's treatment of the Blaskets contrasts sharply with Ó Criomhthain's in both content and form, both ultimately partake of some of the same spirit. For, in different ways, both writers point to a life outside of representation beyond modernity's edge.

Emerging in the midst of significant political turbulence and transition, the early Blasket texts illustrate the profundity of the shift that has taken place in postcolonial Irish culture over the first decade of independence and that will, in turn, set the stage for the fierce battles over "tradition" to come in the 1930s and 1940s. As we consider what this means for the development of modern literary form, we can see how these writers who have long lingered on the margins of literature offer a forgotten link in the history of Irish modernism that at once illuminates the legacy of the Revival and shows how the aftermath of empire brings key aspects of an earlier modernist practice to crisis from within.

CHAPTER TWO

Sean O'Faoláin and the End of Republican Realism

With good reason, a wide array of scholars tend to view Sean O'Faoláin as the overarching figure of the first generation of Irish writers coming to maturity in the wake of the Irish Civil War and the establishment of the Irish Free State. Whether as editor of the *Bell*, animating force within Yeats's Irish Academy of Letters, or irrepressible commentator and polemicist on a wide range of Irish cultural, literary, and political affairs, O'Faoláin serves as a social, professional, or intellectual nexus for a staggering array of Irish writers and thinkers in the early decades of Irish postcoloniality, from Bowen to Behan to Beckett and quite literally almost everyone in between. Indeed, it is difficult to find Irish writers or thinkers who emerge from the 1930s onward without engaging with O'Faoláin or his work in some way. Though he is perhaps best known for his short stories and his editing of the remarkable journal the *Bell* during the 1940s, he remains an extraordinarily prolific writer over some fifty years, producing a wide variety of prose that includes novels, stories, criticism, biographies, histories, travel narrative, and drama.

Despite his large body of work and publication in a variety of journals on both sides of the Atlantic that included important modernist venues such as Eliot's *Criterion* and Scott-James's *London Mercury* along with others like the *Yale Review* and *Virginia Quarterly*, O'Faoláin now scarcely registers within modernist studies, and few scholars working outside of a specifically Irish focus will likely have any familiarity with him. Within Irish studies, O'Faoláin has largely been reduced to a placeholder in recent debates over the legitimacy of colonial analyses of Irish history, literature, and culture. As a result, the breadth of his work has received comparatively little critical attention from scholars over the past twenty-five years and his contributions to the emergence of a distinctly postcolonial vision of late-modernist writing have not been fully appreciated.

Especially neglected have been O'Faoláin's earlier writings, which offer extensive reflections on questions of modern literary form. O'Faoláin's criticism from the early 1930s at once considers the shifts under way in Irish literature in the aftermath of the nationalist revolution and frames the work of the first generation of postcolonial writers in relation to a much broader history of European literary form. He thus positions his own work and that of his fellow Irish writers as coming not just in the wake of Joyce and the Revival but also in the wake of British and French literatures whose sweep from the nineteenth century onward he sees charting the consolidation of an integrated capitalist modernity increasingly defined by what he refers to in a 1934 essay as "machines for producing uniformity" ("Plea" 192–93).

Such insistence on apprehending Irish postcolonial writing in terms of international literary contexts and a response to the coalescence of capitalist modernity roughly align O'Faoláin's vision with the typical outlines of modernism's larger project. At the same time, O'Faoláin's critiques of both Joyce and the Revival signal an effort to develop a radically new aesthetic capable of superseding a persistent affinity for objectification and detachment that he finds marring the more established practices of Irish modernism. He diagnoses this tendency in terms of naturalist features that to his view adhere in different ways to Joyce's work and the primitivist constructions of Revival writers. In their place, O'Faoláin seeks to articulate the bases for a literature responsive to the new political and social realities of Irish postcoloniality and attuned to the ways that the emergence of the postcolonial partakes of a larger moment in the unfolding of a reconfigured global modernity.

O'Faoláin thus becomes the leading advocate of an Irish postcolonial realism that in a broad sense comes to define the literature of the early postcolonial period. Indeed, O'Faoláin's daughter, Julia—herself an accomplished novelist—notes that her father returned to Ireland in 1933 charged to "be its Balzac" (21) by no less a figure than Edward Garnett, who had shepherded the early careers of Joseph Conrad and D. H. Lawrence. Indeed, it is the prospect for a realist aesthetic and the failure to establish its viability in the postcolonial Irish literature he was helping to define that ultimately constitutes one of the most abiding themes of O'Faoláin's work as a novelist, historical biographer, and literary magazine editor in the late-modernist era of the 1930s and 1940s.

This turn toward a realist mode contributes to a sense among many readers that most of the writing—and especially the fiction—produced by this first generation of postcolonial Irish writers was—at least formally—uninspired or even retrograde. In this regard, Terence Brown, one of the most authoritative historians of twentieth-century Irish culture and literature, succinctly renders the prevailing critical view of O'Faoláin and his impact in his 1995 essay "Ireland, Modernism, and the 1930s":

> O'Faoláin was determined to be true to that common life [that O'Faoláin had described Yeats as living "a foot or two, or more" above] and to employ realism as the instrument of his integrity. In rejecting the idealism of Yeats and his confederates, O'Faoláin and others who shared his post-revolutionary disillusionment also . . . rejected the forms in which that idealism had . . . most readily expressed itself—saga, heroic narrative, translated antique text, folklore and myth. . . . It was as if the challenge to realism effected by both the Revival writers and the modernist movement had not taken place. (37–38)

Considered in terms of a singular British literary history that runs from classic Victorian earnestness to the purposeful anachronisms of the Revival and the Pre-Raphaelites that in turn lead to the more radical fragmentations of high modernism, Brown's perspective on O'Faoláin's embrace of realism as a backward leap makes a certain sense. As one takes into account O'Faoláin's sophisticated treatments of the history of literary form, however, a claim like "it was as if the challenge to realism . . . and the modernist movement had not taken place" needs to be viewed with more suspicion.

Considering his effort to develop a postcolonial realism as a project informed by an ongoing engagement with the history and politics of literary form rather than a more naïve application of political principle, we can begin to see how O'Faoláin's work shows postcolonial Irish writing to be constituted from the convergence of multiple literary histories. This understanding of Irish postcolonial literature and form integrates the more "standard" British literary history of late-Victorian and modernist writing with other European strains and with an awareness of the striking gaps and divergences that distinguish Irish literary history from this broader current. Most important for appreciating O'Faoláin's approach is the glaring *lack* of a nineteenth-century Irish realist tradition. As a result, the effort to bring forth a postcolonial realism in the 1930s means something quite different in an Irish context than a British one and can be seen to arise from a particularly attentive reading of literary history rather than a neglect or willful ignoring of its lessons. Similarly, the huge political and cultural shifts within postrevolutionary Irish society mean that forms and aesthetics that carried a radical charge during the first decades of the twentieth century may resonate differently within a postcolonial context as evidenced by the way that the legacy of the Revival is overtaken by the bourgeois nostalgia of "tradition." At the same time, to the extent that O'Faoláin perceives the emergence of Irish postcoloniality in relation to broader shifts in European and global history, we can see how a reassessment of his realist project is important not simply for the new understandings of Irish literature it can yield but for what it suggests about the impact of postcoloniality on the development of modernist form more generally.

Thus, rather than a naïve aesthetic that would seem to arise in ignorance of the seismic artistic and intellectual shifts that had preceded it, O'Faoláin's postcolonial realism constitutes at once a critique of mainline modernism and an alternative late-modernist practice. His primary critique of the two main strands of Irish modernism as represented by the Yeatsian Revival and Joyce—at least up to and including *Ulysses*—is that both in different ways end up producing a false sense of completeness. With the Revival, the problem arises from its tendency toward primitivism and investments in a Symbolist-derived universality, whereas with Joyce the problem arises from a surfeit of detail endowed with meaning by a mythic framework and an alienated modern subjectivity. From O'Faoláin's perspective, this results in both of the major historical formations within Irish modernist writing being overtaken by a strong naturalist tendency to which their modernist aesthetics might in many ways be seen to be opposed.

This ascendance of naturalism constitutes part of a larger historical phenomenon of capitalist modernity that O'Faoláin sees affecting modern literary form as a whole and that he hopes to disrupt through a new mode of realism. Though for the most part O'Faoláin's realism coincides politically with a more classic nineteenth-century realist aesthetic, especially as framed by the famous account of Georg

Lukács, O'Faoláin's approach notably departs from what Naomi Schor labels "Hegel's organicist ideal" underwriting "the aesthetic contract binding the part and the whole" (59). Though O'Faoláin is interested in tracing dynamic relationships between "the part and the whole," he seeks to do so in ways that ultimately unsettle a sense of totality rather than affirm its organic coherence. This is what marks O'Faoláin's postcolonial realism as a distinct late-modernist initiative that departs from a more familiar nineteenth-century version. Driven at once by his sympathy for modernist dissolution of bourgeois social and aesthetic norms and by his opposition to what he sees as the arrest of the anticolonial revolution by the Irish Free State, O'Faoláin seeks to develop a realism that can negate the pull toward naturalism that he sees afflicting the primary expressions of modernism and at the same time draw on modernism's aesthetic energies and critical orientation to reveal the dynamic clash of forces animating the modest materials of the everyday. In its emphasis on a dissolution of the quotidian, O'Faoláin's realism is thus closer to the sensibilities and objectives of a Joycean modernism than those of a more straightforwardly "non-modernist" realism or unreflective naturalism with which critics such as Brown would seek to associate it.

O'Faoláin's concept of realism does not work to sustain a vision of a solid materiality but, ironically, reveals how the materiality of "common life" is chronically incomplete, constantly in flux, and incapable of being definitively apprehended. Profoundly disappointed in the results of the Irish nationalist revolution and animated by a sense of the ongoing necessity for disrupting an atmosphere of political and aesthetic arrest in the postcolonial era, O'Faoláin does not permit himself the more typically modernist move of a mythic or aesthetic resolution that might sustain an effect of final mastery or a more rounded closure. His realism instead compels us to consider the dynamism lingering beneath the seemingly most stereotyped, rigid, and familiar figures of modern Irish culture.

O'Faoláin's more ragged realism can thus be understood as a late-modernist practice that dissolves the stability of bourgeois solidity more effectively and subversively from within so that the fluidity of material reality appears more inherent and inevitable rather than the product of a dizzying artistic alchemy. Its reflection on the naturalism of the earlier modernist modes and its ironic redeployment of material emphases as a means of countering their naturalist effect likewise mark it as a late-modernist practice by virtue of its reflexivity.

The keen awareness of the history of narrative form demonstrated in O'Faoláin's critical writing reinforces all of this still further by showing his realism to be consciously and anachronistically deployed in a way that cannily undermines the straightforward and "naïve" quality that most critics attribute to it. As the intricate structure of his first novel, *A Nest of Simple Folk*, illustrates, O'Faoláin precisely arranges the elements of his realist practice so as to establish strategic contrasts with the various modes of naturalism he seeks to displace.

The distinction between realism and naturalism is crucial to understanding O'Faoláin's intervention. As Brown's earlier account illustrates, the term "realism" is often used rather loosely in critical discussions of O'Faoláin and his generation to signal a departure from Revivalist portrayals of a mythic past. "Realism" in this overly broad sense connotes a turn from the realm of faeries and flaming swords to those of "facts." As O'Faoláin's early critical essays consistently show, however, he views an unreflective immersion in "fact" as the signature of a naturalist aesthetic that he rejects and, indeed, seeks to interrupt. His approach can thus be better understood as a modification of an earlier nineteenth-century version of classic realism that precedes the rise of naturalism and is marked by a sense of revolutionary possibility rather than the modern capitalist vision of an overwhelming world of objects that frames the latter.

The political resonances of O'Faoláin's realism in the early postcolonial era provide an important means for tracing the revolutionary character of his aesthetic and his sense of its role within a wider historical framework. Most immediately in an Irish context, the vision of historical dynamism and an unsettled materiality aligns O'Faoláin's realism with a left-republican perspective that would see the Irish Free State as an illegitimate or incomplete product of the anticolonial revolution both in terms of its acceptance of Northern partition and its failure to address the profound material disparities within Irish society. Opposition to the Free State had, of course, erupted most searingly during the Irish Civil War of 1922–23, and the unresolved divisions that persisted meant the new state placed a premium on cultural and political expressions of stability, as the discussion in chapter 1 of the Blasket texts and "tradition" helps to illustrate.

Anxiety about governmental stability and particular uneasiness about the activities of the IRA continue to pervade the political atmosphere, however, even after the election in 1932 of a Fianna Fáil government led by Éamon de Valera, the symbolic leader of the

Republicans defeated in the Civil War and the repository of many republicans' political hopes in its aftermath. Indeed, many leading members of the new government had fought against Free State forces in the Civil War only a decade earlier, as had O'Faoláin himself, serving for some time as director of publicity for the Republicans as well as having filled more modest roles in and around Cork.[1] Disappointment with de Valera's embrace of "tradition" and his effective reliance on the bourgeois interests that republicanism had long opposed provides a key basis for most of O'Faoláin's writing during the long period of 1932–48 that de Valera's Fianna Fáil party remains in power. While a republican orientation thus constitutes a crucial underpinning for his realist project and its place within Irish cultural politics, its vision of a more radical postcolonial nationalism also helps to clarify how O'Faoláin posits a postcolonial framework as an important means for articulating an alternative account of an emergent global modernity.

The increasing pessimism about such an effort and growing doubts about the viability of a postcolonial realist aesthetic that mark O'Faoláin's writing by the late 1940s help, in turn, to frame the late-modernist character of his early work and underscore its relationship to a particular phase of postcoloniality whose end coincides with that of the modernist era as a whole. Though the end of the modernist era can obviously be dated in a number of ways, the most salient factors to consider in this instance would be the broad geopolitical and economic shifts in the wake of the Second World War that lay the groundwork for the more wholesale replacement of the structures of empire by those of multinational capital.

O'Faoláin comments quite presciently on these shifts in a series of editorials for the *Bell* toward the end of the war as he warns against the emergence of "Imperialism . . . under a new guise" of new multinational alignments and holds out the prospect of a more progressive postcolonial nationalism as a productively discrepant force in the new global order.[2] As he comes to see his left-republican vision of Irish postcoloniality effectively smothered beneath a bourgeois official nationalism tacking to align itself with these wider global currents, though, O'Faoláin reluctantly acknowledges the failure of his postcolonial realist project and his wider effort to resist the relentless tide of naturalism. Viewed historically, however, the ultimate failure of O'Faoláin's experiment in realism can itself help to illuminate our understanding of modern literary form and the aftermath of empire as much in the ways that it highlights the contours of two distinct moments in Irish postcoloniality as in the ways it helps explain the formal tendencies produced by each.

An appreciation of the fundamental break in O'Faoláin's aesthetic orientation at midcentury helps to clarify the bases of two key strands in late twentieth-century Irish literature. On the one hand, we can more easily see Beckett's work—and especially his remarkable postwar novel "trilogy"—as addressing a fundamental shift in the nature of postcoloniality and its relationship to the new global and material orders that will come to undergird postmodernity. At the same time, the late-modernist aspect of O'Faoláin's experiment in realism "before the break" shows Beckett's thought to be less discontinuous with his generation of postcolonial Irish writers than it typically is presented as being even as that gap will grow significantly as the century unfolds. On the other hand, to the extent that O'Faoláin's critical writing from the end of 1949 onward provides the primary intellectual framework for the development of a more robust and distinguished tradition of naturalism in Irish literature during the second half of the century, as Joe Cleary has convincingly argued in *Outrageous Fortune* (146–54), we can see how this burgeoning postwar naturalist aesthetic stems in no small part from a frustrated republican critique rather than the more general hostility to nationalism, with which it tends to be identified.

In this regard, we can see how a reexamination of O'Faoláin's contributions to the leading literary periodicals and debates of the early decades of Irish postcoloniality can provide important new insights about the trajectories of Irish intellectual and aesthetic history in addition to illuminating larger questions about the relationship between postcoloniality and modernist literary form. Though O'Faoláin now tends to be viewed as the key critical forerunner of a broad antinationalist critique that acquires a particular prominence in Irish studies under the rubric of "revisionism" in the 1980s and 1990s, a careful consideration of the experiment in realism that drove his efforts in multiple genres of writing during the first two decades of his career shows that he sought to develop a form that could advance a critique of official nationalism from within nationalist thought itself.[3] Indeed, the persistence of what I am calling O'Faoláin's aesthetic of republican realism over the first quarter century of Irish postcoloniality reminds us how richly contested the cultural expression of Irish nationalism remains during this period.

Most considerations of republicanism in this era understandably tend to focus on the IRA both in terms of its internal politics and the pressing issues of internment and the proclaiming of the IRA as an illegal organization. As O'Faoláin is known to have been critical of the IRA and dismissive of its attempts to impose military discipline via courts-martial, contemporary scholars generally tend to place him entirely outside a republican ambit by the time his writing career had begun in earnest in the 1930s.[4] Such narrowly defined understandings of republicanism and O'Faoláin's relationship to it as an intellectual, cultural, and social force ultimately obscure and distort key features of the era's critical discourse, however. As Nicholas Allen has recently argued, the rise to power of de Valera and Fianna Fáil and their shifting policies over the 1930s significantly complicate what "republican" means in this period (168). The Spanish Civil War likewise lends a new urgency to republicanism in Ireland as do the alternative initiatives from within the IRA ranks such as those posed by leftists like Peadar O'Donnell, George Gilmore, and Frank Ryan. Most notable in this regard is the abortive 1934 effort to organize the Republican Congress as a leftist republican organization that could draw from IRA supporters but be independent of an unsympathetic IRA leadership.

Indeed, O'Faoláin's own writings mark one of the earliest efforts to contest the institutionalization of republicanism in the immediate aftermath of the Irish Civil War. Maurice Harmon notes in his biography how O'Faoláin objected in October 1924 to any sentimentalizing of republicanism and insisted that it must instead define itself in terms of a robust engagement with the problems and cultural realities of the day: "The reiteration of principles, he declared, was unnecessary, the reiteration of propaganda offensive. The people needed facts. They needed Reason and Intellect. One could read *Sinn Fein* for a long time and not realize that Republicanism was an intellectual movement" (62).

This understanding of republicanism as an intellectual movement opposed at once to a sentimental or mythic apprehension of nationalism and to a command culture ensconced in the institutions of either the Free State *or* the IRA is one that continues to mark O'Faoláin's thinking and writing until the end of the 1940s. Harmon defines O'Faoláin's political orientation at the beginning of the 1930s as "midway between the extreme Republican stand of those who wanted to continue the protest against the Treaty in arms and the constitutional policy of De Valera" (*Critical Introduction* 33). The simultaneous rejection of physical force and the fatally compromised republicanism of de Valera underscores the complex and multifarious nature of republican thought and politics in this era. As O'Faoláin's writings and associations illustrate, however, such positions should not be taken as rejections of either nationalism or republicanism since he continues to champion both until the end of his editorship of the *Bell* in 1946. Rather, they are reminders of the extent to which these terms and their implications remain vigorously contested in ways that our own more contemporary debates have tended to blur and reduce.

Given his close association with Peadar O'Donnell and ongoing castigation of de Valera for having ironically consolidated the bourgeois counterrevolution of the Free State founders whom de Valera himself had so famously opposed, it is not surprising that O'Faoláin initially joined in the effort of the left-republican journal *Ireland To-Day*, founded in 1936 by the former high-ranking IRA officer Jim O'Donovan.[5] Frank Shovlin notes that the project was largely driven by the energies of a group of disaffected republicans frustrated at once by de Valera and by the institutional forces of the IRA that had effectively blocked the effort to develop the leftist Republican Congress (68–69). Even as O'Faoláin's sympathies aligned him with the *Ireland To-Day* project, his quarrels with O'Donovan and withdrawal from the editorial staff after only a few issues highlight the particular nature of O'Faoláin's republicanism and his objections to adhering to what he perceived as an unhealthy IRA mentality.

Shovlin notes that letters to O'Donovan in late 1936 indicate that O'Faoláin was repulsed by the IRA shootings in Cork and Wexford that summer that gave de Valera cause to reimpose the ban on the IRA as an illegal organization. As Shovlin suggests, the shootings "had convinced [O'Faoláin] even further of the political and moral bankruptcy of [the IRA]" (79). O'Faoláin's intimate knowledge of the brutality of the notorious "Black and Tan" era of the Irish War of Independence and the dark days of the Civil War combined with his sense that the IRA leadership lacked a viable social or political program caused him to recoil from such violence as falsely romanticized acts with no political purpose or moral legitimacy.[6]

In addition to a general reluctance to sanction or romanticize violence, however, an important basis for his rejection of physical-force republicanism would seem to be his distrust of a military command structure and its concomitant tendency toward organizational secrecy and hostility to open debate. O'Faoláin writes to O'Donovan that such unquestionable lethal authority could just as easily be turned against either of them: "You know these chaps. I know them. We worked and fought with them. They'd plug you or me in two seconds in a moment of hysteria" (qtd. in Shovlin 79). Revealingly, in a subsequent letter to O'Donovan two months later, he identifies a perceived inflexibility and unhealthy secrecy with an IRA mentality when he criticizes O'Donovan for what O'Faoláin saw as his autocratic management of *Ireland To-Day*: "Don't be so bloody exclusive and IRA-ish . . . to think some of these are not your, our, mine, his, way of thinking" (qtd. in Allen 194). Even as they convey O'Faoláin's frustration, these comments suggest an intimate familiarity with O'Donovan and with the IRA that underscores the extent to which O'Faoláin speaks with an insider's confidence and sense of urgency as he calls for a more expansive and dynamic understanding of republicanism and postcolonial Irish thought.

O'Faoláin's objections to physical-force republicanism should thus be understood as at once ideological, moral, and tactical, with the tactical concerns amplifying the moral ones. Significantly, however, these objections are generally not expressed publicly and directly in O'Faoláin's writings at the time but must instead be gleaned indirectly from brief moments in essays and depictions in his early short stories. The most compelling evidence of O'Faoláin's distancing of himself from physical-force republicanism in these early decades is actually the absence of commentary on the post–Civil War IRA or issues such as internment of suspected IRA members, even in a coded fashion. When considered alongside his ongoing articulation of a distinctly republican critique of institutional nationalism, this absence looms larger. In place of what he sees as a discredited physical-force republicanism, O'Faoláin pursues a wide-ranging effort to develop a realist literary aesthetic as part of a broadly constituted republican cultural politics capable of disrupting the prevailing condition of historical arrest by other means.

A focus on historical development is ultimately the defining feature of O'Faoláin's writing and thought in this era. As we shall see as we examine his early focus on the prospects for an Irish realist novel, the form's potential value lies equally in its perceived capacity for narrating the forces driving historical change and for making that dynamism available in the contemporary moment. Approaching the novel as a means of apprehending discrete historical forces and narrating those forces' unfolding relationship to each other, O'Faoláin offers an understanding of the genre that resonates strongly with some key aspects of classic nineteenth-century realism. This resonance emerges with a particular force as we examine O'Faoláin's 1930s analyses of the shared shortcomings of earlier modernist and naturalist aesthetics and consider them alongside the accounts of realism and naturalism being developed by Lukács during the same period.

An emphasis on historical dynamism over stasis, which Lukács captures most succinctly in his distinction between "narration" and "description," is the key difference between naturalism and a more progressive form of the novel for both O'Faoláin and Lukács.[7] Though O'Faoláin does not consistently identify that progressive form with "realism" because he is keen to present his vision of a new form of "Catholic novel," the applicability of the term nonetheless becomes clear as we consider the characteristics of the novel he proposes and compare the distinctions and definitions of the form he offers with those offered by Lukács in his comparison of naturalism and realism. This more limited and theoretically precise understanding of realism diverges in significant ways from the more casual usage of "realist" frequently employed to designate virtually any fiction that depicts the experience of the everyday in some detail or with a greater concern for "realistic" verisimilitude.

In three essays on the form of the novel published in 1934 and 1935, O'Faoláin tries to sketch an alternative to the naturalist and modernist forms of the novel that he sees as insufficiently dynamic. He calls instead for a novel animated by struggle and a sense of the significance of human action. In that, we can see some of the crucial distinctions between naturalism and realism that O'Faoláin shares with Lukács. At the same time, O'Faoláin's framing of his alternative vision of the novel as a new form of "Catholic novel" underscores his insistence on producing dynamic forms from the cultural elements most marked by a sense of stasis and rigidity in postcolonial Ireland.

In "Plea for a New Type of Novel" published in the *Virginia Quarterly Review* in 1934, O'Faoláin identifies an excessive literalism as the fatal flaw of the modern novel. He frames the problem primarily in terms of a naturalist method that amounts to "satisfaction with the mere recognisable presentation of a fact" (189) and has the effect of reducing the novel to "a social document" (190). For him, both naturalist and modernist novels offer soul-killing dissections of humanity executed on either the macro or the micro scale and memorably evoked in his account of "the breaking down process, the watch-menders at their evil work" (198). Any hope that Joycean modernism might offer an escape from naturalist literalism is, according to O'Faoláin, destined to end in disappointment. Framing Joyce as a primary practitioner of what he terms "the subjective novel," he suggests that strand of modernist narrative emerges from the same historical tendencies of capitalist modernity and yields the same result as a broader naturalist aesthetic that encloses it, arguing that "one need hope for nothing from the subjectivists but disintegration without added significance. It is a materialist approach to life and man; and in English thought one readily notes the strong material trend" (198). Though O'Faoláin certainly counts Joyce as an Irish writer, the emphasis on his work coming in the wake of the "material trend" of English thought nonetheless signals his sense of how Irish writing must be apprehended simultaneously within multiple literary and cultural histories. Complementing this as he seeks to articulate the bases for a republican realist departure is his hope that the historical rupture of postcoloniality might afford the means for articulating dynamic alternative narrative structures from within that confluence of histories.

As suggested by his reference to a "strong material trend" in English thought, however, O'Faoláin grounds his concerns about an excessively literal aesthetic in a more far-reaching critique of certain problematic tendencies within nineteenth-century English realism that provide the germ for a naturalism that will eventually choke off realism's progressive potential. He decries the influence of Dickens and Thackeray in engraining a "literal idea of character" (191) that does not convey a sufficient sense of dynamism or authenticity and thus appears either predictable or "dishonest" (192). This literalism, in turn, gives way to the "uniformity" of naturalism common to both its English and French variants: "Zola and H. G. Wells and Arnold Bennett—not to mention Maupassant and Gautier—knocked most of the gusto out of slummery; and cheap education, cheap houses, electric light, Lyons' Tea Shops, the internal combustion engine, the cinema, and wireless, finished the job. Fiction hates these machines for producing uniformity" (192–93).[8] Significantly, O'Faoláin presents naturalism as playing an important and active role in reinforcing a culture of uniformity *alongside* the technologies and methods of social organization typically associated with the consolidation of modern capitalist culture. This suggests a keen awareness of the active role of aesthetics in shaping political and cultural realities and a rejection of a mimetic notion of writing. Additionally, in terms of O'Faoláin's relationship to naturalism in particular, it underscores an appreciation of the historical character of naturalism as arising at a distinct moment of capitalist development.

As an alternative to this mimeticism and uniformity, O'Faoláin proposes "the spiritual idea of character . . . the invisible device as opposed to the obvious" (193). In his emphasis on the "invisible," we see an effort to imagine a form of the novel capable of articulating ongoing historical development in a way that might disrupt the particular sense of arrest hovering over the early postcolonial era and realize the potential of a realist form that goes beyond the merely "literal." O'Faoláin does not seek to abandon the material realm entirely but rather to move beyond the surface of appearances to discover the dynamic "invisible devices" that lie beneath or behind the congealed layer of description to drive history and narrative forward.

As one example of this, he expresses a desire to "dispense with character altogether" and emulate the sense of inexorable movement in the structure of Greek tragedy (197). To achieve this in a modern context, he prescribes an infusion of romanticism to the novel form (195). O'Faoláin's call for modern novelists to "turn romantic" (195) can be understood to introduce a measure of dynamic uncertainty or "mystery" to "an age whose pride is not yet broken, . . . which still fears the undefined, the unreliable, the dark" (199). In a significant way, this emphasis on "mystery" and the "romantic" aligns O'Faoláin with Yeatsian modernism but with the important difference that O'Faoláin feels it necessary for both political and aesthetic reasons to abandon Yeats's stance of artistic heroism and Olympian detachment. As a slightly later essay from 1941 helps to illustrate, O'Faoláin associates that sort of romantic detachment with an earlier historical and aesthetic moment that is no longer accessible to him: "I suddenly remember . . . Yeats's rooms with all the drawings by Blake and Rossetti, so lovely, so mysterious, so ethereal, so remote; and I think of this crude world of common life, and I envy from the bottom of my heart that exquisite world of the senses in which the imagination of the poet fed and contemplated itself hourly" ("Ah, Wisha" 273).

We are reminded here of O'Faoláin's intimacy with Yeats and his experience of occupying some of the same intellectual milieux while nonetheless inhabiting an entirely different historical moment. Though O'Faoláin deeply admires Yeats's ability to plumb the depths of such mystery, he nonetheless cannot embrace Yeats's proud detachment from the more immediate concerns of the everyday. In that regard, a Yeatsian modernism is at turns too naturalist in its detachment and descriptive renderings of objects, places, and people serving primarily as backdrops or prompts for contemplation and too totalizing in its rendering of the contemplative poetic mind seeking to commune with an eternal world of universal symbols.

By contrast, O'Faoláin's emphasis on the "invisible device" and the need to reconcile its relationship with materiality by way of a careful admixture of romanticism strikingly coincides with much of Lukács's writing on realism during the same period. In his preface to *Studies in European Realism*, Lukács echoes O'Faoláin in his criticism of the parallels between naturalism's "coarse biologism" and "the psychologists' punctilious probing" that underlies a modernist emphasis on psychological interiority and a unified subjectivity (8).[9] The result, Lukács suggests, for those who would take either Upton Sinclair or Joyce as their model is a similar failure to render "living beings" (8). Similarly, in "Realism in the Balance," Lukács focuses on the need to "understand the correct dialectical unity of appearance and essence" (33) so as to be attuned to "the underlying essence, . . . the real factors that relate their experiences to the hidden social forces that produce them" (36–37).

Like O'Faoláin, Lukács suggests that a key animating feature of this more dynamic vision of realism is its romantic element. He argues in "The Zola Centenary" that the failure to appreciate the importance of a romantic element leads Zola to misapprehend Balzac and Stendahl (86–89) and produce a false "'scientific'" realism hobbled by "the undialectic conception of the organic unity of nature and society" (86). The result, according to Lukács, is Zola's well-intentioned but "narrowminded" notion of "'harmony' as the essence of social being" (87). This underwrites the essential stasis of naturalism and robs Zola's fiction of a progressive aesthetic character as "the elimination of antagonisms is regarded as the motive power of social movement" (87) and the writer is "reduced to a mere spectator" (90).

Though Lukács elaborates his vision of realism in a far more ideologically rigorous way than we see in O'Faoláin's essays, the political implications Lukács traces for realist and naturalist aesthetics nonetheless have much in common with the critique of naturalism that underlies much of O'Faoláin's exploration of the postcolonial novel form. A key concern for Lukács in the Zola centenary essay is naturalism's reduction of the individual historical agent to a soulless "mechanical average" (91). He contrasts this "mechanical average" with the "type" that enables realism's dynamism and dialectical coherence (91). Lukács presents the "type" as the mainspring of realist form producing a narrative where "the co-operation and clashing of human beings who are both individuals and at the same time representatives of important class tendencies" can be perceived in their full complexity (91).

The official nationalism of the postcolonial state exerts a very similar pressure to reduce the "types" of anticolonial struggle to a politically inert "average" underpinning a state of historical stasis and social "harmony." Indeed, the cloaking of the private interests of bourgeois nationalism in a celebration of the communal via a reified "tradition" only exacerbates this problem by making over the historical actors of earlier moments in Irish history so as to transform them from dynamic "type" to static "average," whether under the guise of the generic "rebel" or "the plain people of Ireland."

As O'Faoláin develops his critique of naturalism and proceeds to sketch a form of the novel more capable of fulfilling a progressive cultural function, we see the terms of his critique increasingly transposed onto a religious schema. Thus, in "It No Longer Matters, or The Death of the English Novel" published in T. S. Eliot's *Criterion* in 1935, the dynamic struggle between the "literal" and the "essential" is recast as an endless struggle between "man" and "Heaven," and the emphasis on the romantic element is rendered in terms of Catholic "mystery" (53–54). Similarly, an investment in a sense of agency and the possibility and necessity of ongoing historical development mingles with religion to yield a sustained focus on how to restore "belief" and a sense of the spiritual significance of human action to the novel.

O'Faoláin thus sketches the framework of a new "Catholic novel" as an alternative to the "objectivizing" and withdrawal that he sees becoming more pronounced as naturalism increasingly comes to express itself through modernist forms in the twentieth century: "The earlier naturalist novelists had at least some sense of elation. They did not specify their hopes but they had some sense of power and some belief left in man. Their successors . . . have little of that fond hope. The young men like Joyce and Lawrence are already sitting back from life, shrugging their shoulders, or with a last brutal despairing effort objectivizing with a grand courage what they so hate" (51). O'Faoláin's identification of Joyce as one of the leading exponents of this tendency reinforces the sense that he is positioning a new postcolonial initiative in Irish fiction as a late-modernist corrective of the previous generation of Irish modernist writers as well as a more far-reaching intervention in the development of twentieth-century form that is enabled by Ireland's comparatively early entry into postcoloniality.[10]

The late-modernist character of O'Faoláin's reinvented realism also inflects his critique of the convergence of modernism and naturalism in a distinct way. Unlike Lukács, O'Faoláin is not repudiating modernism and is not interested in reinstating "the organicist contract" that Naomi Schor distills as the essential structural feature of Lukácsian realism (60). The problem for O'Faoláin is not modernism's disruption of an organic wholeness but an apprehension of modernism as being inevitably charged with crafting new means for assembling a comparable totalizing vision.

The parallels between O'Faoláin's vision of a new sort of Catholic novel as an inherently dynamic form and his earlier calls for the abandonment of the "literal" become more evident when he describes his vision of the Catholic novel by remarking that "the revivification of literature by a spiritual view of life [is not] anything more than an acknowledgement that tragedy at its highest is an *annotation* of the religious idea. It is far from seeing life as a verification of dogma. It is far from seeing literature as a handmaid of edification" (53, emphasis in original). Reiterating his earlier investment in tragedy's conflict and inexorable movement as a model for the novel, O'Faoláin makes it clear that his interest in developing a new version of the Catholic novel lies entirely in its potential for solving a problem of modern literary form rather than in advancing the interests of the Church. He takes great pains to distinguish his vision of the Catholic novel from a more orthodox version of Catholic writing amenable to the interests of church and state. Indeed, he argues that the orthodox Catholic novel merely repeats the descriptive tendencies of naturalism in its "oversimplified" puritanism and zeal to expose a perceived "evil" in the world (54).

Reiterating his concern in another 1935 essay, "The Modern Novel: A Catholic Point of View," that the naturalist novel "objectivises" a world that it sees as "chronically incurable" (342), O'Faoláin proposes that the Catholic novel and the communist novel emerge as imperfect heirs of the realist novel in their comparable capacity to restore a sense of "significance" to human action (344–45). He rejects the tendency of more orthodox Catholic novelists to be overtaken by "a timidity evident in their fear of the senses, a priggishness and a solemnity" that proves "fatal" to their craft as writers and makes the mistake of "pretending that art can be a charwoman for religion, cleaning up life with her broom" (345). O'Faoláin summarizes this as "the folly of the Catholic writer who adopts the technique of . . . naturalism while contesting its general effect" (349). Laying out the bases for an alternative Catholic novel, he argues for a form capable of seeing "man" "as midway between everything and nothing" and "as both more noble and more terrifying for being . . . the antagonist of the Gods" (344–45). This, according to O'Faoláin, "restores at once to human action a significance it lost in the novel of the 'eighties . . . [and] is also the strong point of the Communist [novelist], for to him, of course, life also takes on new significance in taking on new hope" (345).[11]

This understanding of a more progressive Catholic novel form again strongly invites comparison to Lukács's account of the novel, especially his early suggestion in *Theory of the Novel* that "[t]he novel is the epic of an age in which the extensive totality of life is no longer directly given . . . yet which still thinks in terms of totality" (56) and his more famous pronouncement that the novel is "the epic of a world that has been abandoned by God" (88). Though Lukács's thought is not immersed in the complex social and historical resonances of religion with which O'Faoláin must necessarily contend, the relationship they draw between religion and the novel has the same essential contours. For both, the animating force of the novel arises from the conflict between individuals living in a disenchanted and broken world where one must struggle to define a larger order and one's place within it even as the only certainty is the struggle and ongoing process of "becoming." Thus, whether defined in terms of being "the antagonist of the Gods" positioned "midway between everything and nothing" or in terms of the once divinely guaranteed form of the epic persisting in "a world . . . abandoned by God," the novel expresses the formal tension and dialectical potential arising from an ongoing and irresolvable confrontation between individual and totality at a moment when the precise terms of that totality can no longer be relied upon.

An appreciation of the larger philosophical or theoretical orientation of O'Faoláin's vision of "the Catholic novel" helps reinforce a perception that he is not simply seeking to give voice to a particular Irish constituency but is instead focused on resolving a formal problem that has important implications for postcolonial literature as well as for Irish literature's place within twentieth-century writing. He acknowledges in "The Modern Novel: A Catholic Point of View" that the communist and Catholic novels "are neither capable of writing *of* as wide an audience or *for* so wide an audience as their predecessors [from nineteenth-century realism], because they are limited by the common acceptance of their own beliefs. But they are something and they are worth considering" (344, emphasis in original).

Such modest language belies the volatile mixture of elements that O'Faoláin's account of the Catholic novel represents in the context of 1930s Ireland. Beyond the obvious flouting of the Church's strong anticommunist stance, which would become increasingly evident in Ireland a year later with the outbreak of the Spanish Civil War, the comparison of the Catholic and communist novels reinforces the republican dimension of his analyses of Irish historical development and arrest. O'Faoláin's vision of the novel form thus provides a means of disrupting the institutional authority of both the Catholic Church and the Free State while simultaneously insisting that radical critiques of both can be launched from within the discourses of Catholicism and nationalism themselves.[12]

Through his concept of the Catholic novel, O'Faoláin consolidates the means for an ironic subversion of the official nationalism of the Free State as he challenges at once the portraits of peasant simplicity inherited from the Revival and the overlay of rigid Catholic virtue subsequently applied to adumbrate any traces of Anglo-Irish fantasy and render them elements of authentic nationalist "tradition." He thus targets the invocation of Catholicism as the defining feature of Irishness by both Daniel Corkery and the more reactionary Irish-Irelanders such as D. P. Moran. In doing so, however, he neither cedes the cultural and intellectual influences of Catholicism to such perspectives nor endorses the exclusionary sectarian tendencies that so easily extend from them. O'Faoláin refuses to accept that either Catholicism or nationalism can be truly apprehended as a static phenomenon in Irish history and culture. Instead, we see how his engagement with the era's broader questions of form constitute part of a far-reaching effort to discover the means for a dynamic narration of ongoing anticolonial critique secreted within the very forms sustaining postcolonial arrest.

The term "republican realism" usefully encapsulates the broad bases and implications of this effort. Though not a term used by O'Faoláin himself, it draws together the republican strands of thought that constitute implicit and explicit components of his writing over most of the 1930s and 1940s and come into particular focus through his ongoing concern with realist form. The republican critique he pursues most evidently in his essays and commentaries finds its aesthetic counterpart in the form of the modified realist novel that occupies so much of his attention as a critic and fiction writer in the period. Republican realism thus signals an effort to address a perceived problem of form in late-modernist culture in a way that has a parallel effect of injecting a new dynamism into the narration of Irish nationalism in the context of an emergent postcoloniality.

O'Faoláin's republican realism can be understood as an effort to displace both the lyrical fable of "tradition" and the naturalist document that is its dark twin. His first novel, A Nest of Simple Folk, makes clear the parallelism of the two modes in both form and function, with each marked by a tendency toward description and fixity that underwrites an aesthetic of historical stasis. Published in 1934, A Nest of Simple Folk is actually best understood as a novel that realizes its narrative force by way of its repeated disruption of those twinned modes. As we consider the structure of the novel, we can see how O'Faoláin cannily positions his realist aesthetic as a late-modernist intervention that at once demonstrates how the energies of an earlier generation of Irish modernist aesthetics have lost their disruptive force and stages a series of strategic juxtapositions to ironically leverage those energies in new ways.

A family chronicle of five generations of an extended family in Limerick and Cork running from the 1850s to the outbreak of the 1916 Rising, A Nest of Simple Folk effectively fulfills many of the political functions of classic realism in charting historical development by way of a perceptive narration of the interplay of emergent class tendencies.[13] As it moves from the post-Famine era through the late nineteenth and early twentieth centuries, the novel charts the decline of a colonial model of Anglo-Irish landlordism and its replacement by an order of imperial bureaucracy and modernizing reform. In a gesture toward the Big House novel tradition that was so central to nineteenth-century Irish fiction, we see the primary Big House of the novel, Foxhall, progressively falling into greater disrepair and debt only to be taken over by a local Catholic farmer methodically expanding his holdings. The historical scope of the novel reveals itself to be much broader, however, as we see other landlords' Big Houses newly occupied by the imperial bureaucrats of coroner, judge, and district inspector of police, and the rural populace adapting to this modernizing trend through successive generations' migrations to town and city.

The development of a native police force in the form of the Royal Irish Constabulary (R.I.C.) constitutes a key feature of this larger historical process in the novel. With the R.I.C. cast as a means of "rising in the world" for ambitious farmers' sons hoping to claw their way from rural poverty to the lower ranks of the new Catholic bourgeoisie, O'Faoláin uses it as a means of exploring the internal political and class tensions within a rural Catholic populace still reeling from the trauma of the Famine and the memory of the 1798 United Irishmen Rising amid the simmering tension of the Land Wars and the rise of physical-force nationalism that mark the late nineteenth-century political landscape. At the same time, O'Faoláin insightfully presents the internal hierarchy within the R.I.C. and paranoia over advancement and promotion to depict the ironic mixture of condescension and anxiety that drives and sustains the inner workings of the imperial power structure.

Opposing this bureaucratic order of the rapidly modernizing state, the novel depicts a disparate array of nationalist conspiracies extending from the Fenians and the Land Leaguers to the Irish Volunteers. In the ongoing account of the imperial state's increasingly efficient effort to surveil and fix expressions of insurgency by means of informants and intelligence reports, the novel stages nationalist history as one constantly haunted by arrest, both literally and figuratively, and shaped at once by the actions, betrayals, and generosities of the individual and by the structural pressures of a shifting social and political order. As the confrontation between these two forces plays out unevenly over the course of the novel and ends amid the crackling tension of the Easter Rising, O'Faoláin produces a novel whose republican realism inheres in its blending of the individual and the social dimensions of history and its refusal to render the nationalist historical impulse as a fully resolved portrait.

Even as *A Nest of Simple Folk* effectively serves some of the key functions of classical realism, we can also see some of its late-modernist features in the ways that O'Faoláin's version of realism represents a sort of anachronistic return or spectral "living on" of realism outside of its proper nineteenth-century historical contexts. As his essays on the novel make apparent, O'Faoláin is exquisitely conscious of formal elements and their relationship to the social and material contexts of different periods as well as to the history of the novel itself. Thus, his version of realism is necessarily very historicized in its deployment and its incorporation of divergent aesthetic strands.

Indeed, we might say that in his first novel O'Faoláin uses the staccato pulse of republican realism to "write against the grain" of the fixed aesthetic forms that sustain historical arrest in the early Free State. His careful structuring of these competing aesthetics provides a means of apprehending the tendency toward arrest as a recurrent and necessary motif in a longer historical narrative. In this way, A Nest of Simple Folk discloses in unexpected ways a more radical undercurrent beneath the ascendant bourgeois narrative of institutional nationalism that would position itself as the culmination of the historical process.

O'Faoláin renders the fixed vision of "tradition" in A Nest of Simple Folk by way of what might best be termed lyricism, a mode that recurs throughout the novel but is progressively overtaken by the narrative energies of republican realism. Lyricism in the novel is an eminently descriptive and contemplative mode that immerses the text in external space, either natural or human-made, and conveys an overwhelming sense of temporal and narrative arrest. In many ways, we might understand the novel's lyrical mode as expressive of the lingering aesthetic effect of the Revival in the postcolonial era as it has been deprived of its inherent tensions and complexities and been reduced to an inert nostalgic quaintness.

Most striking in terms of the late-modernist character of his writing and an indication of how carefully O'Faoláin structures the novel is the predominance of the lyrical mode in the opening pages of each of the three books that comprise A Nest of Simple Folk. This emphasis on the lyrical is, in turn, complemented at the end of the first two books by the inverted lyricism of the prison that encloses the novel's protagonist and brings to an end each of the first two phases of the nationalist history narrated by the novel. Breaking this pattern with the radically open-ended account of the 1916 Rising that concludes the novel, O'Faoláin thus highlights the sense of unresolved historical potential he attaches to that revolutionary era.

In the novel's opening pages, we are introduced to the rural setting of the Deel River plain in County Limerick that serves as the backdrop for most of the events in book 1—entitled "The Country"—and the point of narrative departure for the novel. Presenting the Deel plain as a place where "there is and always has been a kind of sultry sloth, dead and overpowering and drugging to all the energies of the spirit," with the result that "even the years seemed to fall asleep" (4), O'Faoláin makes the anesthetizing effect of the lyrical mode quite explicit.[14] The impact on any sense of historical dynamism or, indeed, history of any sort, is likewise made clear: "History has reverberated only in the distance, and even then but rarely and too far away to be heard . . . it is a place into which news of the world's calamities has seeped by rumour and dying echo, and been felt in the end only for some small secondary cause. So, before Waterloo, Rachel Foxe had stormed for hours against the French because she had not got sugar from Limerick for three weeks" (4–5). In its lyrical guise, then, Irish rural space—and subsequently urban space—is one that lies wholly outside of historical time. We see here in part O'Faoláin's commentary on the "antique text" that Terence Brown associates with the ahistorical temporality of the Revival ("Modernism" 37), while the relationship noted between the supply of sugar and the Napoleonic wars functions almost as a muted parody of an excessively "literal" version of the realist novel that O'Faoláin decries in his criticism from the same period.

Accompanying references to more immediate Irish concerns such as "O'Connell, Emancipation, Reform, new Poor Laws, political troubles" (4) that also fail to pierce the general stupor underscore the point that this lack of historical consciousness is not simply a matter of an Irish provincialism. Rather, it is fundamentally a question of narrative framing as the subsequent accounts of Fenian activity and police counterinsurgent intrigue that mark the intermittent eruption of realism contrastingly illuminate. "History" and historical potential, in other words, are still very much alive in the Irish countryside but are by necessity marked by narrative and structural discontinuities both because of the exigencies of insurgent struggle and the need to wrench history from the dead hand of "tradition."

O'Faoláin complements the lyrical mode throughout the novel by means of a naturalism poised to reveal its synchrony with lyricism's vision of history's absence. Rather than serenely standing *outside* of historical time as the lyrical mode does, however, naturalism in *A Nest of Simple Folk* nullifies history and renders any notion of change futile. O'Faoláin's naturalism—and, arguably, Irish naturalism more generally—emphasizes a sense of dark futility instead of the devolution that more readily characterizes French, English, and American naturalism. Thus, in place of a downward narrative trajectory, there is effectively no trajectory at all.

An early example in the novel can be seen in O'Faoláin's account of the Deel plain's inhabitants as news spreads of the impending death

of Long John O'Donnell, father of the book's protagonist, Leo Donnel: "So they moved over the dim fields, like night-cattle gathering to
a drinking pool. All the small ends that made life real to them were
diminished and denied by the endlessness of the grave. Seeing suddenly the futility and hopelessness of their lives, they brimmed up
with pity for the man who had anticipated their common lot" (36).

Along with the nullification of history by way of an emphasis on
"endlessness," O'Faoláin turns to the idea of infinite recurrence that
is to become the key feature of Irish naturalism in the postcolonial
era.[15] He presents the suffocating social and economic structures of
rural life both as an accounting of them for their own sake and as a
means of exploring naturalism's inertness as a critical aesthetic. The
portrait of Leo's paternal aunt, Mag Keene, and her tragic foresight
of her daughters' adherence to the same pattern from which there can
be no escape, helps to illustrate this:

> She sat lonely in her kitchen, surrounded by her little brood, her
> face, although she was not really an old woman, already as lined as
> a Flemish portrait, . . . every wrinkle defined by dirt on her skin, her
> dewlaps beginning to sag below the level of her jaws like two with-
> ered potatoes, and her wearied eyes wandering under the lids from
> side to side of the open hearth where the long remnant of her daugh-
> ters sat bare-legged. . . . A child of her womb was gone from her, and
> surely the rest must soon go, one after one, even her youngest Bid, the
> weakest autumnal fruit of her body. . . . One by one they would go,
> all of them but Nonie the Bull, . . . who must remain on the farm and,
> like her mother, slave the round of the years, growing heavy with
> each successive child until she, too, saw them go from her, "rising" in
> the world, as people say, as she dragged on to her end.
>
> God knows it was a weary round of life, and if the good God in
> heaven did not requite them all in the life to come, surely it was a
> cruel life as well. It was a cruel world and there was surely little rea-
> son to it. (128–29)

Beyond the standard naturalist features that are readily apparent,
what is striking about this passage are the ways it reflects a sense of
prefiguration in both form and content that is crucial for O'Faoláin's
treatment of naturalism in the novel. Thus, Mag's appearance is
already anticipated by Flemish painting and the story of her life and
that of her daughters already told and retold. This is true as much for
O'Faoláin as for Mag and her foreknowledge of the shape of Nonie's
life that will take the place of her own. O'Faoláin does not pretend to
any originality in this regard and, indeed, to the contrary, reiterates

the same story a short time later in the novel with Leo's sisters similarly "flung . . . from one slavery [on their natal "homeplace" farm] into another [through marriage]—for herself and her children, now, as before for herself and his sisters" (161–62).

Similarly, the notion of "'rising' in the world" that might break the cycle and retroactively lend some narrative dynamism and purpose to the relentless round of toil and loss so as to shift it from mere description to true narration is also undermined by an emphasis on convention that reduces the prospect of escape through "rising" to a reassuring phrase that "people say." This is underscored by the subsequent turn to "the life to come" as the only space of requital and that which affords any narrative coherence or "reason." Ultimately, however, the effect of this endless recurrence is to render null the possibility of narration—as opposed to description—under naturalism and to show instead how naturalism might work along with lyricism to convey a sense of historical stasis that O'Faoláin sees as the central problem of both postcolonial Irish culture and modern narrative form.

The effective protagonist of A Nest of Simple Folk, Leo Donnel, helps clarify O'Faoláin's approach to discovering the possibility of history and narration amid such static descriptive modes. As evidenced by the dark fate of his siblings and cousins, Leo has strong familial connections to the disenfranchised and impoverished peasantry that make up the most important historical and political constituency of late nineteenth-century Ireland. At the same time, Leo has still closer connections to the increasingly shabby gentry of the Anglo-Irish Big House by way of his mother and maternal aunts, who effectively adopt him after the death of his father early in the novel. Marked by a sense of profound social dislocation, then, Leo Donnel stands at the nexus of two histories and two rival social formations. The plot of the first book of the novel focuses on Leo's movement from the role of hedge-school pupil to that of rakish landlord and then an affiliation with the Land League and the abortive Fenian Rising that culminates in a fifteen-year sentence in Portland Prison for attempted murder of a member of the R.I.C. The rest of the novel then intermittently traces Leo's involvement with shadowy Fenian intrigue as he moves to the town of Rathkeale and then to Cork City after another stint in prison for Fenian activity. The third and final book closes in the midst of the Easter Rising in Cork with Leo gone to Dublin to take part in the events there and his nephew, Denis, wandering Cork's deserted streets.

Leo Donnel thus inhabits an emblematic place in the novel as heir of two rival histories that are passing away and thereby serves as a striking embodiment of discontinuity and dislocation, especially in the first book of the novel. In this way, he becomes the primary means by which a new vision of historical dynamism can be haltingly introduced via a realist mode that builds in momentum and impact over the course of the novel. Leo's intertwining functions—as *end* and intermittent *source*—lie at the heart of O'Faoláin's effort to put forth a vision of history and form that can serve as a dynamic alternative to models based on the continuity of "tradition" and aesthetics centered around fixity and recurrence.

Leo's paternal grandfather, a veteran of the 1798 Rising of the United Irishmen tellingly named Theo, is the repository of native tradition in the novel that finds its end in Leo. A wandering hedge-school master in his earlier days, Theo is by the beginning of the novel an old man seated by the hearth of his daughter Mag Keene, and given to reciting Latin poetry and posing riddles in Irish to his bewildered grandson Leo. Though Theo's personal history as a republican veteran of 1798, follower of Daniel O'Connell, and survivor of the Famine that swept away his wife and most of his children remains important for Leo and for the novel, Theo's role as a link in the chain of an unbroken tradition and timeless cultural memory is distinguished from that material history and presented far more negatively. Commenting on Theo's store of knowledge "inherited with increasing irrelevancy from his father and grandfather," O'Faoláin describes it as a "bottomless memory, linked with these in their turn bottomless memories, [that] reached back so far that in their one decaying brain one might see, though entangled beyond all hope of unravelling, the story (as well as the picture) of his country's decay" (28).

In refusing to credit the importance of "bottomless memory" and, indeed, reading it as an "entangled . . . story . . . of his country's decay," O'Faoláin weaves together the impulses of naturalism and "tradition" and calls into question the model of history championed for different purposes by the writers of the Revival and a conservative postcolonial nationalism growing out of the Irish-Ireland vision of an Irish cultural purity. One of the most sophisticated and famous expressions of the latter had been offered by O'Faoláin's early mentor Daniel Corkery in *The Hidden Ireland*, published ten years earlier to much acclaim in 1924. Corkery's model of history proposes a seamless continuity between an ancient Gaelic world and a modern nationalist project. By separating Theo's personal history of action from this deeper "bottomless memory," however, O'Faoláin challenges an understanding of history and resistance as dependent on a wholly continuous line of unbroken culture and suggests instead the need to view historical agency as eminently material and contingent, attuned to the problems and potentials of a given moment within a broader dynamic system rather than being overshadowed by the abstraction of an idealized and incompletely apprehended past.

In this approach to history, we can see the signature of O'Faoláin's republican realism and clearly see its similarities to a more classic nineteenth-century realist tradition that O'Faoláin and Lukács contrast with a descriptive naturalism. At the same time, we can discern O'Faoláin's critique of Revivalist aesthetics that would rely on the retrieval of ancient texts and myths and the construal of an unbroken folk tradition as sources for a literature that could offer an alternative to the uniformities of empire and capitalist modernity. This spotlighting of the parallel reliance by Yeats and Corkery on the notion of the colonized as a fixed ahistorical object is indeed an innovative critical contribution O'Faoláin uses to sharp rhetorical effect against Corkery in debates that were of critical importance in the intellectual life of early postcolonial Ireland. This insight nonetheless tends to be overlooked in critical accounts of O'Faoláin even as more recent postcolonial critics have traced the contradictory implications of an official nationalism heavily reliant on the notions of an imperial primitivism.[16] In the overlapping critique of official nationalism and Revivalist aesthetics, however, we can see the intersection of the republican and late-modernist characteristics of O'Faoláin's realism.

Leo Donnel's angry exchanges with his maternal aunts, Rachel and Anna, make clear, however, that this alternative vision of historical agency should not be confused with a sense of historical amnesia or a disavowal of the material realities of power in defining the shifting contours and conflicts of particular social formations. While the "relevance" of old Theo's storehouse of traditional memory is questioned, the alternative tradition of Anglo-Irish glory is vehemently repudiated in the novel and countered by the material history of Theo's life. Thus, when Rachel and Anna try to regale Leo with stories about his maternal great-uncle David Quested, who was a shipping merchant, Leo responds sharply, "I know all about Quacky!," using the derogatory nickname that he has learned from his paternal uncle Nicholas. Leo then repeats the story of Quested's having killed Leo's other great-uncle, Theo's brother, by throwing iron bolts at his head as he swam out to Quested's boat to beg some grain during the Famine (86–87). Similarly, when shown the sword and epaulettes of another maternal great-uncle who was a captain of the yeomanry in 1798, Leo "growl[s] with venom" and describes how Theo had been flogged in 1798 for his participation in the Rising (88).

The battle between Leo and the aunts culminates in a bitter dispute over Leo's use of the word "crokered" to describe the permanent damage inflicted on Leo's back by the flogging. Dismissing "crokered" as "'Some Irish word!,'" the aunts insist that Leo "[t]alk proper English!" and say "crookened" even as they also insist that Theo "got no more than he deserved" (88). The struggle over the language used to describe the history of 1798 that Theo carries in his broken body foregrounds the material dimension while showing, along with the survival of Quested's nickname, that a material history need not be sundered from cultural or linguistic practice expressive of difference, collectivity, or resistance. What distinguishes it from the stasis of "tradition" is its contemporaneity, its engagement with what Frantz Fanon refers to as present "realities" (225) such as those embedded in the aunts' insistence on "proper English" and, more strikingly, their verdict that Theo's flogging was deserved.

The precise nature of O'Faoláin's separation of a dynamic historical consciousness from the fixity and continuity of "tradition" is encapsulated most neatly by the account of Leo's early experiences in Limerick city, where he is sent by his aunts to live with a maternal cousin and learn the ways of an Anglo-Irish gentleman while advancing his education. The disdain of his doctor-cousin, Dicky Wilcox, scandalized by Leo's complete ignorance of and disinterest in the various Anglo-Irish Big Houses of the Limerick countryside, reinforces the novel's account of Leo's alienation from a sense of a vibrant Anglo-Irish tradition (116–19).

O'Faoláin shows through Wilcox how this tradition is articulated both by the practice of a ritualized "visiting" of the different houses and by maintaining a shared oral tradition of their features as an index of Anglo-Irish culture and continuity. This knowledge is preserved and conveyed by reciting the provenance of each house and the features that allow each demesne to sustain the performance of Anglo-Irish leisure and dominance, especially through activities such as the foxhunt. The importance of such knowledge as a more indirect or abstract expression of another tradition that is rapidly fading is suggested by Wilcox's own ignorance of who currently lives at "Beechmount" and the revelation, when Leo turns the questioning on his host, that Wilcox has never been to any of the estates whose glories he has recited in such detail by way of admonishing Leo (118–19).

We thus see an account of another increasingly "irrelevant" knowledge that parallels that possessed by old Theo. This account of Anglo-Irish tradition should be understood as more than just a standard expression of Anglo-Irish decline, however, and is instead best apprehended as part of O'Faoláin's ongoing effort to articulate a dynamic vision of history through a realism designed to work against the underlying aesthetic structures of a history mediated by "tradition." By showing how a disintegrating Anglo-Irish culture is itself propped up through a rather desperate rehearsal of tradition, O'Faoláin takes aim at the other pillar of Revivalist modernism that intertwines with and complements its account of a timeless rural periphery. That he accomplishes this dissolution while avoiding a Yeatsian reconstitution of Anglo-Irish greatness through tragedy such as we see in *Purgatory*, "Meditations in Time of Civil War," and other late writings while simultaneously refusing to countenance the more simple-minded dismissiveness and sectarianism that can characterize more conservative nationalist approaches of the Irish-Ireland variety underscores the subtlety of O'Faoláin's aesthetic politics.

The contrasting dynamism of a narrative mode of republican realism makes its first significant appearance in the novel as Leo happens upon a meeting of the Tenants' League, a 1850s precursor of the Land League, when he first arrives in Limerick and visits the shop of another paternal uncle, Frankie O'Donnell. As with subsequent accounts of the Fenians that take on increasing importance in the second and third books of the novel, O'Faoláin provides only a fragmentary glimpse of the meeting, with the result that "true" history is apprehended as a phenomenon that eludes complete representation and always extends beyond the narrative frame.

The discovery of the Tenants' League meeting not only points to an unseen historical dynamism churning beneath the deceptively placid surface elaborated by the lyrical and naturalist modes but does so in a way that pointedly resists the absorption of that dynamism into "tradition." O'Faoláin presents the meeting in a series of incompletely resolved images so that we have "the shouting of a mob of men" and "babbling voices" ensconced in the back of a shop "behind a bulbous wall of bags" and dimly lit "by a mud-spotted skylight" (104). When

Old Tom Mulcaire is called upon to offer "a good land-song," he is praised by two meeting attendees standing on each side of Leo. Yelling above the tumult, one says of Mulcaire, "A man suffered for the cause." while the other adds in Leo's other ear, "Five years in Maryboro Jail!" (105).

The prospect of Mulcaire's being figured as an embodiment of "tradition" is disrupted, however, by O'Faoláin's account of Leo's more detached musing that goes unspoken: "Leo merely looked at the white face of the old man who had been in jail, and wondered why they put him there and what he had done, and what the cause was for which he had suffered" (105). More than simply registering Leo's political naiveté, the description of his "merely" looking and wondering about the details of Mulcaire's personal experience deflates the portrait offered by the others and underscores the tension between material history and the reifying effects of "tradition" that would render that material history into a vague exhortation for "the cause."

Heightening this tension is Mulcaire's refusal to sing a land song. He instead takes the opportunity of an attentive audience to recite a satirical poem on the merchants of Limerick entitled *The Divil's Address to the Merchants of Limerick* (105–8). The satire greatly displeases the shopkeeper-host, Frankie O'Donnell, who once again asks Mulcaire for a land song, to which he replies: "What's the land to me, now . . . until I get my own land back. It's the merchants are my enemies now! . . . And the enemies of many besides me" (110). In Mulcaire's retort, we see O'Faoláin's insistence on a view of historical and political engagement that refuses to allow an aestheticized politics of resistance to displace the immediately pressing concerns of a more materially oriented republicanism capable of adjusting its focus on an ongoing basis. The potential for a reification of the nationalist "cause"—necessarily of significant concern in the early 1930s—is made explicit in the scene by Frankie O'Donnell's "very serious" comment that the Tenants' League meeting "is the first time I sold sixpence worth in this bar for a month" (111). With that, the interests of bourgeois nationalism and the reasons for Frankie's investment in Mulcaire's "land song" are laid bare.

As the novel continues and Leo joins the Fenians only to be sentenced to fifteen years for his activities surrounding the 1867 Rising, we see the accounts of his subversive nationalist activity again offered in glimpses that undercut a more expansive and totalizing lyricism conveying a false impression of historical stasis. Thus, after a description of the harrowing experience of silence and isolation in prison that combines elements of naturalism and lyricism at the end of book 1 (156–60), Leo appears at the beginning of book 2 as a man prematurely old and seemingly lost in a haze of semi-retirement in the town of Rathkeale.

O'Faoláin explicitly invokes the lyricism of the novel's opening as we again see the river Deel as an evocation of a soporific timelessness: "[I]n an old flat-bottomed boat of the doctor's, [Leo] . . . trailed his gold-ringed hand in the water or over the tips of the flat reeds. . . . With a tag of Virgil he pulled the white cups [of the lilies] up from—so he spoke of it—the omphalos of the river god, and held them in his pale hand and looked at them. Then he walked home . . . smoking a cool pipe, and stopped at the first pub in the street for a cool drink" (199). O'Faoláin's combination of classical references to "omphalos" and Virgil with an atmosphere of lyrical arrest seems to offer a muted commentary on a perceived quietism accompanying the emphases on classical sources within Irish modernism. The Joycean resonances of "omphalos" and a river deity are particularly striking in this regard. Within the context of the novel's lyricism and depiction of the Deel as a site of historical stasis, their inclusion here seems a means of signaling how notions of centeredness and recurrence within the broader aesthetic or historical structures of the earlier generation of Irish modernist writers stand at odds with the more radical and dynamic notions of history O'Faoláin feels the need to develop through his late-modernist practice of republican realism.

This becomes immediately evident as beneath this placid narrative surface a different reality dimly emerges from secondhand scraps of stories of Leo meeting shadowy figures under hedges and on railway platforms (202). The extent to which this furtive activity constitutes one aspect of a dynamic and far-reaching historical process at work in ways largely unseen becomes increasingly clear over the second half of A Nest of Simple Folk. O'Faoláin illustrates how this historical process is one constituted as much by physical-force nationalism as by the rise of a Catholic bourgeoisie that enables and is enabled by a reorganization of colonial power through a more efficient model of imperial inclusion and cooptation. The references to "rising in the world" that abound in the novel serve as a shorthand for the new historical impulse that drives this phenomenon. Cumulatively, these references seem to constitute a sardonic wordplay on the disappointing results of the 1916 Rising and the notion of "a risen people" tragically immured in the same discourse of reform and modernization that underlies the structures of institutional nationalism and the Free State even as they may be camouflaged by invocations of "tradition."

In a chapter entitled "An Ambitious Man," O'Faoláin distills the operative mechanisms governing the Catholic bourgeoisie's relationship to this larger process by way of a masterfully rendered scene that depicts the young constable Johnny Hussey on an errand to the district inspector of police, now occupying the Big House of Mount Massey. Though Johnny had poached on the estate as a boy, he is now entirely cowed as he approaches the house directly on official business as an imperial subordinate (221). As the scene unfolds, O'Faoláin shows how the new imperial relationship of a mediated intimacy compels obedience and subordination in a way that a more crude and complete exclusion never could.

The district inspector deftly manages a series of unspoken threats and implied promises to induce Johnny to identify his interests with those of "the Force." Keenly aware of Johnny's anxiety and sense of being "at a loss for the correct routine of behaviour" (221), he heightens that sense of unease by inviting Johnny into his study for an interview that punctuates flattering attention with sudden and uncomfortable questions about Johnny's uncle, the Fenian Leo Donnel. This leads Johnny to seek to restore the sense of intimacy with his superior and assuage any concerns about his loyalty by disavowing Leo and, indeed, any other personal connection that might give offense to the inspector (225). O'Faoláin perceptively captures this dynamic with his description of Johnny as "gradually becoming dog-loyal to this man, who was so natural and condescending, and yet kept all the correct manners and the proper distance of a gentleman and a superior talking to a policeman" (222).

The realist aspect of the scene inheres most notably in the ways that we can see O'Faoláin actively articulating the positions of these two new class formations of imperial gentleman-bureaucrat and aspiring Catholic bourgeois rather than presenting them as simply fixed social phenomena. Here again we can see illustrated Lukács's distinction between "narration" and "description." The uncertainty of Johnny's position is emphasized to him and the reader alike as it suddenly becomes clear that the inspector already knows a great deal about his activities and Johnny realizes he can be as much a subject of state surveillance as he can be its agent: "The question gave Johnny exactly the same feeling as the sight of the two night police had given

Leo Donnel when he saw the might of the law towering above him. Johnny felt the same immense and pitiless forces closing about him; he saw he was being watched and reported on" (224–25).

Besides being a reminder that Johnny necessarily remains in a subordinate position within the institution of the R.I.C., the sense of "immense and pitiless forces" looming behind the more visible structures of imperial authority endows them with an irreducible dynamism. O'Faoláin cleverly narrates the relationship between the seen and unseen in imperialism's canny structuring of power by way of his deft combination of "the Force" as the embodiment of authority and its reliance on a vast array of undetectable "forces," rendered in the plural and lowercase.

Unlike naturalism, which would eliminate the unpredictable agency of the individual and any possibility of change, the realist mode displays the potential for "rising" laid before Johnny and the uncertainty as to whether and how that potential will be realized. With the inspector a dynamic agent and more practiced player within the same system, we see how he relies on the mixture of anxiety and desire that animates imperial power as he notes with a calculated offhandedness that he has heard Johnny will soon be applying for promotion:

> "I hear," said the inspector—and Johnny wondered what was coming next—"that you are having a shot at the acting-sergeant's examination?"
>
> "Well, I *was* thinking of it, sir, but—"
>
> He had been so humbled that it now seemed a presumption on his part to aim so high.
>
> "It's in July, isn't it? That's next month! You know they always ask me for my opinion of the man?"
>
> "Do they, now, sir?"
>
> That "they" was filled with awe.
>
> . . . The inspector rose.
>
> "I need hardly say that counts for a lot."
>
> What "that" meant Johnny was unable to say. (225–26)

O'Faoláin perceptively illustrates how the vagueness of the inspector's comments that are at once threatening and promising reveal the nature of imperial power. Beyond the banal promises of promotion and pension and the constant reminders about the insecurity of both that play such a crucial role in binding the individual to the imperial bureaucracy, O'Faoláin's intriguing underscoring of the amplifying effect of the lack of clear referents for "they" and "that" adds the vital element of "mystery" that distinguishes realism from naturalism. Rather than a faceless institution that proceeds automatically to reduce and devour the individual, the imperial order and its modes of power are instead configured in terms very close to those of religion.

This sense of a world of invisible forces that are in constant struggle effectively drives the rest of the novel. Thus, we have the inspector warning Johnny that Leo Donnel is "very deep" and "a member of the Irish Republican Brotherhood—a secret society" (226), with the result that as Johnny imagines Leo, "he saw now, as he had never seen before, a cunning in that smile and a secret in those small, peering eyes" (227). This shift in awareness that allows Johnny to perceive a secret lingering beneath the surface recurs throughout the latter part of the novel as we begin to notice secret Fenian tattoos and handshakes and must speculate about likely coded meanings in letters to Leo that Johnny has intercepted.

Rather than a sense of certainty that might emerge as we have this "secret world" unveiled to us, the late-modernist character of the novel's antimimeticism becomes more apparent as we are instead plunged into a vertiginous and paranoid relationship to reality. We are presented with only glimpses of events and things and must suspiciously consider each item and person we encounter and speculate as to their significance or true relationship to each other. The narrative voice that would attempt to string them together within the novel itself is that of the police report being composed by Johnny Hussey. O'Faoláin emphasizes how the form of the police report is necessarily gapped and marked by formulae and self-serving suppositions that clearly mark it as unreliable and, indeed, coercive in its narrative structure (255–57).

While the realist narrative mode comes increasingly to the fore in the latter half of *A Nest of Simple Folk*, O'Faoláin also continues to render it by way of contrast and ironic disruption of static descriptive modes. As the novel moves to the urban setting of Cork in the last of its three books, therefore, we see the lyrical mode invoked again at the outset with Cork depicted under an "evening sky . . . dappled with warm pink and a soft fire burn[ing] on the gilt halo of the Virgin on the peak of the Palladian façade of Saint Mary's" (295) and the city described the next morning as being "like a bouquet spread along the valley" (299).

By this time, Johnny Hussey has been promoted and is an "acting-sergeant" earnestly trying to build a life of middle-class respectability in the city. Much of that aspiration is channeled into his son, Denis, whose birth opens the final book, and whom Johnny wants to see rising above the "blackguards" (338) and serving "with the highest of the land . . . [where he would] know secrets of 'the financial affairs of the empire'" (357). Through Denis, O'Faoláin offers a largely autobiographical portrait informed by his own experience as the son of a fiercely imperialist and anxiously striving R.I.C. father growing up in Cork in the first decades of the twentieth century and moving from admiration and fear for his father toward confrontation over the young O'Faoláin's growing sympathy for nationalism.[17]

A striking index for Denis's doubts about the pattern of life laid out for him by his policeman father is his relationship to the space of the city and the pointed failure of the lyrical mode to provide a means of reconciling to a fixed order. We thus see the more complete emergence of realism in the last book of the novel coincide with the growing presence and aggressiveness of nationalist politics leading up to 1916. Initially, for Denis, "Cork was . . . a place of endless summer daylight, that cold Irish daylight without shadows . . . faint-falling from a sky that in its whiteness is so like the night-sky before the sun has gone, and the dawn before it has risen, that they seemed to sleep through light into light, and had no memory of the darkness at all" (309). Even as this vision of the city conveys a sense of lyrical stability, we can detect the growing late-modernist character of the novel in the slightly strained inflection of the syntax and the surreal notion of "sleep[ing] through light into light."

The familiar timelessness that O'Faoláin conveys via the lyrical mode throughout the novel contrasts sharply with Denis's vision of the city as he is confronted more fully by his father's determined plans for him and he begins to become aware of the stirrings of a nationalist movement that would contest the imperial order to which his father had pledged both of their futures. As a result, "the city he had known builded of light and loveliness sank before his eyes" (358), and "so faded all the luminous memories of his youth . . . [that] all his images from this on became nocturnal and lamp-lit" (359). The mysterious realm of realism and history thus begins to emerge as Dennis glimpses shadowy figures conducting military drills in the semi-darkness or hurriedly transferring packages of what seem to be rifles in out-of-the-way places.

Rather than presenting this dark world as a descent into lyricism's naturalist obverse, however, O'Faoláin offers an intriguing alternative

vision of the city as a dynamic space of shifting possibilities for Denis
as he wanders its streets in search of something he cannot name:

> Still he kept wandering about the city, searching patiently for what
> had never been. He would deceive himself for a week with some such
> fragment out of that reliquary of decay, as a bellied shop window left
> by the nineteenth century; or an old slum rookery, once a gentleman's
> town house, standing like a jail out of a welter of roofs; or it was a
> church, that had actually been a city jail, now so black and ugly and
> unfitting in its conversion that its stones, its ancient purpose, its new
> tenant, would hold him for long spells of wonderment. (359)

O'Faoláin's prose is again strikingly modernist in its odd combina-
tions and contrasts. In place of the timeless stasis that marked Denis's
earlier apprehension of the city, we now have a strange protean
space decaying into the future. Thus, instead of a historical foundation, Denis is "searching . . . for what had never been" and finding
a remarkable fluidity in the city's very concreteness as the incongruous collections of architectural fragments and buildings' shifting uses
over time seem to jostle against each other and mock all sense of resolution or stability. O'Faoláin reinforces this sense of deferral syntactically by way of a series of clauses that never come to any conclusion
and fail to disclose exactly how Dennis "deceive[d] himself" or what
the precise nature of his "wonderment" might be. Arguably what he
is meditating upon here is the historical process itself as a phenomenon where the forms produced at a given moment are consistently
being overthrown in the next.[18] As with O'Faoláin's earlier account of
the aged United Irishman Theo, and the enduring memories of 1798
and the Famine etched into his body, history is apprehended as at
once eminently material and irreducibly dynamic.

In a move that underscores the directness of O'Faoláin's challenge
to the prevailing mode for apprehending Irish history, he makes the
disruption of the lyrical mode quite explicit as we see Denis "trying
to form the lines of a verse" (359) so as to render his "wonderment"
into a more defined and reassuring expression. In another strikingly
modernist feature of the narrative that departs from anything we have
seen earlier in the novel, three efforts to distill an appropriate poetic
response are each interrupted by an emphatic "No!" that seems to
emanate equally from the omniscient narrator and from Denis himself (359, 360). The jarring effect of these repudiations reiterates the
disjunctive impact of the earlier syntactic deferral and shifts the novel
more fully toward a realist narrative mode as Denis and the reader

alike must contend with a sense of a historical dynamism unable to be definitively mediated or fixed by an enclosing lyrical form.

The contrast between lyrical arrest and the rush of history comes to a head on the Easter Monday of 1916 that brings the novel to a close. Though Denis and his mother and siblings leave Cork for a day in the countryside, the pastoral ease of the landscape cannot be encountered directly but is instead mediated by his mother, Bid's, memories of the river Deel that so consistently conveyed an overwhelming somnolence in the novel's first two books. As a result, Denis and his siblings "saw here not one country-side but two, and filled it not with its own life but with the life of her vanished youth" (387). In a way that shows how much the late-modernist character of the novel has come to the fore, O'Faoláin makes the break between the lyrical and the material realm more definitive as the lyrical is rendered as an image superimposed rather than as a means of apprehending—or failing to apprehend—the immediate reality of space and events as had been the case earlier in the novel.

The drowsy spell of the overlaid lyrical image is quickly broken when Denis and his mother talk about his heated arguments with his father, Johnny, over Denis's growing sympathy for nationalism and the still only dimly perceived political activities of his great-uncle Leo Donnel and his cousin John O'Donnell. O'Faoláin expresses the effect this has on the coherence of the lyrical image in a late-modernist language and logic that seem calculated to defy resolution in a way similar to the earlier account of Denis's musings on the ever-changing Cork cityscape: "[W]hen she spoke the likeness [of the Cork countryside to Bid's memories of the Deel plain] faded, farther even than that to which it was so nearly like" (387). The strange, almost gnostic, quality of this account that disables the key lyrical mechanism of simile disrupts the lyrical mode with a particular force as the arrest of time and history in the immediate moment of the Easter Monday outing and the earlier moments along the Deel are simultaneously dissolved.

Plunged into a more radical immediacy, we thus see the serenity of the country scene interrupted by the pressure of immediate historical events signaled by Denis's hazy imaginings of his great-uncle Leo speeding away into the darkness with two fellow Fenians (388) and the insistence of British military lorries "churning up the dust and back-firing" on the main road (389). The late-modernist doubling and dissolving of the static lyrical image thus combine with the realist eruption of historical immediacy and dynamism to underscore the complementary and mutually amplifying functions of O'Faoláin's republican realism.

When Denis and the rest of the family return home that evening, they are immediately confronted with the events of the day in the form of Johnny with a bloody bandage on his head. Unleashing a shower of abuse on "bloody Sinn Fein" as a "lousy pack of country hooligans" and a "low, uneducated pack from the bogs," Johnny attacks Denis for associating with Leo Donnel and John O'Donnell and thereby compromising the respectability of the family with "my pension in sight. . . . and promotion, maybe to head constable waiting for me" (393). The realist narrative aspect again manifests itself by way of the class division between bourgeois respectability and a nationalist radicalism that must be framed by Johnny in terms of a "low, uneducated" hooliganism threatening his claims of civility and his rise within the imperial hierarchy.

Even more importantly, O'Faoláin uses a realist narrative mode to depict the Easter Rising itself. Indeed, though the reader knows what the event is, the novel itself never identifies it as a discrete historical event and instead presents it in terms of a series of swirling tableaux and a profound sense of anxiety and expectation that remains unresolved as the novel closes.

The glimpses O'Faoláin offers emerge as sudden and confusing eruptions of unrest with little or no framing context and frequent use of second- and thirdhand accounts. The few direct depictions we see consist of scenes of running skirmishes with the police on the streets of Cork. O'Faoláin imbues these scenes with a chaotic air as he describes scattered clusters of rebels throwing stones and bricks at the police and cheering excitedly when one of their group finally succeeds in getting an ancient revolver to fire (392). He represents the more famous events of the Rising in Dublin only indirectly through snatches of news passed around by word of mouth and in Denis's excited imaginings of crouching riflemen looking over the rooftops at a city aglow with flames. Through it all, O'Faoláin shows himself to be intent on capturing the raw energy and uncertainty of the Easter Rising. He literally decenters the conventional nationalist account of the Rising by portraying it from the perspective of Cork rather than Dublin and injects a fresh intensity into the rebellion as historical and political event that contests its reification by the Free State as its founding moment.

Ending the novel abruptly in the midst of a profound unrest that has not yet been named or subsumed into an official nationalist tradition, O'Faoláin seeks to call attention to the narrative modalities of bourgeois nationalism and disrupt them at their point of apotheosis. Rather than processing the revolutionary potential of the moment into a symbolic register of transcendent martyrdom, he wrenches this most sacred moment of Irish nationalist tradition back into historical time by insisting on the radical incompleteness of the Rising both in the sense of its diffusion into a disparate array of moments that resist assemblage into a reassuring whole and in the sense of the Free State's fatally compromised expression of its revolutionary project.

Maurice Harmon partly misapprehends this aspect when he observes of the portrayal of 1916 in *A Nest of Simple Folk* that "Revolution is a kind of mystical presence, an emotive force passed down from generation to generation . . . the causes are many and irrational" ("Man of Ideas" 38–39). Though "mystical," the revolution is not ultimately "irrational" in O'Faoláin's account. Instead, O'Faoláin's target is the reification of the revolution by the new Fianna Fáil regime having just come to power in 1932 that he sees as sacrificing republicanism in favor of a more symbolic nationalism.

O'Faoláin's biography of Constance Markievicz that—like *A Nest of Simple Folk*—was published in 1934 helps clarify some of his thoughts on the shortcomings of this version of nationalism. In *Constance Markievicz*, he focuses on what he sees as the tragedy of James Connolly's dynamic materialist analysis being eclipsed by a deadening fixation on a nationalism apprehended primarily through sentimental abstractions. The result of this, as evidenced most notably for O'Faoláin by Markievicz's political career, was the dominant emphasis on a nationalism mediated through abstract symbolism in the wake of 1916. He harshly criticizes Markievicz for failing to carry forward Connolly's republican legacy by allowing herself to be drawn "away from the cause of the living people" (196) and, in remarkably sexist terms, blames her inherent feminine susceptibility to emotion and hysteria for her succumbing to "the hypnotic influence in the glittering vision of Pearse, and for[getting] the rather humdrum and not at all spectacular vision of Larkin and Connolly" (254). We thus see the political implications of the two aesthetic modes of a Yeatsian lyricism and a republican realism made plain.

O'Faoláin elaborates on the consequences of what he perceives as a thralldom to this "glittering vision" in a well-known and, in its time, extremely controversial essay on Daniel Corkery in the *Dublin Magazine* in the spring of 1936. Many of the complexities of O'Faoláin's critique in the essay unfortunately, though understandably, tend to be overshadowed by the provocative—and rather foolish—suggestion that Corkery's enthusiasm for an Irish literature reflecting a crowd at a hurling match might have Nazi or fascist echoes.[19] Less spectacular but more illuminating are O'Faoláin's arguments for a sense of Irish nationalist history grounded in republicanism and "the ideas that ultimately liberated [the Irish farmer], back to Tone and the effect of the French Revolution" (60) rather than one grounded in "the now dead and forgotten Celtic world" (61).

Importantly, O'Faoláin insists on understanding this republican vision of modern Ireland in nationalist terms as an "indigenous growth" and one that recognizes "the value of the Gaelic tongue to extend our vision of Irish life, to deepen it and enrich it" but does so in a way that pointedly rejects the "aristocratic, effete, world" that characterizes the old Gaelic order celebrated by the Irish-Ireland enthusiasts (60–61). O'Faoláin's larger point that he develops in subsequent essays and his widely misapprehended biography of Daniel O'Connell is that the configuration of a Gaelic cultural sphere as historically continuous and pristine is a profoundly conservative intervention that misconstrues Gaelic and Irish history alike. Though aimed most immediately at Corkery and a conservative nationalist vision, this critique also has significant implications for Yeats's approach to Gaelic culture and his canny intertwining of aristocratic lines through his reworking of the materials of Gaelic saga and myth and his mourning of the more contemporary decline of the Anglo-Irish aristocracy.

As he pursues his attack on Corkery, O'Faoláin refuses to concede exclusive claims of indigeneity to an Irish-Ireland vision that offers but one version of a Gaelic past and present and that he sees as ultimately ahistorical in its advocacy for a Gaelic culture and an Ireland that has effectively remained static for nearly a millennium. For O'Faoláin, this vision is ahistorical both in the sense of not acknowledging change and development in Gaelic culture over time and in its effort to undermine or arrest the progressive historical emergence of an impoverished Irish mass through a celebration of a markedly elitist ancient social order.

The effect, O'Faoláin argues, is to normalize the political marginalization of the masses under the guise of "tradition." As he writes, "To us the Irish fisherman and the Irish farmer and the Irish townsman is the result of about one hundred and fifty years struggle. And that, for history, is long enough for us. To us, Ireland is beginning, where to Corkery it is continuing. We have a sense of time, of background . . . but we cannot see the man ploughing against the sky in an aura of antiquity" (60–61). The emphasis on "continuing" and the image of the ploughman cast against the sky as an emblem of an eternal order strikingly reiterates the key elements of the lyrical mode that recurs throughout *A Nest of Simple Folk* only to be interrupted and rendered discontinuous as a realist narration of "beginning" comes increasingly to the fore. We can also see more clearly here how the mythic approach of the Revival's modernist mode can have a remarkably similar effect to that which is typically attributed to late nineteenth-century naturalism even as the Revival also functions in a British literary context to interrupt Victorian naturalism and didacticism.

Underscoring the crucial importance of form for O'Faoláin in narrating the dynamism of Irish historical development and repudiating the different political and aesthetic ideologies sustaining historical arrest, he proposes that a realist fiction offers a more vigorous and expressive thread of Irish writing in the Free State. In an assertion that insightfully links key underlying assumptions common to conservative nationalism and Revivalist aesthetics and is clearly calculated to infuriate Irish-Ireland enthusiasts who would like to dismiss all signs of Anglo-Irish culture as a foreign and inauthentic presence, he proposes: "Had [Corkery] outlined his ideas twenty years sooner, in the period of the Celtic Twilight that he so despises, he would have had many more followers than he has now. But realism, which has been for some time the cry in Irish fiction, has been against him" (61).

O'Faoláin's review of Liam O'Flaherty's novel *Famine* in *Ireland To-Day* in early 1937 illustrates what he sees as the virtue of this body of Irish realist writing: "In the best sense this is the perfect proletarian novel, because the balance is held between the development of the individual (which the proletarian writer usually neglects) and the power of inexorable circumstance, such as the forms of contemporary society, to mould and limit him, and create a persistent tension about him" (81). This account strikingly accords with the vision of the "Catholic novel" O'Faoláin sketches in his 1935 essays on the future of the novel and with Lukács's delineation of what distinguishes realism from naturalism. Though O'Flaherty is generally read in terms of an unrelenting naturalism, O'Faoláin argues that

Famine is marked by "a pity, [and] a heartrending tenderness unusual in O'Flaherty's novels" (81), with the result that his realism coheres in "his keen memory of intimate life" (82). Indeed, O'Faoláin criticizes O'Flaherty only for his failure to apply that same approach to his depiction of the land agent, Chadwick, asserting that "inhuman as his kind were they remain human beings" (82). Though the antipathy toward the land agent may be understandable, this constitutes for O'Faoláin a lapse in realist practice that mars the aesthetic coherence of the novel in a way that resembles Lukács's more far-reaching critique of Zola and his well-intentioned simplifications.

Despite this exacting sense of what constitutes realist narrative practice, O'Faoláin is himself unable to produce an adequate realist novel after *A Nest of Simple Folk*. His second novel, *Bird Alone*, published in 1936, has the opposite problem of the one for which O'Faoláin takes O'Flaherty to task in his depiction of the land agent. Rather than ignoring the individual, *Bird Alone* narrates the growing detachment of its protagonist, Corney Crone, from his social context. Although Corney's isolation is in many ways painful to him, it is nonetheless presented in terms of a proud integrity and an admirable refusal to yield to a repressive sexual and social orthodoxy. This isolation takes a more exuberant form in O'Faoláin's 1940 novel *Come Back to Erin*, with its treatment of Frankie Hannafey's flight to New York and his navigation of a new and at times bewildering sexual and social liberty. Though Frankie does elaborate an ambitious plan of agricultural cooperatives as a counter to what he describes as a bourgeois hijacking of the nationalist revolution, his pleas for action fall on deaf ears in New York as in Ireland (185–92). In both novels, the isolation of the protagonists coincides with a broader sense of historical stasis in 1930s Ireland and a shift away from apprehending political and historical agency in collective terms. In this regard, both novels can be understood to tend more toward naturalism than realism in their emphasis on an individual posed against a fixed social and historical environment. Even as the novels offer a negative commentary on the historical paralysis and repressive cultural atmosphere of late-1930s Ireland, they nonetheless resonate with the era's larger emphasis on the transcendence of the collective by the individual as the site of political and historical agency in postcolonial Irish society.

In this regard, O'Faoláin's second and third novels follow Joe Cleary's schema of Irish naturalist narrative as being "typically focalized through the consciousness of characters so socially isolated and so temperamentally alienated from their communities, or indeed from any sense of collective agency or solidarity, that any sense of social protest is typically funneled into individual rebellion against a common philistinism" (*Outrageous* 97). Cleary explains, however, that this tendency in naturalist narrative need not stem solely from an inherent conservatism or a failure of nerve on the part of the naturalist writer but may be understood as being shaped by the particular historical contexts of late capitalism: "[W]e can conceptualize naturalism neither as a failed realism nor as a depressed, bleakly dystopian realism, but rather as a mode haunted by a commitment to the expectations and conventions of classical realism in a more advanced capitalist context, where these expectations have become increasingly difficult to realise" (*Outrageous* 123).[20]

This understanding of naturalism is a particularly apt one for O'Faoláin as a writer still committed at this point to the unrealized revolutionary potentials of a left-republican nationalism and one simultaneously very attuned to the historicity of form. His second and third novels bear witness to his growing awareness that a realist novel cannot be sustained in a cultural and political atmosphere so dedicated to relegating collectivity to a fixed "tradition" that can only be "preserved" and is thereby effectively separated from concerns of the present. This framing of collectivity as "tradition" serves a crucial purpose as much in deflecting and delegitimizing a more radical collective politics as in underwriting and camouflaging the more profound historical and cultural shift toward apprehending political agency in terms of the individual. This shift is, of course, a signature feature of an emergent late-capitalist culture.

Given his lack of success in sustaining a realist mode in the postcolonial novel, especially when dealing with more historically contemporary material, O'Faoláin turns in the late 1930s to the genres of historical biography and the literary magazine as the primary means of advancing an aesthetic of republican realism. In different ways, O'Faoláin uses these two genres to maintain the crucial tension between the individual and the more collective dynamism of the age that he was increasingly unable to generate in his novels. The realist novel is nevertheless a form that haunts O'Faoláin's approach to both of the latter genres and is especially apparent in his biographical writing as we shall see in his biography of Daniel O'Connell. The importance of the little magazine for modernist writing and for leftist critique in 1930s Britain—and to a far lesser extent, Ireland—is clearly an inspiration for O'Faoláin and one with which he has no small experience as a contributor, editor, reviewer, and reader. We can thus see his effort with the remarkable magazine the *Bell*—which he establishes with Peadar O'Donnell in 1940—as an immensely important part of his late-modernist practice both in terms of his more direct contributions as writer and editor/orchestrator of the magazine and in terms of his ongoing reflections on the material and historical conditions shaping modernism's ultimate decline.

A look at the 1938 biography of Daniel O'Connell, *King of the Beggars*, underscores the importance of the lack of a nineteenth-century Irish realist novel to O'Faoláin's analyses of Irish literary and cultural history and illustrates his sense that it is precisely that lack that later contributes to the rise of an ahistorical notion of "tradition" in the postcolonial era. Though *King of the Beggars* tends to be viewed in the context of the recent revisionist debate within Irish studies as offering a wholesale rejection of nationalist thought, it can be read in its own historical moment of 1938 as an effort to separate republican nationalism from what O'Faoláin sees as a disabling and purposeful framing of nationalist history in terms of a platitudinous recitation of loyalty to a strategically inert Gaelic "tradition."[21]

Through *King of the Beggars*, O'Faoláin offers an alternative history of nationalism grounded in collective struggle and an engagement with the pressing realities of material degradation. He is keen to trace the ongoing historical development of nationalism and the dialectical ripening of a more radically separatist and republican version of nationalism in response to the resistance of what he identifies as "vested interests" (107) responding at key moments to more modest nationalist claims such as Repeal of the Act of Union or Arthur Griffith's now largely forgotten notion of dual monarchy.

The emphasis on a gradual historical development of nationalism that proceeds in a zigzag and discontinuous fashion underscores the fact that O'Faoláin sees nationalism as a dynamic phenomenon rather than the static notion of restoration or continuity to which various emphases on "tradition" would reduce it. In that sense, nationalism is for O'Faoláin an insurgent modern, and even modernizing, discourse, insofar as it enables and organizes the expression of a collective political agency and the emergence of a progressively greater republican dimension within Irish political discourse. Importantly, though, O'Faoláin at this point presents this vision of nationalism as a radical critique of the atomized understanding of politics and culture mediated through the individual that constitutes a hallmark of *capitalist* modernization. O'Faoláin's subsequent essays in the *Bell*, in turn, repeatedly link this unacknowledged embrace of capitalist modernization to de Valera's betrayal of a collective republican politics in favor of the interests of a new economic elite.

O'Faoláin thus frames O'Connell's importance as resting not on any personal parliamentary achievement such as Catholic Emancipation but on an ongoing process of historical development he helps set in motion.[22] Even with the emphasis on O'Connell as the political and rhetorical genius that serves as the resolving agent of the historical narrative he is presenting, O'Faoláin repeatedly portrays the members of the Irish mass as the central characters of the history he is recounting. They are for O'Faoláin "the romantic heroes" and the "living muscles" of the "Irish Atlas" that O'Connell begins to awaken (232).

In this emphasis on historical development and the balance between individual action and historical circumstance, we can begin to see how the biography carries the imprint of the realist novel that is so central to O'Faoláin's late-modernist aesthetic. O'Faoláin immeasurably amplifies this characteristic tension animating realist narrative by grounding the emergent collective politics of nineteenth-century Irish nationalism in an acknowledgment of the reduction to object status that the Irish colonial subject works individually and collectively to disrupt.[23] Even as he is careful to note that O'Connell was "never a republican" (106) and was, indeed, an elitist quite hostile to the amelioration of the Poor Laws and the demands of an incipient trade unionism in Ireland (214), O'Faoláin defines O'Connell's political genius in terms of his insight for "admit[ting] poverty and nothingness as the true fact from which to build" (290). Indeed, the ironic tensions and contradictions between O'Connell's own elitism and reformist tendencies and the far more radical potential of a collectivist politics he helped enable make him a perfect central figure for a realist historical narrative. O'Faoláin makes this connection quite explicit when he notes that "there is nothing whatsoever of the romantic hero about O'Connell—little to admire or idealize" and suggests that this is why no less an authority on realism than Balzac dubbed O'Connell "the absolute realist" (229).

The overwhelming importance of realist form to the alternative nationalist history O'Faoláin is seeking to advance in *King of the Beggars* is ironically punctuated, however, by the realist novel he is unable

to read or write. In a clear rebuke to Corkery that again has parallel implications for Yeats and the aesthetic politics of the Revival,
O'Faoláin heaps scorn on the late eighteenth- and early nineteenth-
century Gaelic poets not only for their veneration of an aristocratic
order he is glad to see ended but for their parallel neglect of the historical and social circumstances that surrounded them: "[H]ow we
curse those Gaelic songsters who might so easily have brought us by
the hand and sat us down by the hearth of the people, and let us hear
them on what most concerned them—instead of weaving their endless
classical myths into hare-brained visions about the return of James
Stuart" (139). Ultimately, however, he suggests poetry would have
been inadequate and only the novel or drama could have sufficiently
illuminated the inner life of "those millions" O'Connell helped organize (220–21). Without a genre such as the novel, the resulting gap, he
argues, cannot be filled as "they seem—because of our ignorance—to
be in such a morass of non-personality that they never emerge as critical, individual human beings" (221).

   This gap in the Irish cultural archive and the inevitable ignorance
it creates for later writers and historians is a recurrent concern for
O'Faoláin in *King of the Beggars*, and it is clearly something that
troubles him deeply. The depth of his regret would seem to indicate a
sense of loss that is as much about the effective lack of a realist novel
in his own era as in the early nineteenth century. O'Faoláin seems
haunted by a sense that he is unable to do justice to those whose
efforts and courage laid the basis for the nationalist history of collective agency and progressive change he fears is being obliterated by a
perverse caricature of "tradition" that would deny them agency and
full humanity. A lack of access to their inner life makes it impossible
for him to offer a definitive blow to this discourse that would reduce
them to objects and diminish their courage and contribution by framing nationalism solely in terms of an inevitable recognition of a Gaelic
continuity that was always already there. As a result, he can only register their agency indirectly through a repeated confession of lack.

   In a comment that distills his insight about the impoverished understanding of Irish nationalist history and, in a different way, anticipates the sort of novel that Beckett would develop to break through
the formal impasse of naturalism, O'Faoláin says of the unrelenting colonial degradation of the early nineteenth century: "For that
there is, naturally, no record but the absence of record: the emptiness of non-being!" (141). Thus, as much as O'Connell may be "the

absolute realist," the focus on him as the narrative center of the book appears, in a certain sense, a compromise and an ironic expression of O'Faoláin's reluctant acknowledgment of the limits of realist narrative in the context of the Free State. He can only register a collective political agency and a historically dynamic nationalism indirectly and ironically as part of a portrait of an individual and "great man" of history.

O'Faoláin's turn to the form of the little magazine in 1940 can thus be understood as an effort to address this problem and realize the radical potential of republican realism in a way that he was unable to do in the novel or biography.[24] As Frank Shovlin points out, O'Faoláin had been interested in editing a magazine for some time and had been effectively precluded from doing so earlier by the launch of *Ireland To-Day* in 1936, the left-republican literary magazine for which O'Faoláin briefly served as books editor (99–100). When he joined with Peadar O'Donnell to launch the *Bell* in 1940, however, O'Faoláin had arguably absorbed lessons from a variety of leftist magazines in the late 1930s in both Britain and Ireland and was more poised to combine those with his own increasingly precise sense of the problems faced by realism in postcolonial Irish culture.[25]

The failure of O'Donnell's initiative to develop a leftist Republican Congress in 1934 and the even more recent collapse of *Ireland To-Day* in 1938 under the pressure of an intense red-baiting campaign spearheaded by the Catholic Church gave O'Faoláin and O'Donnell good reason to be strategic about their positioning of the *Bell*.[26] Thus, O'Faoláin articulates the vision of the *Bell* in his inaugural editorial, "This Is Your Magazine," in terms of a collective endeavor to give voice to "Life" in Ireland:

> You who read this know intimately some corner of life that nobody else can know. You and Life have co-operated to make a precious thing which is your secret. You know a turn of the road, an old gateway somewhere, a well-field, a street-corner, a wood, a handful of quiet life, a triangle of sea and rock, something that means Ireland to you. . . . Men and women who have suffered or died in the name of Ireland, who have thereby died for Life as they know it, have died for some old gateway, some old thistled lag-field in which their hearts have been stuck since they were children. . . . These are the true symbols. When Pearse faced death it was of such things he thought—the rabbit on the sloping field at Rosmuc, the field lit by the slanting sun, a speckled ladybird on a blade of grass. That is Life. You possess a

precious store of it. If you will share it with all of us you will make
this bell peal out a living message. (6)

Redefining Ireland in terms of "Life" and a dynamic insight realized at
the confluence of individual and collective experience where "You and
Life have co-operated" coincides with the notion of realism O'Faoláin
develops in his earlier essays and reviews. At the same time, his use of
the lyrical vocabulary of the "old gateway" and "a handful of quiet
life" and his invocation of Pearse and those who "have died in the name
of Ireland" are calculated and, indeed, masterful efforts to redeploy
and subvert the sentimental language of "tradition" so as to challenge a
more conservative nationalist rhetoric on its own terms and dissolve the
fixity of "tradition" and "symbol" from within. Rather than timelessness or continuity and a cultural agency operating from the outside to
"preserve" an essential Irishness, O'Faoláin shifts the emphasis toward
"Life" and a "living message" that emerges from a collective cultural
agency in an ongoing present. As Nicholas Allen observes of the opening editorial, "A republican ideal persisted in O'Faoláin's invitation for
public participation" (205). O'Faoláin frames the *Bell* as an effort to
give voice to an Irish vitality and sense of "beginning" growing out of
familiar spaces and typical lives that need not be apprehended solely by
way of "tradition."

The envisioned effect of this "living message" reinforces the connection to O'Faoláin's republican realist aesthetic and leaves no doubt
that he is positioning the *Bell* in its opening editorial in terms of a dramatic cultural and political intervention:

> People will hear these change notes to the north and people will hear
> them to the south, and when they say, in field or pub, in big house or
> villa house, "There is the bell," they will echo the replication of its
> notes, and the air will carry the echo wider and wider. Each note a
> message, each echo an answer, each answer a further message—can
> you not imagine them a linking, widening circle of notes, a very peal
> of bells, murmuring all over the land? . . . When between us all, we
> have struck echoing notes so wide and so far, shall we not have awo-
> ken the innumerable variety of Life itself? (6–7)

O'Faoláin's emphasis on "north" and "south"—both rendered in
lowercase—and his placing of "big house" alongside "field or pub"
clearly frame Irish culture in a way that challenges both the Northern
partition and the separation of the Anglo-Irish from the wider populace to suggest that such divisions are at odds with a more natural and
dynamic expression of "Life."

At the same time, the strikingly modernist image of a nonmelodic change-ringing producing endless permutations and echoes across the countryside surprisingly combines a sense of idyllic rural serenity and the underlying dynamism of a discordant cultural contiguity that is at once "echoing" and "a further message," a "replicating" peal and a dissonant expression of "innumerable variety." Rather than the stasis of "tradition" or naturalism, we see a realist vision of an ongoing and collective elaboration of Irish culture and history. That O'Faoláin's own writing from the 1930s repeatedly demonstrates how difficult such an exchange of ideas could actually be only underscores the fact that he is offering this vision as a tactical intervention.[27] Presenting things in such terms allows the *Bell* to build support from a reader-ship and an array of advertisers conditioned by an official national-ist rhetoric of simplicity and solidarity and makes it more difficult to mount an effective opposition to the magazine as had led to the downfall of *Ireland To-Day*.[28]

The extent to which O'Faoláin consciously approaches his editor-ship of the *Bell* in terms of the development of a broader cultural movement is shown by his private correspondence and by how he defines the *Bell* through both his editorials and the material he chooses to include in its early numbers. A 1941 letter to Frank O'Connor reveals O'Faoláin's strategic and ideological positioning as he makes use of the cultural cachet of an elevated national literature in deal-ings with potential wealthy patrons. Even as he assiduously courts the support of the new economic elite, he seeks to redeploy such sup-port to develop a notion of culture as a popular and collective move-ment quite distinct from a more elite notion of literary culture that he explicitly links with Yeats and the prestige of an earlier generation of modernist writers:

> We must work with the materials available. If I can get William
> O'Dwyer of Sunbeam Hosiery to give me £50 for *The Bell*, in adver-
> tising, by writing to him as a literary man, on behalf of literary men,
> and putting it to him that it is *his* job to help letters, then I am doing
> good work. He is, of course, flattered, and I play on that. . . . I have
> to pay for that in humiliations of various sorts, and it is always a deli-
> cate and vital question, "Am I going too far?" If I can get *The Bell* to
> take in every sort of person from Kerry to Donegal, and bind them
> about you and me and Peadar and Roisin do you not see that we are
> forming a nucleus? Take the long view—bit by bit we are accepted as
> the nucleus. Bit by bit we can spread ideas, create *real* standards, ones
> naturally growing out of Life and not out of literature and Yeats and

all to that. It is going to take years and years. Explosions and rages
get us nowhere. You sit down there on your backside and do the high-
falutin' artist, while up here, painstakingly, I am doing a spot of real
construction. (quoted in Harmon 145)

The notion of standards "growing naturally out of Life" rather than
"out of literature and Yeats and all . . . that" is one that O'Faoláin
will effectively abandon by the postwar era. But in the early years of
the *Bell* before he assumes the guise more familiar in critical portraits
from our own time, he strikes a far more radical pose both in relation
to the earlier generation of modernist writers and in relation to his
sense of what a late-modernist practice of republican realism might
yet be capable of achieving.

The material and political implications of this alternative cultural
ideology become increasingly apparent when O'Faoláin opposes the
"arid traditionalism" promulgated by an Irish political and artistic
elite to a more dynamic and modern culture rooted "in the small
towns and little villages" ("Beginnings" 4, 5). Using the same term
that appears in the letter to O'Connor making the case for a collective elaboration of postcolonial Irish culture, he argues that the space
of the small town and village must be developed as "a nucleus" for
Irish cultural and material life. Cultivating such nuclei, he asserts,
will allow modernization to be "slow[ed] down to a healthy tempo"
and "assuaged" so that Irish people can "partake fully and simultaneously of the life of our origins and the life of our fullest ambitions"
("Beginnings" 5).

To facilitate such a shift, O'Faoláin commissions an ambitious
series in the *Bell* on village and town planning. We can discern in that
effort the combination of the cultural, material, and formal concerns
that make up the republican realism underpinning the *Bell* and see
how his approach to modernization and rural Ireland is more nuanced
than the standard critical portrait would suggest.[29] At the same time,
the in-depth engagement with all the complexities of material culture
and the built environment that the planning series entails illustrates
the remarkable range and fluidity of O'Faoláin's late-modernist practice and his particularly innovative use of the magazine genre as he
takes up modernism's long-standing concerns about the relationship
between modernity and the rural periphery and grapples with how
they might be addressed in ways that combine aesthetic and material
concerns. His emphasis on "the life of our origins" alongside "the life
of our fullest ambitions" points to a republican nationalism oriented

toward the pressing material concerns of a rural Ireland decimated by emigration. Such communities are cruelly mocked, O'Faoláin argues, by celebrating "tradition" in a way that consciously neglects the material basis that might sustain it.

O'Faoláin's effort to develop an alternative late-modernist cultural ideology more attentive to a material dimension can likewise be seen in *Bell* pieces as varied as his article on the manufacture of traditional furniture or Flann O'Brien's accounts of the public house and dog track as well as in the magazine's more famous examinations of crises in employment, housing, and education. Shovlin insightfully argues that O'Faoláin borrows the techniques of documentary realism from 1930s magazines of the British Left such as *Fact* and *Left Review* in a way that consciously rejects a more distanced and sensational naturalist account and is instead part of what Shovlin describes as an effort aimed at "radically changing a society which [O'Faoláin] saw as having failed to live up to the promise of the 1916–21 period" (104).

O'Faoláin himself describes this approach in late 1941 as a rejection of "abstract theorizing, generalized argument, loose impressionism" and "superficial literary perfection" in favor of presenting "living matter" and "experience" with the result that "Life has—as it always does—slowly created a form to hold itself. For creation cannot exist without a form or shape to hold it" ("Attitudes" 6). This notion of form arising organically from "Life" rather than being imposed coincides with O'Faoláin's critique of naturalist pretense and his ongoing search for a means of elaborating a realism capable of narrating Irish historical development. He defines this project for the *Bell* in terms of creating "a technique of living . . . suited to our natural democratic, nationalist, and religious bent" and "project[ing] the theory of the Nation in concrete form" ("Attitudes" 11).

O'Faoláin reinforces the political implications of this emphasis on form when he contrasts the precision of the *Bell*'s realist approach with the formlessness of "Celtophilism" and the "poetic myth of the Noble Savage" that would frame the Irish people as "an incoherent, helpless mass with no political integration and no political pedigree" ("Plain People" 6, 5, 7). Though such a critique is again initially targeted against the benighted and disingenuous invocations of "tradition" and "the Gael" by a postcolonial official nationalism, it applies equally to the "Celtophilism" and "poetic myths" of the Revival. Indeed, O'Faoláin's account of these "poetic myths" is quite striking in the way that it identifies a "formlessness" at the heart of an aesthetic practice so famously dedicated to the elaboration of formal precision. The concern with form on the part of Yeats or Synge is revealed to be a matter of internal focus that relies on an indistinguishable background of primitives or "folk culture" to cast the vision of the artist and his relationship to a longer aesthetic or intellectual history in stark relief. Portraying such mythic constructions as antidemocratic and "self-seeking" efforts to "'take the harm' out of political history by pretending that it does not exist or function," O'Faoláin insists on the importance of a sense of form as a key element of "seeing our people politically" ("Plain People" 7).

During his editorship of the *Bell*, O'Faoláin repeatedly stages the struggle over form as a battle over the historical development of nationalism. Consistently portraying the Free State in terms of a historical arrest resulting from the betrayal of a progressive republican nationalism, he argues that "the final stage of the Revolution around 1922 became . . . a middle-class *putsch*. It was not a society that came out of the maelstrom. It was a class" ("Stuffed Shirts" 187). This *putsch*, he asserts, was consolidated in 1932 under de Valera, whom he relentlessly excoriates for maintaining a pretense of republicanism while wielding a "barren power" supported by the "well-padded shoulders" of big business ("One World" [October] 2).

Frequently citing James Connolly as an exemplar, O'Faoláin asserts that nationalism and republicanism are inextricably linked, with the result that true Irish independence "could only have been carried through on the basis of an economic revolution—and that was something that neither the men of 1922 nor the men of 1932 wanted" ("One World" [October] 9). The resulting false nationalism of the Free State seeks to sustain itself and distract attention from its bad faith, O'Faoláin argues, by the "smoke-screen" of sentiment, myth, and "smuthunting" ("One World" [October] 9). Strikingly, O'Faoláin links the "fake-society" of official nationalism and Fianna Fáil's erstwhile republicans to "the successors of Mr. William Martin Murphy," the notorious business leader who was the primary force among the employers in the 1913 Dublin Lockout. He suggests that it was "the people who rose in 1913" who "were thwarted in 1922" and now constituted a key constituency of a republican nationalism that had been abandoned by the official nationalism of the Free State ("Stuffed Shirts" 191).[30]

In the face of this bourgeois stultification of nationalist historical development, O'Faoláin suggests that realist form can play a key role.

In contrast to the conservatism and censoriousness of an ascendant middle-class sensibility, he argues, "the only real sanity in this island, as far as culture is concerned, is in the novels of our Realists" ("Nasty Novelists" 12). Indeed, citing the example of Balzac's postrevolutionary society, O'Faoláin proposes in the September 1943 *Bell* that Irish postcolonial society provides a particularly remarkable opportunity for realist narrative: "What would a Balzac not have done with it, or a Flaubert? So that if one should say that there is nothing to write about one talks nonsense" ("Silent Ireland" 460). Strikingly, though, even as O'Faoláin is championing the possibilities for a realist literature in postcolonial Ireland, the title of the editorial, "Silent Ireland," and the exhortation to follow Balzac underscore a frustration that this potential is not being realized.

From roughly 1944 onward, O'Faoláin's considerations of Irish historical arrest and related questions of form in his *Bell* editorials increasingly tend to frame the Irish situation in terms of a larger historical moment that positions nationalism and the decline of empire in relation to the emergence of a new era of global capitalism. Significantly, in a March 1944 editorial entitled "One World" (one of a series published under the same title), he once again cites Balzac as a model of a "man of letters" who saw the importance of considering literature in relation to its political contexts and observes "Ireland must be aware of world-trends, or, . . . the world may come suddenly on her like a whirlwind" (471). He suggests that the new centers of political gravity and the arrangement of international capital likely to shape the aftermath of the Second World War seem to be arraying themselves against the notion of national sovereignty, especially for small nations like Ireland. As a result, Ireland must consider its relationship to Britain with regard to larger questions of trade and investments and to the fact that "[w]e shall soon be within bombing range of three continents" (471).

O'Faoláin nonetheless rejects the notion of larger supranational structures and federations as "[i]mperialism . . . under a new guise" (469) and suggests that Ireland can play a key role in this new global order precisely because of its understanding of the progressive potential of nationalism as a political and historical force (472). In an assertion that reflects his understanding of the relationship between nationalism and republicanism in the unfolding of Irish nationalist history, he insists that an international socialist revolution that fails to take account of nationalism exhibits "a false theory of revolution" and cites no less an authority than Lenin in support (472).

This wider historical orientation likewise informs one of O'Faoláin's most searing polemics against de Valera in the April 1945 *Bell*. Condemning de Valera's government as "a despotism disguised as a democracy" and the Northern partition as "the dismemberment of our country [that] has become a frozen problem," he suggests that Ireland's place within the international circuits of labor and migration might offer the only hope in yielding what he terms a "Marxist . . . 'historic moment'" that would disrupt the historical and political impasse within Irish nationalism ("Eamon De Valera" 18, 16). As Irish emigrants return after the war, he speculates they may bring with them a new consciousness less susceptible to the repressive effects of "our gombeen-men's ambition" and "de Valera's notions of what a 'good' Irishman is." If not, O'Faoláin predicts, "then the picture of to-day is the picture for ever" ("Eamon De Valera" 17).

Posing Ireland's future in such stark terms perhaps inevitably leads toward a deeper awareness of late capitalism's reconfiguration of politics away from collective agency which Cleary identifies as the crucial historical and material background for naturalism (*Outrageous* 123). Thus, in what is effectively a farewell to republican realism, O'Faoláin writes an editorial entitled "Romance and Realism" for the August 1945 issue of the *Bell*, one of the last few he would edit. Once again, he shows realism to be constitutively intermingled with romanticism. Here, however, he draws from Yeats's famous pronouncement in "September 1913" to declare Ireland's romantic element gone—if not yet definitively "dead." The absence of the romantic aspect in Ireland is framed as part of a larger problem of the age with the global phenomenon of "will . . . barely hanging on by its finger-nails," manifesting itself in Ireland via a "Sentimental Ireland . . . made of pound notes" and "Cathleen ni Houlihan as a pin-up girl" (382).

The notion of an entirely commodified "Sentimental Ireland" and Cathleen ni Houlihan as a mechanically reproduced sex symbol underscores O'Faoláin's sense of the growing efficiency of official nationalism's cultural mechanism and its virtual hegemony as part of a much larger historical phenomenon of capitalist modernity to which Ireland is becoming increasingly synchronized.[31] Though he still holds out the possibility of the return of realism and romance, the markedly subdued tone and cold Yeatsian abstraction that conclude "Realism and Romance" suggest that O'Faoláin has lost his faith in the potential of a republican realist aesthetic and has begun his turn toward the more pessimistic naturalism that Cleary elucidates in his discussion of O'Faoláin's later work.[32]

Eight months later, in the April 1946 issue, O'Faoláin writes his valedictory as editor of the *Bell* and invokes Yeats once again as the basis for a bitterly harsh judgment on what he has done with the journal: "Yeats would not much care for this magazine (and I should not blame him), where politics and social problems intrude, and there is much that he would think purely on 'the surface of life.' It may be that as he did—and was sorry for it—we have gone too much into the arena, come too close to the battle. It may be that poetic truth, which lives remote from the battle, is more to be sought for than political truth" ("Signing Off" 2). O'Faoláin thus effectively surrenders the vision of the *Bell* that had driven the project over most of the preceding years. A more removed Yeatsian "poetic truth" takes the place of the collective endeavor O'Faoláin had described so breathlessly to O'Connor five years earlier in terms that explicitly rejected the standards and priorities of "Yeats and all . . . that." What had previously been the potential materials of "Life" in all its complexity and vitality was now merely "surface." Thus, we find the vision of a late-modernist practice predicated on discovering the underlying dynamism and "mystery" of quotidian reality to be linked to an initial phase of postcoloniality that is impossible to sustain in the wake of broader historical change.

As the 1940s give way to the decade that will famously be marked for Ireland by the full embrace of the values and structures of capitalist modernization by de Valera's chosen successor as leader of the government and the Fianna Fáil party, Seán Lemass, O'Faoláin can be seen to argue that an emphasis on "surface" in Irish writing and culture is the inevitable result of the inherent superficiality of postcolonial Irish society. In "The Dilemma of Irish Letters," which appears in the December 1949 issue of the English journal *Month*, O'Faoláin borrows from Henry James to declare Ireland "a thinly-composed society" that renders a realist novel impossible (373). The cultural and political "formlessness" he had previously contested in the early volumes of the *Bell* as a false imposition, he now declares as undeniably real. The result, according to O'Faoláin, is that "the novelist or the dramatist loses himself in the general amorphism, unthinkingness, brainlessness, egalitarianism and general unsophistication" (376).

As Terence Brown notes in "After the Revival" (574), O'Faoláin is perhaps commenting on his own experience with *A Nest of Simple*

Folk as much as on the experience of Joyce and George Moore when he remarks in "The Dilemma of Irish Letters" on the impossibility of sustaining an Irish realism: "I think it is obvious that realism as a technique for dealing with such material soon arrives at a dead-end. The realist . . . will get one powerful book out of its surges and thrustings and gropings. After that he will either have to repeat himself endlessly, or stop" (376–77). Surrendering thus to naturalism and all that he had decried in his mid-1930s essays on the novel, he suggests that postcolonial Irish society provides "stuff for the anthropologist rather than the man of letters" (376).

In an observation that nonetheless makes clear that his abandonment of realism cannot be separated from his sense of Ireland's increasing synchronization with the political and cultural modalities of an emergent global capitalism, O'Faoláin speculates that the challenges for novelists may extend beyond Ireland and be only part of a larger mid-twentieth-century crisis for the novel genre ("Dilemma" 378). If we recall his earlier protests against the disabling of a republican politics by a cynical elite far more modern than it would ever admit, O'Faoláin's framing of the failure of Irish realism as a symptom of a global historical phenomenon impels us to read his critique of Ireland's cultural and political "amorphism" as a statement of modernization's ascendance in Ireland rather than its absence. Such an understanding of modernization and its effects on postcolonial politics and aesthetics significantly challenges the standard diagnoses of Irish "backwardness" and helps to explain the limitations of a reinvigorated naturalism and the more ambitious government modernization programs that define late twentieth-century Irish culture. Acknowledging the need for a new set of political, intellectual, and formal tools, O'Faoláin thus observes of the failure of realism and the novel, "All we can do, in this period of pause, is to experiment with it . . . to incite writers coming after us, by our very failure" ("Dilemma" 377).

O'Faoláin thus construes failure as productive insofar as it might illuminate the "dead-ends" within Irish postcoloniality and the ways in which political and literary forms based on nineteenth-century paradigms prove to be inadequate for an Ireland increasingly defined by its place within a newly energized capitalist modernity. As one who has spent the better part of two decades trying to elaborate a republican realist aesthetic in a series of vigorous initiatives yielding a prolific array of work across multiple genres, however, this acknowledgment of failure is nonetheless one that exacts a toll on O'Faoláin. He settles uneasily—if quite successfully—into a naturalist aesthetic to which he can never fully reconcile himself given his many years of scrutinizing its shortcomings.

It would take a writer like Beckett to make failure truly productive. Beckett elaborates a radically new form of the novel capable of getting behind the surfaces of a global capitalist modernity that Irish naturalism is only able to reproduce and dilate as dark backdrops for increasingly bitter accounts of stagnation and disempowerment.

Despite its ultimate lack of success, however, O'Faoláin's pursuit of a postcolonial Irish realism over the 1930s and 1940s constitutes an important initiative that helps to fill a gap in the formal history of postcolonial Irish writing while also shedding new light on the trajectory of late modernism during the early postcolonial era. From the perspective of form, a better understanding of O'Faoláin's realist project and the reasons for its failure helps illuminate the relationship between the Irish postcolonial novel and a process of modernization that was under way long before Seán Lemass would come to embrace it as state policy in 1959.

Seeing Irish naturalism as a formal tendency arising from an *excess* rather than a paucity of capitalist modernization highlights the need for the radical formal break O'Faoláin calls for in 1949 as a means of speaking to Ireland's place within an emergent global order. This, in turn, makes it easier to see how Beckett's 1950s "trilogy" can be read in the context of postcolonial Irish writing as an important intervention emerging at the juncture of the national and the global. As we shall see, Beckett's novels provide a means for elaborating the phase shift within postcolonial culture and politics as the modalities of power slide from those of empire and nationalism to the more insidious disavowals common to an incipient globalization and a postcoloniality entering on its maturity.

CHAPTER THREE

Unnaming the Subject

Samuel Beckett and Postcolonial Absence

Until relatively recently, many scholars have been reluctant to consider Samuel Beckett's Irishness as much more than a curious biographical footnote. Though critics as varied as Vivian Mercier, Seamus Deane, Hugh Kenner, Declan Kiberd, and David Lloyd—to name a notable few—have all turned aspects of Beckett's Irishness to useful scholarly account, consideration of Beckett's Irishness has for the most part been the province of specialists in Irish literature.[1] It has typically not been taken up by the larger body of Beckett scholars as a matter of great concern for those seeking an understanding of his place within modernism or those attempting to interpret any but his earliest works.[2] The oft-quoted anecdote of Beckett's reply of "Au contraire" to the French journalist who had asked if he was English offers an intriguing example of Beckett's complex wit. The frequency with which the anecdote is repeated as evidence of Beckett's attachment to his Irishness may only reinforce the sense of its significance to his writing being rather slight, however. Beckett's long exile and his use of French as a primary language of composition for much of his most important work obviously reinforce the sense of the marginal importance of Irish literary concerns to his writing.

As a result, Beckett tends to be apprehended as the ultimate cosmopolitan artist, a writer who demonstrates the growing irrelevance of national boundaries and national literatures. Such understandings of Beckett are not without legitimate bases and extend quite naturally from his stark portraits of characters wandering across blank, undefined landscapes or trapped in strange interstitial spaces.[3] The importance of his reflections on twentieth-century literary form, moreover, lend his work a centrality that would seem to defy any merely local or national conception of his writing.

Despite the huge purchase of Beckett's work, however, it would be a mistake to downplay its Irish dimensions both in terms of its contribution to the development of Irish postcolonial writing and as a means of framing its key contributions to the elaboration of late-modernist form. Rather than reducing his Irish aspect to the biographical realm or to references carrying a distinctive Irish gloss, the Irishness of Beckett's writing is most fully and legitimately perceived when read in concert with an appreciation of his place in the broader history of twentieth-century literature. As Seán Kennedy has observed, the tendency toward partitioning Beckett into an "Irish Beckett" or a "European Beckett" is of a piece with oversimplified notions of Irish backwardness and nonmodernity and European sophistication and artistic freedom ("Ireland/Europe" 5–6) that conventional accounts of Beckett and Irish modernism have tended to reinforce.

From the perspective of postcolonial studies, Beckett's distinctive position as a writer poised between the national and the international spheres significantly coincides with the trajectory of Irish postcoloniality at midcentury as it moves toward a more explicit embrace of a far-reaching program of modernization and the rearticulation of Irish space in relation to global capital flows. With the end of the Second World War and "the Emergency" in Ireland, the late 1940s and early 1950s were marked by significant electoral upheaval and a reorientation of political priorities as the sixteen-year rule of de Valera and Fianna Fáil came to an end in 1948. In the decade that followed, a series of comparatively short-lived governments struggled to develop economic policies that could address growing concerns about Ireland's relationship to the new alignments of international power and multinational capital emerging in the war's aftermath.

The extent to which Irish postcolonial politics followed the course of a broader global phenomenon that increasingly saw power mediated through assertions of presence within the circuits of global capital rather than the fading terms of empire and anti-imperial nationalism is strikingly indicated by the fact that it was ultimately Fianna Fáil that emerged as the party of free trade and the policies of modernization that redefined Ireland from 1957–59 onward. Fianna Fáil had, of course, been formed as "the republican party" in 1926 and had initially come to power in 1932 on a campaign that questioned the middle-class orientation of the earlier Cumann na nGaedhael modernization program. To accentuate the contrast, Fianna Fáil called for implementing the proposal of the leftist republican Peadar O'Donnell to withhold land annuities paid by Irish small farmers to the British government. This approach had led, in turn, to de Valera's "Economic War" with Britain and an economic protectionism posed in anti-imperialist terms in the years leading up to the Second World War. It is thus a telling signal of the profound shift in the orientation of Irish postcoloniality that the architect of that protectionist policy, Seán Lemass, becomes the face of modernization and global capitalist integration as he takes the reins of government in 1959.

Indeed, as debates about such a new departure had been simmering within Irish politics since the early postwar years, we can see the period from the late 1940s to 1958 as an important era of transition where the fundamental terms of Irish postcoloniality effectively shift from those of "tradition" and anti-imperial nationalism toward those of an incipient globalization. Beckett's writing offers one of the most searching analyses of this wider moment in the articulation of a global modernity.

At the same time, given that Beckett orients his work in relation to a deeper history of Irish modernist thought, his relevance to an understanding of the development of Irish postcolonial writing within a late-modernist idiom is obviously of central importance. Indeed, as we shall explore, the critique of certain tendencies within the dominant expressions of Irish modernism that he offers in his early writing coincides in significant ways with O'Faoláin's critique of Joyce and Ó Criomhthain's critique of the Revival. Beckett develops the means for dramatically amplifying the antimimeticism of these more popularly inflected late-modernist narrative modes and produces a novel form by midcentury that has made the quantum leap from a naturalist-inflected modernism that O'Faoláin had called for but been himself unable to realize.

Explaining Beckett's status as a late-modernist writer in both historical and political terms, James McNaughton writes: "Beckett arrived late to the Irish revival and late to modernism: he came of age after the First World War and was 16 during the civil war in Ireland. Perhaps we should not be surprised that his predominant literary signature is aftermath" (56). Underscoring how Beckett's aesthetic explorations fit in with a "second-generation" modernist practice, McNaughton argues that Beckett's use of "aftermath" provides a key means "to evaluate the failures of modernism to accomplish its promise of critique" (56). Importantly, the sense of "aftermath" that McNaughton elucidates in Beckett's writing is at once the aftermath of the initial iteration of modernist literary aesthetics and the aftermath of the anticolonial revolution in Ireland.

Using Beckett's early letters and writings to demonstrate the falsity of the critical commonplace that the intellectual and literary circles of 1930s Ireland were effectively not conscious of modernism, McNaughton asserts that Beckett's accounts of the disappointments of this era of aftermath "reveal the repetitiveness and derivativeness of the [modernist] movement itself" (59). Rather than a simple repudiation of the backwardness of early postcolonial Ireland launched from the perspective of the aspiring European sophisticate, then, McNaughton shows how Beckett "uses Irish provincialism to work out anxieties about modernism's ineffectiveness" (60).

Connecting this sense of aesthetic exhaustion and ineffectiveness with a diagnosis of the ways that a radical political discourse of republicanism had been emptied out and reduced to platitudinous repetition by the official nationalism of the 1930s Fianna Fáil regime, McNaughton insightfully observes:

> The ideological components that revitalized republicanism, under the cover of an increasingly meaningless political cliché, gave way to an outcome opposite to the original connotation. These events staged for Beckett a number of important ideas that became relevant as modernism faced the challenge of fascism in the 1930s: how interpretive models can linger long after their usefulness has expired; how revolutionary language, particularly as it loses any meaningful relationship to historical reality, not only mars political intelligence, but provides cover for reactionary tendencies; and how the artist's imperative to explore . . . also contains a political imperative that language be reevaluated against the historical reality it supposedly describes. (58)

The extent to which this exhausted discourse of official nationalism produces a similarly exhausted and prescriptive aesthetics of "tradition" in early postcolonial Ireland helps to explain, McNaughton suggests, the different challenges faced by an avant-garde in Ireland and Europe during this same period: "The European avant-garde tried to disrupt a disinterested aesthetic tradition that contributed, in Peter Bürger's words, to 'the artist's loss of any social function.' Yet in Ireland . . . the opposite was true. The loss of social function of the Irish artist derived from an 'interested' yet limited political aesthetic that in one form eventually buoyed a rigorous censorship" (62). In this regard, we can see how Ireland's comparatively early entry into post-coloniality helps produce a literature that in many ways anticipates a concern with the aestheticization of politics that would subsequently take on a greater importance within other European and postcolonial contexts. At the same time, McNaughton's analyses of the exhaustion of earlier discourses and forms of political and aesthetic radicalism help to explain the failure of O'Faoláin's effort to breathe new life into older ideological and aesthetic formations via republican realism.

Though their very different social formations provide some fairly obvious reasons for their differing approaches to the sense of aesthetic and political calcification that they diagnose in early postcolonial Ireland along remarkably similar lines, the late-modernist practices of O'Faoláin and Beckett also can be understood as being driven by their respective orientations toward an early or late postcoloniality. O'Faoláin's early critique of modernist "subjectivists" who essentially turn naturalist description inward parallels Beckett's concern with the perils of leading modernist aesthetics and their insufficiently skeptical relationship to language. Ultimately, however, by the end of the 1940s, O'Faoláin resigns himself to what he perceives as the inevitability of postcolonial historical arrest now copper-fastened by Ireland's integration with a robust global capitalism and the submergence of nationalism as a historical force in the new global alignment of power. This surrender coincides with an acceptance of naturalism as the defining mode of Irish writing from the midcentury onward. By contrast, Beckett's innovations in novel form, especially as exemplified by his novels of the early 1950s, offer a radically negative critique of this consolidating order and a vision of "absence" that goes beyond O'Faoláin's weary account of fixity and arrest to offer an alternative narrative mode more attuned to the modalities of mid-twentieth-century capitalism.

Ironically, the degree of Beckett's formal radicalism may be a significant part of the reason why he is not as readily accepted by many critics and literary historians as an Irish writer and still less as a *postcolonial* Irish writer. As his narrative form departs so significantly from the work of other Irish writers of his generation, it has been difficult to position Beckett in the arc of the standard literary histories of the postcolonial era. In large part, however, as we have been exploring, this stems from a misapprehension of the main body of early Irish postcolonial writing as naively mimetic. Greater appreciation of the aesthetic complexity and intellectual sophistication of early postcolonial literature makes it easier to see the connections with Beckett's work, especially in its critique of a more "descriptive" modernism tinged by the methods of anthropology and naturalism.

A crucial aspect of Beckett's approach—especially important when considered in regard to Ó Criomhthain—is his relentless interrogation of subjectivity. Rather than the Revivalists' focus on an alienated or dissociated subjectivity that might find solace or resolution by merging with the reified object of an imagined primitive consciousness, Beckett charts how subjectivity itself exerts a reifying effect that structurally limits representative agency. At the same time, he refuses to follow the path of Joyce's own critique of Revivalist modernism by taking refuge in an exuberant proliferation of representative possibility. Instead, the withering eye Beckett trains on the reified objects and surfaces of a burgeoning late-capitalist culture signals a reflexive late modernism already in the process of transition to postmodernism.

Integrating our understanding of the different phases of Irish postcoloniality with a consideration of the broader history of capitalist development enables us to see Beckett's late modernism and a more familiar mid-twentieth-century Irish naturalism as two divergent responses to Irish postcoloniality's accelerating immersion in modernization and the object-world of late capitalism.[4] Viewed in this way, we can better understand the character and function of the strong naturalist response within Irish literature and see how its critique serves as an ironic aesthetic complement of Lemassian modernization.

Beckett's radical intervention in the form of the novel and the narration of subjectivity thus emerges as important at once for its central role in the history of late modernism and for the light it sheds on critics' overemphasis on naturalism as the inevitable vehicle of an oppositional aesthetic within late twentieth-century Irish literature. What Beckett's aesthetic illuminates and naturalism tends to obscure is how the phenomena of late twentieth-century political stasis and disempowerment in Ireland stem more from the intersection of Irish postcoloniality and late-capitalist modernity than from a lingering fidelity to nationalism or a countermodernity that discourses of "tradition" have grown increasingly efficient at subsuming.

Patrick Bixby's account of the radical reworking of the structure and function of the *Bildungsroman* in Beckett's three novels from the early 1950s helps clarify the importance of understanding the conjunction of postcolonial and capitalist historical formations in the

midcentury era. As Bixby observes, "Even as these novels evoke the
familiar features of the *Bildungsroman* . . . they consistently deny the
image of a subjectivity progressing from a stable origin towards an
ever more substantial presence, replacing this trajectory with a narrative in which identity is relentlessly in flux" (28). Bixby identifies the
Bildung narrative as "the literary form that most plainly announces
the ideology of European capitalist modernity" (33). Nonetheless, he
insists that Beckett's work "participates in a specifically *postcolonial*
critique of modernity, related to, but distinct from, his profile as an
avant-garde or postmodern writer" (33, emphasis in original).

An important aspect of the postcolonial dimension of Beckett's
work not to be overlooked in the emphasis on the forward motion of
Bildungsroman—and which Bixby is careful to note—is its simultaneous critique of "a stable origin" that I have been suggesting can be
connected at once with the primitivism of Revivalist modernism and
with the notion of "tradition" nurtured by the institutional nationalism of the postcolonial state. So Beckett offers a critique not simply of
the ends of the *Bildung* narrative but also of its groundings. The relationship between these two intertwining aspects of his critique arguably only comes into complete focus in the midcentury era as the Irish
postcolonial state's project of institutional nationalism merges more
explicitly with that of capitalist modernity.

Bixby similarly connects the regime of subjectivity narrated into
being by the *Bildungsroman* with "the authority of the bourgeois
nation-state" (8) and asserts that "[t]he Beckettian 'no man's land'
functions as a counter-site to modernity, where the voice of his nar-
rators contests the teleological movement from savagery to civility,
otherness to sameness" (39).[5] Though a terminology of "counter-site"
risks confusion in its suggestion of a more stable space of absolute
inversion, Bixby's formulation of a "teleological movement from savagery to civility, otherness to sameness" usefully renders the main
thrust of Irish postcolonial narrative evident from the Blasket texts
onward. Understanding Beckett's intervention in this way also provides an important alternative to the naturalist novel that begins to
emerge as the dominant form in Irish writing from the midcentury
onward. Viewed alongside Beckett's writing, the naturalist novel's
affinity for a robust program of modernization becomes more evident.

For all that, coming as he does from a middle-class Protestant family, raised in the exclusive Dublin suburb of Foxrock, and educated at
the elite Portora Royal School and Trinity College Dublin, Beckett's

class and religio-ethnic formation can sometimes work as a barrier toward perceiving him in an Irish or postcolonial light. As one who shared much of the same early formation, including attendance at Portora and Trinity a few years behind Beckett, Vivian Mercier's comments about Beckett's social and cultural milieu offer an interesting perspective on the question of his relationship to colonial power in Ireland:

> Beckett grew up—happily, as he insists—in Foxrock, then one of
> the more distant and exclusive Dublin suburbs. His neighbors were
> mainly well-to-do professional people, many of them Protestant,
> living in comfortable houses set in their own grounds. A few were
> retired British Army officers. Golf was part of their way of life at a
> time when Irish golf clubs were less democratic than they are now.
> The males and some of the females of the typical Protestant family
> took the train every weekday to office, school or university in Dublin.
> In all these places they were likely to be associating almost exclusively
> with fellow Protestants—as Beckett did at Earlsfort House School
> and later at Trinity College. Irish Catholics, rich or poor, played
> walk-on parts in their lives. The females who stayed at home spent
> their leisure time with other Protestant ladies, though their maids and
> gardeners were usually Catholic. If one preferred to think of oneself
> as English, there was really no reason not to.[6] (*Beckett* 28)

This description would suggest that Beckett was likely to be intimately familiar with the experience of a distinct colonial elite, whatever he may have felt about it. Indeed, Mercier describes himself and Beckett as "colonials" and claims that "we find it hard to shake off the wariness and mistrust of the natives proper to a foreign garrison" (*Beckett* 27).

Beckett's deep immersion in a "colonial" background makes it difficult to ignore the ways in which the specters of empire may linger in his subsequent meditations on power and representation.[7] The status of the Anglo-Irish in postcolonial Ireland as a marginalized but not wholly disempowered elite would seem to make transactions of power in the colonial and postcolonial spheres an even more likely influence. For in the shifting fortunes of the Anglo-Irish, Beckett could see perhaps more clearly than many the disconnection between representation and power and the consequences of continued investiture of authority in stagnant forms and institutions.

It might seem most obvious, therefore, to propose a postcolonial reading of Beckett rooted in the experience of Anglo-Irish marginalization after 1922 and focusing on the concomitant critique of a repressively orthodox postcolonial state incapable of fulfilling its claims of representation. Indeed, much interesting work remains to be done along these lines. Though we have seen considerable discussion of Beckett's attacks on the censorious atmosphere of the Free State and his antagonism toward an Ireland that drove him into exile, these matters have generally not been considered in terms of a postcolonial rubric. Beckett's famous claim that it is the British government *along with* the Catholic Church that should be seen as most responsible for the profusion of great Irish writers in the late nineteenth and twentieth centuries (Bair 492) illustrates the extent to which he sees the repressive institutions of postcolonial Irish society as being intertwined with colonial precursors.[8]

To the extent that such work focuses on the specific content of Beckett's objections and his historical relationship to Ireland, however, it seems likely to have very little impact on either the canons of Beckett criticism or the broader fields of modernist studies or postcolonial studies. Far more useful, seemingly—and far more resonant with Beckett's own method—would be a consideration of how he addresses the logic of power upon which postcoloniality and an emergent global capitalism constitute their relationship at midcentury. Besides offering a reading of Beckett more intellectually consistent with his late-modernist aesthetic, such an approach opens a wider political dimension for modernism and postcolonialism alike. Modernism can be seen more clearly as an aesthetic movement emerging—at least in part—from the collapse of empire and the rise of a new order of global power. At the same time, a postcolonialism viewed through the prism of Beckett is one more deeply infused with the energies of an intellectual and aesthetic radicalism and less easily conflated with a caricature of nationalism.

The complexity and promise of such an approach to Beckett's work is perhaps nowhere more evident than in the last of the three novels he publishes in the 1950s. *The Unnamable* offers a thoroughgoing critique of the mediation of power by discourses of representation. The precise rendering of the mechanisms of modern discursive power and the means by which they reconstitute themselves in the face of resistance makes *The Unnamable* especially relevant to analyses of postcolonial subjectivity. At the same time that it calls into question the extent to which a rapidly modernizing postcoloniality represents a substantive change from an imperial mentality, Beckett's account also offers a sense of the unrealized potential of an agency outside the bounds of subjectivity previously hinted at by Tomás Ó Criomhthain.

The terms of Beckett's critique of power are essentially the same as those of the primary critiques of representation he offers in the broad realms of language and art. In each, his focus tends to be on the stability of the object of representation and the ways in which claims of coherence distort and deny an underlying dynamism. An early critical work such as his study of Proust, originally published in 1931, reveals his contempt for literature that "describes" and is "content to transcribe the surface" (59). Dismissing such work as "the penny-a-line vulgarity of a literature of notations" (57), Beckett champions Proust's "involuntary memory" as a means of accessing "the real" (20). Thus, rather than a shift into a realm of complete abstraction, we see a residue of "the real" that persists throughout Beckett's work and lingers beneath the surfaces of representation. In this regard, we can see how his project coincides with the antimimeticism of O'Faoláin's early work even as Beckett focuses on the exhaustion of language and politics rather than the prospect of their revivification through republican realism as O'Faoláin does.

From the 1930s, the two pieces of writing that offer some of the clearest articulations of Beckett's general critique of representation are his 1934 essay "Recent Irish Poetry" and the well-known "German Letter of 1937," both collected in *Disjecta*: Miscellaneous Writings and a Dramatic Fragment. In each, we see him apply his analysis of the object's stability to a consideration of the role of literature in a strikingly programmatic way. The deep theoretical continuities between the two make it clear how much Beckett's engagement with the politics of postcolonial writing in Ireland lingers behind his vision of a late-modernist literary aesthetic. That these ideas remain so prominent in a work like *The Unnamable* illustrates how postcolonial concerns can be seen to penetrate to the very heart of a late modernism that has typically been perceived by critics as being more focused on matters deemed more "purely aesthetic."

The intersection of these two aesthetic and political agendas can be seen quite clearly in "Recent Irish Poetry." Published in 1934 under the pseudonym of Andrew Belis and only attributed to Beckett in 1971, the essay offers a fascinating perspective on how some of Beckett's key theoretical foci emerge in the context of debates within Irish modernism during the early postcolonial era. Essentially a critique of the mythic emphases of the Revival, "Recent Irish Poetry" decries their continuing influence under the regime of "tradition" fostered by the Free State. He suggests that the future of Irish poetry lies with a more radically experimental writing that he sees being crowded out of Ireland by an influential cadre of older writers generally affiliated with Yeats. Beckett terms these writers and their younger followers "the antiquarians" and includes among their number people such as James Stephens, Austin Clarke, Padraic Colum, and George Russell. His most prominent target, however, is Yeats himself. Even as his portrait is not completely lacking in respect, Beckett repeatedly takes Yeats to task for his role in fostering an Irish literature obsessed with celebrating figures of Irish legend. Implied in this criticism is a broader attack on a perceived imperative for Irish writers that Beckett sees as privileging a literature tending toward allegory and the reified objects of "tradition."[9]

As its title makes clear, "Recent Irish Poetry" locates these concerns within an established Irish debate even as Beckett also tries to push toward a broader reconsideration of the aesthetic politics of an anthropological modernism by means of an examination of the materiality and the stability of the object. Reading "Recent Irish Poetry" in the context of other contemporaneous discussions of the Revival and its influence, John Harrington remarks that Beckett's critique "was not news" (31). Harrington argues that its similarity to other critiques of antiquarianism within Irish writing suggests the essay be taken simply as a sign of Beckett's depth of awareness of and involvement with Irish literary culture. He notes, in fact, that Yeats himself had adopted a similar position in the 1890s in his criticism of Young Ireland ballads and Charles Gavan Duffy's New Irish Library (33). Harrington's point in this regard is crucially important. Not only does the familiarity of Beckett's argument suggest significant engagement with a tradition of Irish literary culture, but the level of his knowledge and engagement must necessarily complicate the typical understanding of the early Beckett as being formed almost entirely under the influence of more "continental" thinkers such as Descartes or Dante or, in a different way, the later Joyce (30).

Greater attention to the theoretical bases of "Recent Irish Poetry" may suggest, however, that in addition to demonstrating an engagement with a tradition of Irish literary criticism, Beckett is consciously revising or updating it. In other words, the lack of novelty of Beckett's critique of the Revival may be precisely the point. The very familiarity of the critique makes his more subtle points about the stability of the object stand out more clearly. In other words, Beckett is not simply intervening on the matter of the Revival and its influence but, more profoundly, on the way the critique offered *by* the Revival fails to contend adequately with the underlying intellectual and aesthetic problems of representation framed by empire. He identifies as a primary concern "the degree in which the younger Irish poets evince awareness of the new thing that has happened, or the old thing that has happened again, namely the breakdown of the object, whether current, historical, mythical, or spook" ("Recent" 70). Beckett's reference to "the new thing that has happened, or the old thing that has happened again" simultaneously acknowledges the lack of novelty in his critique and subtly chastises Revivalist thought for its failure to attend to the metaphysical dimension of "the object" in its analysis. It at once finds fault with the Revivalist critique and makes that critique itself coincident with the object that must be seen to disintegrate.

Beckett's strong concern to distinguish his analysis in "Recent Irish Poetry" from the earlier Yeatsian critique identified by Harrington would seem to be indicated by his early observation that those who see "the stuff of song as incorruptible, uninjurable and unchangeable, never at a loss to know when they are in the Presence, would no doubt like [the breakdown of the object] amended to breakdown of the subject" (70). Beckett immediately adds, however, that the breakdown of the subject "comes to the same thing—a rupture of the lines of communication" (70). For Beckett, the fragmentation of the subject cannot be seen as its own phenomenon but must be viewed as a secondary extension of a more far-reaching critique of the stability of the object. Here, we can see a key point of connection between Beckett and the late modernism of other Irish postcolonial writers. In this focus on the stability of the object as primary, we can detect the resonances with Ó Criomhthain's response to the Revival's construction of the timeless Gael and O'Faoláin's antimimetic realism.

Though Beckett insists that "the breakdown of the object" has a broad metaphysical purchase that extends beyond the spatial and temporal specificities of postcolonial Ireland, the phenomenon is one that has a particular urgency and significance in that context. Noting that disdain for those who would insist on the importance of the breakdown of the object is "not peculiar to Ireland or anywhere else" (70), he nonetheless suggests that a failure to engage with the matter is a problem that is "especially acute in Ireland, thanks to the technique of our leading twilighters" (71). Beckett's particular interest in calling attention to "the breakdown of the object," an interest that remains an abiding concern throughout much of his later work, must thus be seen as being driven in no small part by its prominence within a larger postcolonial problematic.

In "Recent Irish Poetry," those unwilling or unable to take adequate cognizance of this breakdown suffer a full measure of Beckett's famously acerbic wit:

> [T]hose who are not aware of the rupture, or in whom the velleity of becoming so was suppressed as a nuisance at its inception, will continue to purvey those articles which, in Ireland at least, had ceased to be valid even before the literary advisers to J. M. Synge found themselves prematurely obliged to look elsewhere for a creative hack. These are the antiquarians, delivering with the altitudinous complacency of the Victorian Gael the Ossianic goods. (70)

Beckett's acid reference to the "the velleity of becoming [aware of the rupture]" being "suppressed as a nuisance" makes clear the extent to which he sees the matter in explicitly political terms as an aesthetic serving particular and consciously chosen ends. His wry description of "delivering . . . the Ossianic goods" with "the altitudinous complacency of the Victorian Gael" puts a particularly sharp point on this critique of an oversimplified cultural coherence condescendingly imposed by exoticizing Revivalists. Bringing together Macpherson's Ossian controversy and Yeats's poetic exploitation of the legends of Oisín, Beckett's sly reference to "the Ossianic goods" brilliantly encapsulates his sense of the fraud being perpetrated by the commodification of "tradition."

Beckett's point in this regard would seem to be twofold. Most fundamentally, he argues that an emphasis on the stability of the object constitutes a false imposition and "a flight from self-awareness" (71) that would enclose art and self alike. At the same time, he takes particular exception to the Revival's disingenuous hearkening to "tradition" for more materially and culturally "pure" elements out of which this vision of stability might be cobbled together. Not only does this evade the problem of the breakdown of the object by cynically invoking the imagery of a supposedly more intact past, it does so in a way that projects the reifying efforts of the Revivalist writer onto the Gaels themselves.

This double evasion lies at the heart of the key term "antiquarian" that Beckett deploys so devastatingly in the essay. As a phrase such as "the altitudinous complacency of the Victorian Gael" deftly conveys, the turn toward Gaelic material is at once a flight from the pressing conditions of modern dissolution and an assertion of power over a Gaelic other. The "altitudinous complacency" is a mask facilitating a performance of exceeding assuredness and mendacious disinterest. It is precisely just such a performance that undergirds the anthropological discourse of the Revival and—as the Blasket texts make so clear—the Gaelic fetish of the Free State that succeeds it. Thus, Beckett does not simply illuminate the falsity of the object's stability as part of an aesthetic critique of a particular modernist expression but, in fact, shows how such expressions inevitably intertwine with a larger discourse of power that would seek to naturalize and displace its underlying interests.

A parallel concern for Beckett with the "antiquarian" poetic lies in the concomitant neglect of an underlying maelstrom of self that exceeds the bounds of the subject. He poses the issue in terms of a shifting "centre" of self that contrasts with an objective "edge" or "circumference." The antiquarian poets concern themselves exclusively with this edge and endeavor to trace the solidity and durability of its contents: "At the centre there is no theme. . . . But the circumference is an iridescence of themes—Oisin, Cuchulain, Maeve, Tirnanog, the Táin Bo Cuailgne, Yoga, the Crone of Beare—segment after segment of cut-and-dried sanctity and loveliness" (71).

Beckett's assessment makes it clear that the problem with the antiquarian's "circumference" is not simply its false stability and cohesiveness as object but its lack of vitality or distinctiveness. Though marked by "iridescence" and "loveliness," it remains "cut-and-dried" and repetitious in "segment after segment." The intact but desiccated result underscores the anthropological aspect of the antiquarian aesthetic in both its reduction of the colonized other to an easily definable object and an accompanying investment in a universally intelligible symbolism. In opposition to the "centrifugal daemon" or "Celtic drill of extraversion" (73) that he sees driving the antiquarians, however, Beckett presents an emerging school of Irish poetry who take "self-perception" and "the centre" for a theme and show the influence of the French surrealists and poets such as Eliot and Pound. In this group, he places poets such as Thomas McGreevy, Brian Coffey, Denis Devlin, and Lyle Donaghy (74–75), most of whom he knew well as fellow Irish exiles in Paris.[10]

Beckett's emphasis on the importance of these poets' work on "self-perception" and a shifting "centre" illustrates the crucial connection between "the breakdown of the object" and "the breakdown of the subject" that he mentions at the beginning of "Recent Irish Poetry" and yokes together under the heading of a "rupture of the lines of communication." The near-identity of the two—the breakdown of the object and the subject—and the pronounced need to turn toward a theme of "self-perception" constitute a remarkably complicated problem that continues to drive Beckett's work for some time.

Beckett's notion of "self-perception" might be best understood as a perception that supersedes both subject and object and, indeed, exposes subject *as* object. Importantly, this superseding of the subject is not oriented toward a nihilistic emptiness but rather a paring away of reification. This is why self-perception constitutes such an important aspect of the breakdown Beckett charts; the breakdown of subject and object is coextensive with the self's coming to consciousness.

The failure to appreciate this fully goes a long way in explaining why Beckett is so often mislabeled as "apolitical." If one takes seriously the Irish context of "Recent Irish Poetry" and considers the ways that the late-imperial contexts of the Revival overshadow both its language and its theoretical claims, however, the political implications of Beckett's aesthetic project come into sharper focus. As Seán Kennedy notes, the analyses of "Recent Irish Poetry" are "conducted in pursuit of 'the nucleus of a living poetic in Ireland,' and, what is less often acknowledged, in arbitration between available Irish alternatives" ("Ireland/Europe" 7). Beckett's language of "the nucleus of a living poetic" strikingly coincides with the language O'Faoláin will use to describe the mission of the *Bell* a few years later and again reminds us not only of Beckett's engagement with the unrealized potentials of postcolonial Irish writing but also his persistent interest in a mysterious or undefined center or "nucleus" that can thrive as the shell of both object and subject fall away. The challenge to the Revivalists' definition of the object and its linkage to the elaboration of the subject highlights the role that a primitivist aesthetic plays in constructing the false self of the Revival writer's own subjectivity and subsequently that of the postcolonial "primitive" emerging into modernity as we see in the Blasket texts and as Beckett himself will proceed to treat in *Watt* and the novels of the "trilogy."[11]

Locating a self beneath the surface of the "antiquarian" discourse of the Revival's anthropological modernism and the official nationalist discourse of "tradition" that constitutes its more homely reiteration in the postcolonial era, Beckett provides the basis for an aesthetic and a politics that radically destabilizes the dominant categories of postcolonial identity. Thus, although Beckett maintains an idea of a self or center, his emphasis on absence, silence, and violent discontinuity starkly contrasts with the elaboration of a newly centered national culture that Jed Esty traces in English late modernism during the same period (7). Rather than filling in an absent center at the imperial core now coalescing as a result of "demetropolitanization," Beckett instead indicates a center that had been covered over by the false presence of definitions generated by the "metropolitan perception" of empire and repeated to the point of exhaustion by an official nationalism emptied of any potential for critique. As James McNaughton's analysis of the function of postcolonial Irish political discourse for Beckett helps to illustrate, this critique of an evacuation of meaning through repetition is part of a broader aesthetic problem Beckett is addressing and should not be mistaken for a disengagement from postcolonial politics (66–67).

This understanding sheds crucial light on the further elaboration of these ideas that we see Beckett present in his famous "German Letter of 1937" written to Axel Kaun three years after the publication of "Recent Irish Poetry." In the letter, language itself seems to have taken on many of the objective and falsely representational aspects that he earlier decries in the antiquarian poetic: "It is indeed becoming more and more difficult, even senseless for me to write an official English. And more and more my own language appears to me like a veil that must be torn apart in order to get at the things (or the Nothingness) behind it. Grammar and Style. To me they seem to have become as irrelevant as a Victorian bathing suit or the imperturbability of a true gentleman. A mask" (171). We can see here strong echoes of his language from "Recent Irish Poetry" in his references to "a Victorian bathing suit," "the imperturbability of a true gentleman," and "[a] mask." Beckett once again frames the problem in terms of a Victorian propriety that creates a false sense of disinterested authority and a superficial sense of self coalescing from acts of overly confident external description.

This ongoing naming that Beckett finds so wearisome closely parallels the anthropological orientation that would purport to delineate the features of the primitive and distill the "tradition" of "the folk." While Beckett has already linked this orientation to an aesthetic of "cut-and-dried . . . loveliness" in "Recent Irish Poetry," his deeper interest here in "the things" or "Nothingness" beneath the surface of language recalls the insights offered by the Blasket writers, especially Tomás Ó Criomhthain, as they empty out the figure of the Gaelic primitive. The assault on language that Beckett proceeds to develop thus can be understood as significantly intensifying the critique of anthropological modernism that we have seen in the earlier late-modernist expressions of postcolonial Irish writing. Just as the Revival and Joyce provide the impetus for the alternatives presented by the Blasket writers and O'Faoláin, we see both fulfilling a similar function for Beckett in his early efforts to establish the bases for his own late-modernist aesthetic, even as he ultimately pushes modernism to its very limits.

Beckett's concern with English is, of course, profoundly different from the classic chafing under the colonizer's language or even something akin to the more complicated differential relationship to language that Joyce renders so economically in the famous "tundish" passage in *Portrait of the Artist*. Beckett takes issue more fundamentally with language's basic representational function. His antipathy to language is perhaps best understood as an extension of his earlier disaffection for the iridescent "circumference" of the antiquarians. By the time of the "German Letter," Beckett has begun to see language itself as inevitably implicated in the problem of representation and a failure to come to terms with the breakdown of the object.

This failure can no longer be attributed to a particular poetic for Beckett, even one that might present the especially egregious instance of blithe evasion that he detects among the Revivalists. His measure of relief at being able to turn to German in his letter to Kaun—and, of course, French in his later work—results from the slight but crucial alienation from language afforded by working in a language other than his native tongue. This linguistic displacement facilitates his critique of language's representational status and radically advances the antimimetic project of the late-modernist aesthetic practices running through early postcolonial Irish writing. Just as the turn toward "self-perception" constitutes an inescapable aspect of the consideration of the breakdown of subject and object, we see that Beckett poses his attack on the representational stability of language in terms of accessing a state beyond representation.

Thus, describing to Kaun his vision of what the writer must do in the face of a reifying language, Beckett offers a brief but stark manifesto:

> As we cannot eliminate language all at once, we should at least leave nothing undone that might contribute to its falling into disrepute.

> To bore one hole after another in it, until what lurks behind it—be
> it something or nothing—begins to seep through; I cannot imagine
> a higher goal for a writer today. . . . Is there something paralysingly
> holy in the vicious nature of the word that is not found in the ele-
> ments of the other arts? Is there any reason why that terrible mate-
> riality of the word surface should not be capable of being dissolved,
> like for example the sound surface, torn by enormous pauses, of
> Beethoven's seventh Symphony, so that through whole pages we can
> perceive nothing but a path of sounds suspended in giddy heights,
> linking unfathomable abysses of silence? (172)

Though the calls to bore holes in language and make every possible
effort to bring it into disrepute are perhaps the most arresting part
of this oft-quoted section of the letter, Beckett's emphasis on "what
lurks behind" language constitutes an important motive for his critique that tends to be neglected. Still more overlooked is the way that
his invocation of Beethoven positions this assault on language in the
context of a broader aesthetic project. Beckett is clearly not attack-
ing language as part of some sort of nihilistic effort. The point is not
the destruction of all but rather the more targeted destruction of the
edifices of representation that might enclose and distort self, art, or
agency. As H. Porter Abbott observes of the negativity of the "German Letter" and its assault on language:

> The fascination with an *hors-texte* which he expresses in this letter
> is a fascination with possibilities, not an assertion of actualities. By
> contrast, a skepticism that accepts the absolute absence of knowledge
> outside of the text is to that extent not skepticism but certainty. In
> its finality, it assures. However bleak, such an absolute stance con-
> veys greater "metaphysical comfort" than does the full import of the
> adverb "perhaps," which . . . Beckett has called the most important
> word in his work. (55)

Beckett's invocation of Beethoven summons the power of artistic
precedent and a broader aesthetic impulse to amplify the call for a
disruption of reification. Simultaneously, the references to the "something or nothing" that lurks behind representation points to a substantive alterity that we can see from "Recent Irish Poetry" to have a
significant postcolonial inflection.

   To raise the possibility that it is "nothing" that lurks behind representation to await a "seeping" release is certainly not to suggest that
the project of boring holes in language may prove fruitless. Indeed, it
is not even to propose that the effort may inadvertently give way to
nihilism if a nothingness might seep through to corrode and obliterate

all. An extremely important term in Beckett's work, "nothing" should be understood not as emptiness or meaninglessness but as a sort of absence akin to the "unfathomable abysses" he admires in Beethoven. Not only is this a substantive "nothing" for Beckett, it is one whose substantiality combines significantly with the other possibility of a "something" behind language to ensure that language and representation do not simply reconstitute themselves in the form of a more purely representative "anti-language" of silence. The two possibilities of "something" and "nothing" interpenetrate and mar each other productively in a way that preserves a creative negativity.

The extent to which Beckett's project goes beyond a simple argument about the artifice of language and instead constitutes a more far-reaching critique of representation and its ends becomes apparent by the end of the "German Letter." After conceding the necessity of a gradual approach and distinguishing his aim from a Joycean "apotheosis of the word" (172), Beckett lays out his objective in more polemical terms: "On the way to this literature of the unword, which is so desirable to me, some form of Nominalist irony might be a necessary stage. But it is not enough for the game to lose some of its sacred seriousness. It should stop" (173). Beckett's impatience with "sacred seriousness" and his desire to obliterate the larger structure of "the game" rather than simply mitigate its effects reads as a wholesale repudiation of an overarching order of representation. This repudiation can be understood as a "second-generation" refinement of modernist aesthetics and an effort to face the full implications of an antimimetic writing practice. At the same time, within 1930s Ireland, the immediate contexts of censorship and prescriptive notions of literary and cultural expression based—somewhat ironically—on retreaded versions of Revivalist imagery provide ample illustration of the politically and culturally stultifying effects of a literature that traffics in such reconditioned objects.

Indeed, the problem of an overinvestment in a politics of representation is quite acute in early postcolonial Ireland, and Beckett's analyses in such essays as "Recent Irish Poetry" and "Censorship in the Saorstat" show it to be a matter that greatly exercises him. His regular visits to Ireland and his experience of having his works banned by the Irish censorship authorities would make it impossible for him not to be cognizant of the pressures on Irish artists to produce work compatible with an exceedingly narrow vision of a "representative" Irish culture. Though Beckett's exile may have afforded him more space to contend with such pressures, it certainly cannot be said to have rendered them insignificant. Indeed, as Patrick Bixby notes, Beckett's early correspondence and published writings as much as his physical and linguistic exile can be understood as part of an effort to discover a postcolonial writing that does not reproduce "the formal consistency between Irish cultural nationalism and imperialist ideology" (163) but instead "focuses on the tension between redemption and reification" (184).

Seamus Deane's comparison of Beckett's work to that of Joyce in *A Portrait of the Artist* offers an elegantly concise elaboration of how Beckett's origins shape his response to the censorious atmosphere fostered by the cultural ideologies of official nationalism in the early postcolonial era: "Joyce's text is a manifestation of a will to power by someone who has felt enslaved. Beckett's are refusals of that will to power by someone who has seen the disappearance of the Gaelic language as an historical premonition of his own plight. If the Anglo-Irish could only achieve the dumbness of the Gaelic Irish, that would be a mercy" (130). Beckett not only refuses the heroic pose and cold Olympian detachment of an Anglo-Irish modernist such as Yeats, but, as Deane suggests, he finds in the tenuous postcolonial position of the Anglo-Irish echoes of an Irish history of marginalization and dispossession previously presided over by the Anglo-Irish themselves.

Beckett's relationship to his particular Irish social formation is obviously a complicated and contradictory one that ultimately eludes simple declarative statement. Deane's elliptic comment about the dumbness of the Gaelic Irish constituting "a mercy" for the Anglo-Irish, however, captures much of the complexity of the move beyond representation that Beckett explores in his remarkable reflections on silences of different sorts. At once resonating with the critique of Revivalist fetishization that echoes across the gaps and silences of Ó Criomhthain's writing, Beckett's work amplifies those silences and transposes them to a more rarefied social and aesthetic register marked by a parallel sense of obsolescence.

David Lloyd traces a similarly complex and disjointed sense of inheritance for Beckett in his groundbreaking analysis of Beckett's *First Love (Premier Amour)* as a study of postcolonial subjectivity. Stressing the necessary indebtedness of the subject (50), Lloyd argues that the postcolonial subject is at once indebted to the "alien absent presence" of the colonizer and that of the "paternal" precolonial origins that must be reassembled as part of nationalism's attempt to "restore authenticity to the colonized subject" (*Anomalous States* 54). As Lloyd points out, such an effort is necessarily futile in that the subject's differential formation and reliance on a dispersed and fetishized originary identity inevitably renders it inauthentic and alienated from the self.

Postwar works like *Premier Amour* reflect the vision of linguistic estrangement we see in the "German Letter" even as they also come more immediately in the wake of Beckett's famous 1945 Dublin epiphany where the value of a method of writing based on "subtracting" made its most significant impression on him.[12] Indeed, though James Knowlson quotes Beckett as saying that it was at that point that "*Molloy* and the others came to me" (319), we can nonetheless find the key elements of this subtractive method and the awareness that it offers an alternative to Joyce articulated in the "German Letter" written almost a decade earlier. As Lloyd's and Deane's analyses reveal, we can also connect these insights to Beckett's ongoing reflections on postcolonial displacement and alienation.

The crisis for Irish postcolonial subjectivity arguably comes to a head in this same postwar era as the global realignments of power signal a gradual eclipse of the structures of empire by those of multinational capital. This key period for Beckett at midcentury is thus also a crucial transitional period for Irish postcoloniality. Marked by significant governmental instability between 1948 and 1957, this transition ultimately culminates with the embrace of the new international order and a shift in emphasis from nationalism to capitalist modernization as the dominant official ideology by 1959. As Beckett probes the limits of late-modernist narrative form in *Molloy*, *Malone Dies*, and *The Unnamable*, therefore, we also are reaching the end of the initial phase of Irish postcoloniality. A striking indicator of this transition within postcoloniality and modernism is the ongoing reference to ethnographic representation that Bixby traces throughout the three novels and that becomes increasingly implicit and abstract in each successive volume (185–89). The result, as Bixby writes, is that "the spaces of Beckett's fiction are haunted by what we might call after Jean-Michel Rabaté 'the ghosts of modernity' especially the specter of Man, which returns over and over in the traces of anthropological discourse and the novel tradition strewn throughout the trilogy" (191).

As *The Unnamable* arguably stands as one of the key limit-texts for the modernist novel—and perhaps modernism more generally—we find it registers a particular crisis within postcolonial subjectivity. From the first page of *The Unnamable*, ultimately published as the third part of Beckett's *Three Novels*, Beckett addresses the situation of the subject in terms of the question of representation. He interrogates the subject on both mimetic and ontological grounds and insists on their inseparability. This linkage builds on the essential point of "Recent Irish Poetry" where the breakdown of the object and the breakdown of the subject are seen to coincide.

Thus, from the outset of *The Unnamable*, we see Beckett call into question the "I" that speaks and the signified subject that is "spoken":

> I seem to speak, it is not I, about me, it is not about me. These few general remarks to begin with. What am I to do, what shall I do, what should I do, in my situation, how proceed? By aporia pure and simple? Or by affirmations and negations invalidated as uttered, or sooner or later? Generally speaking. There must be other shifts. Otherwise it would be quite hopeless. But it is quite hopeless. I should mention before going any further, any further on, that I say aporia without knowing what it means. (291)

The status of "I" assumes a central importance here and will continue to prove a critical means of tracing the trajectory of subjectivity over the course of the novel. At the most basic level, however, "I seem to speak, it is not I" reads as a sort of "affirmation and negation" where the "is not" builds on the initial uncertainty of "seem" and completes the refusal of the "I" presenting itself through speech. This refusal of what initially seems true serves as an example of the repudiation of definitive meaning and, as we shall see, lies at the center of an effort to cast doubt on the legitimacy of language's objective reality. The speaker's proposal of proceeding "by aporia" indicates that this instability of meaning is not isolated or circumstantial but in fact functions as a constitutive element of the text. The subsequent confession that the meaning of "aporia" is itself not known only makes a stable ground of meaning—even that of indeterminacy—still more impossible.[13]

The emphasis on "proceeding" and "shifts" instead frames meaning in terms of an inherent dynamism. Beckett reinforces this jarring sense of dynamism through the speaker's propensity to correct and rephrase comments and engage dialogically with a statement that has just been made. Such destabilization of meaning might be seen as one of the primary "technical" means by which Beckett challenges representation as similar deployments of language throughout *The Unnamable* stage the continued failure of mimesis.

The destabilization of "I" is of particular importance in this regard, of course. For more than any simple repudiation of mimetic closure, the fact that it is the position of the narrating "I" that is being challenged raises fundamental questions about the agent of speech in the text. If "I" is not speaking, then who is telling us "it is not I"? How can the speech of the text be executed without recourse to some "I" as a basis for articulation? Is the speech completely severed from a speaker and simply imagined by the reader?

In *The Unnamable*, the "I's" seem to proliferate and refer uncertainly to one of a series of narrating subjects or to no subject at all. Beckett's constant recourse to an "I" that insistently invokes its linguistic presence through repetition even as it disavows both narrative authority and clear referentiality as a sign functions to undercut the novel's typical function in confirming the mutually constitutive subjectivity of narrator and reader.

Ultimately, however, this destabilizing of "I" as a sign is properly understood as a consequence of the breakdown of the object or the failure of language. Though the breakdown of subjectivity lies at the center of Beckett's articulation of a radical late-modernist vision in *The Unnamable*, it constitutes more of an application of the basic conditions that give rise to the critique. As "Recent Irish Poetry" and the "German Letter" might prepare us to expect, however, it is the inward turn and "self perception" rather than "Nominalist irony" that proves most important for Beckett. Though Bixby argues that "the quest to reclaim home, identity, and memory" (189) remains a crucial focus of *The Unnamable*, each of these arguably provides a point of closure or grounding that facilitates the enclosure of self within subjectivity.

Thus, even as we appreciate the destabilization of "I" as a sign, we can also read a line such as "I seem to speak, it is not I, about me, it is not about me" as inaugurating an analysis of the subject itself and not simply its representation in language. The denial of the initial impression that it is "I" who speaks is also a denial of the capacity of the subject or "I" to express agency. It suggests that the speaking "I" functions as some sort of ventriloquist's dummy that falsely projects agency and an appearance of self-representation. "Speaking" here connotes a sense of an authentic representation of the self; the political aspect of representation features more prominently than the mimetic at this point. The "I" does not speak both because the speech may originate elsewhere and because the "I" is alienated from the self.

To put it differently, we might say that "I's" speech is at once alienated from itself and from *a* self.

Beckett amplifies this sense of alienation in the passage with a succession of elements that combine to convey a subtle impression of coercion and subordination. The references to "general remarks" and "generally speaking" not only suggest an imprecision at odds with "true" representation but a concession to a more general will or discourse. Sentences like "These few general remarks to begin with" or "Generally speaking" literally mean next to nothing and serve merely as gestures that recognize and reinscribe discursive convention. As part of that, "general" speech suggests expression that originates outside of the individual subject. The ongoing questioning of what to do and how to proceed only reinforces this perception of the subject's subordination as does the repeated use of "should" in the passage.

Completing this alienation from representation is the split between "I" and "me." Though this split is scarcely noticeable at this point in *The Unnamable*, it will prove increasingly significant as the novel continues. The observation that "I's" speech "is not about me" is more than just a repetition of "I's" alienation. It should also be understood to signal a profoundly different status for "me" from the outset. The difference between "I" and "me" is not simply that attaching to the grammatical difference between the subjective and objective cases, as David Hesla suggests. Though this key distinction in grammatical case proves crucially important for his method, Beckett's manipulation of case ultimately goes far beyond Hesla's observation that "the Unnamable is not the same person or being in the objective case as he is in the nominative" (118). The unnamable self simply cannot be articulated in nominative terms except by means of a series of complex mediations. Similarly, the objective status of this unnamable self is much more complicated and fractured than Hesla's analysis admits. Neither nominative nor objective and, equally, neither hybrid nor duality, it rather emerges in the failure of the transaction between the two. Hesla's observation that the division between "I" and "me" marks an important split in identity (118) is somewhat more to the point in this regard. It is the split itself that is most important, and it is a split that cannot be made whole by any act of representation.

What is of primary importance at this early stage of the novel is that we begin to see the various ways that Beckett denaturalizes subjectivity and its "most natural" articulation by means of the pronoun "I." As Daniel Katz notes: "If the very proper name or pronoun 'I'

which sets in motion the figural chain is itself a figure . . . then a poetics of self-revelation and self-scrutiny, even visionary self-scrutiny,
becomes impossible. . . . The positing of subjectivity itself becomes
one figure in the chain and no longer the chain's origin or destination"
(15). Katz's use of a specular language of "revelation" and "scrutiny"
is quite appropriate here in conveying how the subject's function
within a regime of discipline—and especially self-discipline—is disrupted by Beckett's approach. This disruption does not extend so far
as Katz suggests, however, to render "consciousness" entirely figura-
tive as well (17). Not only does that rob Beckett's method of a great
deal of its political import but, more importantly, such a reading vio-
lates its critical logic by imputing a nihilism that is ultimately positive
in its certainty.

It is for that reason that "me" becomes such an important term for
Beckett's handling of the subject in the novel. His assault on the subject is not directed against the self. To the contrary, it is the distinction of the two that provides both motive and means for his project.
As will become more apparent over the course of Beckett's critique
in *The Unnamable*, "me" provides a key means of referral to the self
that is always indirect and framed outside the terms of subjectivity.

Amid the novel's vertiginous play of signs and unrelenting destabilization of meaning, "me" stands as a remarkably stable sign through
most of the text. This stability may perhaps be attributable to the fact
that its sign comprises a signified that is not entirely consistent with a
typical sense of the term. For "me" signifies a self quite literally outside of representation. As such, some other term such as "indicator"
may ultimately be more appropriate for "me" than "sign." However
it is ultimately termed, the importance of "me" as a nonrepresen-
tational but nonetheless significant means of registering self in *The
Unnamable* cannot be underestimated. "Me" provides Beckett a crucial means of balancing and clarifying his critique so that he can sys-
tematically and ruthlessly pursue an attack on the subject and representation while leaving the self relatively unscathed.

Such a short passage warrants such extensive commentary because
it helps to explain how immediately and subtly Beckett begins to establish the overlapping techniques and terms of the critique he pursues
through the rest of the novel. Not only does the split between "I" and
"me" play a hugely important—if insufficiently appreciated—role in
The Unnamable, but the tension between the two modes of reading
sketched above remains operative throughout the text. Consideration

of the "inward turn" and Beckett's analysis of subjectivity tends to require a more "literal" interpretation of the text somewhat at odds with the earlier appraisal of its destabilization of meaning. Ultimately, however, the literalism of the former mode only underscores the treatment of "aporia" under the aegis of its deconstructive counterpart where even the meaning and preeminence of aporia are not assured.

The two aspects of Beckett's critique that one might associate with these two modes of reading are indispensable to its functioning and thus continue to play off of each other over the course of the novel. As suggested previously, however, the destabilization of meaning simply expresses Beckett's subscription to the notion of a breakdown of the object. Though he applies the idea creatively to the language and structure of the novel, he does not develop it to quite the extent that he develops his critique of the subject as a disciplinary structure. Rather than dwelling on a series of examples of the destabilization of meaning in *The Unnamable*, therefore, it is perhaps more useful to consider it primarily in terms of the progression of his more structural critique of the subject.

This more direct examination of the subject also allows us to attend more fully to the matter of "self-perception" that Beckett emphasizes in "Recent Irish Poetry" and with which he proceeds to concern himself so intensely in the three novels of the early 1950s. Though self-perception and "self-accounting" obviously constitute significant themes for *Molloy* and *Malone Dies*, neither can really compare with *The Unnamable* in terms of the depths of self that Beckett plumbs and the thoroughgoing critique of the subject he provides. It is for this reason that the latter text stands as one of Beckett's most important novels from the perspective of midcentury Irish postcoloniality even as—or perhaps especially *because*—it may be one of his least explicitly Irish works.

After initially calling into question the authenticity of the speech of "I," Beckett proceeds in *The Unnamable* to consider the subject's relationship to the various personae—Murphy, Moran, Molloy, Malone, Mercier and Camier—that he has spoken of or through in previous novels. Are the various figures subordinate to the speaker's authority and/or imagination or is she/he/it subject to theirs? Are they somehow more free or fully realized as they wheel periodically through the speaker's field of vision and impress themselves on his/her/its consciousness or are they all the more subordinate or illusory? Where might Beckett himself figure amid all of these voices? To what extent is *The Unnamable* autobiography or an intensely personal meditation on writing and the position of the writer? Though such questions, of course, touch on central issues for modern literature and its interrogations of the author and of fictionality, they are of particular importance for postcolonial writing as a means of addressing the ways that postcolonial identity and representation are inauthentic and alienated by virtue of mixed inheritance—or "indebtedness," as Lloyd might more precisely put it.

After presenting Malone and Mercier and Camier in *The Unnamable*, Beckett thus offers an analysis of their relationship in a way that foregrounds the political aspect of postcolonial representation:

> Why did I have myself represented in the midst of men, the light of day? It seems to me it was none of my doing. We won't go into that now. I can see them still, my delegates. The things they have told me! About men, the light of day. I refused to believe them. But some of it has stuck. . . . There were four or five of them at me, they called that presenting their report. One in particular, Basil I think he was called, filled me with hatred. Without opening his mouth, fastening on me his eyes like cinders with all their seeing, he changed me a little more each time into what he wanted me to be. Is he still glaring at me, from the shadows? Is he still usurping my name, the one they foisted on me, up there in their world, patiently, from season to season? (297–98)

The initial account of being "represented in the midst of men, the light of day" locates representation in alienation and visibility; it involves simultaneously a submersion of self in collectivity and a definition of discrete limits such that one might be visible in "the light of day." As becomes increasingly clear over the course of the passage, this entry into representation is at once a matter of submission to the authority of external "delegates" and acceptance of a reconfiguration or, indeed, *figuration* of self in the prescribed form of the subject.

Beckett deftly conveys the deflection of agency this process involves in the ambiguity of "have" in the first sentence. The phrase "have myself represented" can refer either to something commissioned or to something suffered. In neither case is agency fully preserved or fully surrendered. The status of "I" obviously complicates this further. Given that Beckett has marked "I" from the outset as a term of subordination and alienation, its function here as the originator or vector of representation means that agency is inherently compromised no matter how much the subject or the "I" may be seen to authorize delegation and insertion into "the midst of men." The observation that "it seems to me it was none of my doing" reinforces this still further and reminds us of the profoundly different status of "me" as more indicative of self and never able to be subsumed or represented by "I."

The passage's emphasis on an institutional element underscores the degree of alienation from "me's" realm of self that we see being brought into effect by representation. The references to "delegates" and "presenting reports" combine to leave an impression of the processes of subject formation and representation as intensely bureaucratized and depersonalized phenomena. Indeed, describing the presentation of the report in terms of "four or five of them [being] at me" makes the process seem quite overwhelming. The efficacy of this institutional formation would seem to be considerable, however, given that "some of it has stuck" despite its being disbelieved.

The hint of violence underlying this transformation continues with the account of Basil and his burning eyes "glaring" through the darkness. Agency is once again made somewhat ambiguous as we are left to wonder about the significance of Basil "fill[ing] me with hatred." Is the hatred an expression of "me's" judgment and agency? This would certainly be plausible given "me's" status as a nonsubjective self. One may question if this really constitutes agency, however, if it is so explicitly reactive to Basil and his hateful staring. Might it, in fact, be the means of thwarting "me" and erecting the subject on the foundation of a congealed hatred that overlays the dynamism of the self? The structure of the sentence easily admits of the possibility that the "hatred" not only originates with Basil in a reactive sense but is in fact entirely attributable to him and is never wielded by "me." In other words, Basil is quite literally "filling" "me" and not simply prompting a response. However one might read that sentence, the succeeding lines make it clear that a great deal of the agency must be attributed to Basil as he gradually but surely reshapes "me."

Basil's endeavor is clearly the wrenching of self into subject. Not only do we see the typical articulation of the subject in opposition to a starkly defined other, but we have this associated with the process of naming and entry into bureaucratized representation. Though it is somewhat unclear from the passage whether this process entirely obliterates or taints the self of "me," it later becomes more apparent that "me" emerges relatively unscathed, and the subject merely claims representative status for a self from which it is completely alienated. Indeed, we see a hint of that in this passage as well with the mention of a "foisted" name that is then "usurp[ed]" by Basil "up there in the world." The latter phrase suggests the continuation of a mode of existence distinct from the realm of subjectivity and representation. The description of the name being at once foisted and usurped would seem to reiterate the narrative of representation offered over the course of the passage; the subject is so aggressively substituted for the self only so it can be used to anticipate and underwrite representation by even more remote "delegates."

Beckett seems to target his critique of representation at this point against a state formation that would seek to enclose the self in succeeding layers of bureaucratized reification. Though such a critique could be applicable to virtually any modern liberal state and Beckett is one who had much experience of bureaucracy in a variety of national contexts—especially during the war—its analysis is particularly relevant to the postcolonial state and its uniquely pronounced assertion of representative status. Beckett's choice of name for the chief enforcer of subjective representation would appear to underscore this even as it gestures to a demonic colonial precursor that at once makes use of hateful opposition and bureaucratic envelopment to generate subjects for its purposes. As an especially English or Anglo-Irish name, Basil seems the perfect choice for such an agent.

The hegemonic character of Basil's influence becomes more apparent as *The Unnamable* continues. Not only does Basil effectively enclose the self with the subject but he insinuates himself into the subject he brings into being. This compromise constitutes, of course, one of the classic problems of subject formation. If anything, the problem only becomes more acute after decolonization when the self of the formerly colonized would seem to be most fully realized. Beckett's account of Basil's shifting presence illuminates this problem for the postcolonial subject particularly well:

> Decidedly Basil is becoming important, I'll call him Mahood instead, I prefer that, I'm queer. It was he told me stories about me, lived in my stead, issued forth from me, came back to me, entered back into me, heaped stories on my head. I don't know how it was done. I always liked not knowing, but Mahood said it wasn't right. . . . It is his voice which has often, always, mingled with mine, and sometimes drowned it completely. Until he left me for good, or refused to leave me any more. I don't know. Yes, I don't know if he's here now or far away, but I don't think I am far wrong in saying that he has ceased to plague me. When he was away I tried to find myself again, to forget what he had said, about me, about my misfortunes, fatuous misfortunes, idiotic pains, in the light of my true situation, revolting word.

> But his voice continued to testify for me, as though woven into mine,
> preventing me from saying who I was, what I was, so as to have done
> with saying, done with listening. (309)

We might profitably read the first part of this passage in terms of
a refinement of the subject's disciplinary function. Mahood softens
Basil and facilitates a stepping away from the violence of the burning eyes that characterized the earlier moment. Here, in addition to
providing a means for conveying a "softer" and more omnipresent
authority, Mahood enables a further projection of power through
his mingling of voice and consciousness with the speaker. Beckett's
description of the drowning of voice and Mahood's constant movement back and forth illustrates how such beneficent interest and representation in story functions to facilitate subordination and alienation from a self outside the bounds of subjectivity. Bixby connects
these efforts to mold the speaker to a standard imperial "education"
meant to facilitate "assimilation to and acquiescence in the culture of
the colonizer and, above all, the humanistic, Enlightenment ideal of
Man" (196).

It is not entirely surprising, therefore, that it is difficult to ascertain
whether Mahood has "left me for good, or refused to leave me any
more." This latter might be read as elucidating the fate of the colonial
subject as empire gives way to postcoloniality. As Bixby notes, "The
overriding effect of the education imposed on the narrator . . . is his
experience of linguistic dispossession, his sense that the language he
speaks is always that of another, and the attendant sense that the self
he speaks of is always inauthentic" (197). Beckett's account would
suggest that traces of imperial discourse linger most deeply in representation itself. Importantly, however, this is not to obliterate self
entirely. Even as Mahood "has ceased to plague me" and there has
been an effort to reclaim the self from his reifying stories, we find
Mahood's voice "woven into mine" and subjectivity hopelessly entangled in ongoing negotiations of power.

The result, significantly, is a common but discrete alienation for
the subjective "I" and for "me." In the wake of Mahood's ostensible
departure, "I" seeks to overcome its alienation from "me" but finds
itself barred equally from "me" and from the power of representation.
Mahood's voice continues to emanate through the speaker, and "I"
cannot even articulate itself much less provide access to "me." "I's"
double isolation from self and the power of representation encapsulates the rather pathetic condition of the postcolonial subject quite

well. Given that, the desire to move beyond representation toward silence that is hinted at in the wish "to have done with saying, done with listening" is quite understandable.

Beckett's continued elaboration of this point immediately afterward would seem to leave doubt neither about the hopelessness of "I's" situation nor its peculiar aptness as an account of the postcolonial subject. The problem clearly remains a structural one:

> And still today, as he would say, though he plagues me no more his voice is there, in mine, but less, less. And being no longer renewed it will disappear one day, I hope, from mine, completely. But in order for that to happen I must speak, speak. And at the same time, I do not deceive myself, he may come back again, or go away again and then come back again. Then my voice, the voice, would say, That's an idea, now I'll tell one of Mahood's stories, I need a rest. Yes, that's how it would happen. And it would say, Then refreshed, set about the truth again, with redoubled vigour. To make me think I was a free agent. But it would not be my voice, not even in part. That is how it would be done. Or quietly, stealthily, the story would begin, as if nothing had happened and I still the teller and the told. But I would be fast asleep, my mouth agape, as usual, I would look the same as usual. And from my sleeping mouth the lies would pour, about me. No, not sleeping, listening, in tears. But now, is it I now, I on me? Sometimes I think it is. And then I realize it is not. (309–10)

Considered in relation to the initial stage of postcoloniality, we can see how decolonization would appear to leave imperial discourse no means of renewal as the increasing assertions of an institutional nationalism and the installation of the postcolonial state aspire to displace imperial authority definitively. Yet, despite such aspirations, it rapidly becomes clear that imperial structures of power are not so easily shunted aside and, indeed, official nationalism has little interest in doing so.

In order to displace the imperial discourse, the postcolonial subject must try to "speak" and assert power over the mechanisms of representation. As soon as that happens, however, we see Mahood begin to "come back." He comes back all the more insistently and insidiously by "go[ing] away again and then com[ing] back again" and asserting his authority indirectly through the institution of representation rather than direct articulation. Official nationalism's particular susceptibility to such "sympathetic" fetishizing of "tradition" as we see bedeviling the Blasket texts emerges in "I's" mistaken belief that telling one of Mahood's stories about the colonized self of "me" can be a means of articulating "free agen[cy]." Again, we hear an echo of Beckett's critique of the antiquarian and find that "I" not only reinscribes the objectification of the colonized but can actually be seen to rehearse its own alienation from representational power once more.

The delusion of the postcolonial subject lies in its initial belief that it can speak of the new national self and be at once "the teller and the told." Indeed, its greatest delusion is its belief that it can speak at all. For it can only speak in a voice distinguishable from that of empire insofar as it can articulate a means of more direct access to a colonized self that has been reified and distorted by imperial discourse. As Beckett's analysis shows, however, a derivative subject such as we see with official nationalism always stands "mouth agape" as it tries to represent postcoloniality. The postcolonial subject cannot speak. Even as its "lies" continue to separate it from the colonized self of "me," it cannot enjoy the consolation of being reconciled to representation. Instead, subjectivity remains empty, the discarded skin of the imperial serpent left behind to distract and awe.

Beckett intensifies his critique of a more derivative or institutionalized subjectivity as the speaker continues to relate stories of Mahood. Mahood's prolonged tale (315–25) of a struggle to return home across vast wastes on crutches obviously recalls *Molloy*. That his journey is motivated in no small part by a desire for revenge and destruction seems especially significant here in the wake of Beckett's critique of a derivative subject, however. The lurid scene of Mahood stomping on the rotting corpses of his family when he arrives home might be seen as suggestive of an unseemly wallowing in the demise and ruination of the reified objects of "tradition." Such necrophilic cavorting is not unknown to official nationalism as the elegiac aspect of the Blasket texts demonstrates so lamentably.

In this case, the simultaneous disposal of three generations of family and the mixing of their entrails into one undifferentiated mess would also seem to convey the extremity of the postcolonial subject's alienation. No connection to family or identity remains whether in a past, present, or future iteration. As the speaker puts it, Mahood "represented me as rid at one glorious sweep of parents, wife, and heirs" (323). The subject is completely isolated from any notion of genealogy or metonymic continuity and must dwell within a temporal nullity. In this regard, we can also see how postcolonial subjectivity is increasingly confronting the transition at midcentury from an initial phase of postcoloniality emphasizing nationalism and a sense

of metonymic continuity with "tradition" toward a late postcoloniality oriented toward a global modernity. Under the influence of
Mahood, the subject not only finds itself divested of whatever metonymic chains through which it might hope to invoke a claim of representation but even has this utter isolation advanced as the representative—and exultant—state of "me."

The relevance of Beckett's critique to the project of institutional
nationalism becomes perhaps even more explicit as the speaker relates
a subsequent story of Mahood's that would seem to offer an important frame for the earlier narrative of the arduous sojourn to the family home. Recalling *Molloy* again, we find that the length and difficulty of the journey may have more to do with the psychic distance to
be traversed than any significant barriers of geography:

> I might as well tell another of Mahood's stories and no more about
> it, to be understood in the way I was given to understand it, namely
> as being about me. . . . I'll try and look as if I was telling it will-
> ingly, to keep them quiet in case they should feel like refreshing my
> memory, on the subject of my behaviour above in the island, among
> my compatriots, contemporaries, coreligionists and companions in
> distress. . . . To tell the truth—no, first the story. The island, I'm on
> the island, I've never left the island, God help me. I was under the
> impression I spent my life in spirals round the earth. Wrong, it's on
> the island I wind my endless ways. The island, that's all the earth I
> know. I don't know it either, never having had the stomach to look at
> it. When I come to the coast I turn back inland. And my course is not
> helicoidal, I got that wrong too, but a succession of irregular loops,
> now sharp and short as in the waltz, now of a parabolic sweep that
> embraces entire boglands, now between the two, somewhere or other,
> and invariably unpredictable in direction, that is to say determined by
> the panic of the moment. (326–27)

The topographic description of the place as an island marked by
bogland of course strongly suggests Ireland, as is often noted. Though
this resemblance is significant, the passage's value as a reflection on
postcolonial nationalism looms as a potentially far more important
aspect of its relevance to Ireland. Here, once more, we have the subordination of the subject as Mahood is again the sole agent of representation, and "I" is "given to understand" the story and find itself
coerced into enunciating it. "I's" only glimmer of agency lies in the
resolution to "try and look as if I was telling it willingly." Such is the
refuge of the postcolonial subject and the postcolonial state: to "try
and look" as if one is exercising one's own original authority.

The significance of locating the story's origins with Mahood increases as one considers the extent to which it is a story of institutional nationalism's alienation from—and, indeed, lack of interest in—the local components that comprise the nation. We find that the subject has "never . . . had the stomach to look at it" and turns back toward the center as soon as it finds itself close to the periphery. Such aversive ignorance obviously coincides with the account of "tradition" that we can discern in the Blasket texts and O'Faoláin's essays or see sketched with such devastating ridicule by Myles na gCopaleen in *An Béal Bocht*. Institutional nationalism's neglect of—and even antipathy toward—the national periphery haunted by the subaltern is here repeated in terms suggesting a profound alienation from self.

In this way, Beckett might be seen to connect the somewhat abstract structural problems of postcolonial subjectivity to the more materially immediate issues attaching to postcolonial geography and the state's articulation of postcolonial national identity, especially in this moment of transition. The earlier disruption of the familial metonymic chain is now given a spatial dimension as the speaker conveys a discontinuous landscape known only by way of a halting and "unpredictable" itinerary "determined by the panic of the moment." As before, this disruption renders representation by the postcolonial subject impossible. Representation by a subject or subjects unable to "stomach" engagement with the actualities of the periphery and ignorant of the spatial relationships of the territory it would purport to represent must obviously be viewed as illegitimate. The postcolonial subject is isolated in space as well as in time.

Beckett expresses this splendid isolation by means of the Mahood story in *The Unnamable* that is probably best-known and most memorable in its imagery: that of Mahood reduced in body to a limbless trunk and encased within a large glass jar (327–37). Mahood and his jar are prominently displayed atop a pedestal and constitute "a kind of landmark" (328) for those in the area. Festooned with lanterns and plastered with menus for the chop-house across the road, Mahood's jar becomes an item of significant interest and study for passersby. Mahood himself is almost entirely ignored, however, except for the "proprietress of the chop-house" (328), who dutifully cleans the jar each week and puts a covering over his head in the rain and snow. The interest directed Mahood's way is almost entirely an interest in the jar as an imposing structure and a space for notices and advertisements; the occupant of the jar is unnoticed and unimportant. Seemingly

quite aware of what is going on around him and capable of effectively
wielding language to articulate his own thoughts internally, Mahood
stands nonetheless incapable of representation and simply watches all
in silence.

In this, he embodies almost perfectly the vision of the postcolonial subject that has been emerging over the course of the novel and
which resonates particularly with the midcentury shift from a jaded
discourse of institutional nationalism and "tradition" toward one of
global capitalism. Privileged over the self is the surrounding edifice;
the external shell of the subject, like the menu-plastered glass of the
jar, is all that signifies or represents. Though the subject might appear
immediately accessible, we find it is actually trapped behind a transparent wall and overtaken by commercial discourse. Mahood's gross
corporeal reduction and complete inability to tend to his most basic
needs suggests a parallel alienation from self. The subject can claim
significance neither on the basis of authentic connection to self nor on
the idea that the subject enables some real purchase on power within
the system of representation. Whatever prominence Mahood has in
his jar is due entirely to his position atop the jar's pedestal and the
attention directed to the advertisements projected onto the jar; even
then, he is scarcely noticed.

Portraying Mahood's absolute reduction to a silent isolation, Beckett turns more directly to the matter of alienation from self. This turn
is not at all surprising, of course, given the thrust of Beckett's work
apparent as far back as "Recent Irish Poetry." Nor is it ultimately
discontinuous with the account of Mahood in his jar. Mahood's
alienation from the outside world within his jar and from his own
corporeality with the disintegration of his body prompts an understandable inward turn in search of self. *The Unnamable* thus shifts its
primary focus from Mahood to Worm. The speaker presents Worm
as an alternative to Mahood, a better means for "the masters" to pla-
cate the dissatisfied voice and fully incorporate the speaker into their
structure of power by securing access to "me."

One description of Worm suggests he fills a very different position
than that which we earlier saw associated with Mahood:

> Worm, to say he does not know what he is, where he is, what is hap-
> pening, is to underestimate him. What he does not know is that there
> is anything to know. His senses tell him nothing, nothing about
> himself, nothing about the rest, and this distinction is beyond him.
> Feeling nothing, knowing nothing, he exists nevertheless, but not for

himself, for others, others conceive him and say, Worm is, since we conceive him, as if there could be no being but being conceived, if only by the beer. Others. One alone, then others. (346)

Worm is at once "for others" and completely buried within himself, devoid of all knowledge and sensual perception. He is not, at least from his perspective, one who engages with the external world. Nor is he one who consciously rejects or avoids it.

Unaware of being "one" at all, Worm is, in some sense, pure unalienated being. Raising the possibility that being may consist entirely in "being conceived," the speaker begins to chart a dramatically different course than that which had been proposed previously. Worm essentially poses the possibility of an anti-subject. Being is posited in terms of such complete alienation from self and others that it is neither agentive nor "authentic" in the sense of self-awareness. The idea of Worm is one that completely inverts the earlier notions of realizing being through subjectivity and representation and thereby turns alienation into a virtue. Here, we can see another version of Beckett's critique of a Revivalist modernism's investment in an unadulterated "primitive" consciousness.

Even as the speaker lays out this vision of Worm, however, Beckett simultaneously undercuts it with the speaker's critique of the ends to which the idea of Worm might be directed and the misconceptions it might provoke. In particular, the speaker considers Worm's relationship to Mahood and "me" more critically: "To think I thought [Worm] was against what they were trying to do with me! To think I saw in him, if not me, a step towards me! To get me to be he, the anti-Mahood, and then to say, But what am I doing but living, in a kind of way, the only possible way, that's the combination" (346). Here we see a fairly straightforward evaluation of the prospect of the anti-subject. After some initial enthusiasm for Worm as a way out of the matrix of representation through which modern authority consolidates power, the speaker begins to view Worm as an even more insidious vehicle for enclosing self and agency.

Instead of the earlier focus on "I," the target of this approach turns out to be "me." Rather than enabling a reconciliation with the self of "me," however, the speaker suggests it is ultimately a means of substituting "me" for "I" as the subject of a different ontological discourse conceived as more authentic or "the only possible way." The "combination" or method to gain assent to this alternate mode of subjectivity is to first make it appear as a repudiation of the reified structure of the subject and then have this less explicitly public notion of being take on representative status both for the being itself and for being in general.

This results, ultimately, in a more direct and complete consolidation of authority in that "me" is drawn into the web of representation in a mimetic sense even as the possibility of individual or local political representation is foreclosed as a possibility. In a strange sense, this can also be understood as a prescient commentary on the new "alternative" subject of the late-capitalist consumer, who ostensibly expresses his or her freedom or individuality through choices of what to consume. As the initial postcolonial emphasis on "tradition" gives way to an emphasis on insertion within an emergent late-capitalist modernity, then, Beckett's portrayal of Worm suggests that neither a withdrawal into a fantasy of premodern detachment nor dehistoricized individual consumption provides a means of self-realization.

This critique of Worm and his potential role within structures of power continues with a fuller consideration of the speaker's own relationship to Worm that builds on the discussion of Worm as one position within a field of ontological possibilities. The speaker develops the critique of Worm's function by turning to the central question of voice:

> Is there a single word of mine in all I say? No, I have no voice, in this matter I have none. That's one of the reasons why I confused myself with Worm. But I have no reasons either, no reason, I'm like Worm, without voice or reason, I'm Worm, no, if I were Worm I wouldn't know it, I wouldn't say it, I wouldn't say anything, I'd be Worm. But I don't say anything, I don't know anything, these voices are not mine, nor these thoughts, but the voices and thoughts of the devils who beset me. Who make me say that I can't be Worm, the inexpugnable. Who make me say that I am he perhaps, as they are. Who make me say that since I can't be he I must be he. That since I couldn't be Mahood as I might have been, I must be Worm, as I cannot be. But is it still they who say that when I have failed to be Worm I'll be Mahood, automatically on the rebound? . . . And is it still they who say that when I surprise them all and am Worm at last, that at last I'll be Mahood, Worm proving to be Mahood the moment one is he? (347–48)

Beginning with a reminder of "I's" alienation from speech and representation, the speaker nonetheless proceeds to consider "I's" positive ontological status as alienated subject. "I" has "no voice" and "no reason" and merely serves as a conduit for the voice and reason of "they," the "devils" who wield authority. At the same time, however, "I" does seem to exist independently of "they" or at least is not identical with "they" even if "I" does rely on "they's" structures of representation. "I" might be understood as a distinguishable, if dependent, *effect* of this larger system. This sense of being through alienation would seem to give "I" a certain sort of self-awareness as subjective shell even if it remains alienated from the self of "me."

And it is this self-awareness, the speaker suggests here, that crucially separates "I" from Worm for Worm "wouldn't know it, . . . wouldn't say it." This is the other—Cartesian—side of Worm's disciplinary role affirming the inevitability and legitimacy of the subject. Since "I" is able to conceive of its complete alienation, it exists and, more than that, realizes authentic identity in its awareness of alienation. If, on the other hand, this is all a lie or manipulation orchestrated by "they" and "I" is *not* actually aware of its alienation, "I" becomes Worm and fully enters into "they's" power by way of the anti-subject sketched above. As the speaker suggests, both paths lead to Mahood, either "on the rebound" in the first instance or through the ignorant defiance of the anti-subject in the latter case.

The relevance of all of this to the postcolonial situation may be fairly apparent. Just as the postcolonial subject is alienated from both direct representation and the colonized self, the anti-subject of the imagined primitive of "tradition" is also alienated. Though the alienation from the power of representation is perhaps not surprising given the anti-subject's complete lack of consciousness, the alienation from self might be somewhat less expected in that anti-subjectivity would seem to involve a move inward. It is that belief in a nonalienated self that drives Synge's primitivist fantasy and the subsequent postcolonial investment in "tradition" and the permeability of "modernity's edge" for a postcolonial national consciousness that can ostensibly maintain "authenticity" in the midst of modernization. Here, we can thus see how Beckett's late-modernist critique of the subject responds at once to the legacy of Yeatsian modernism and to the expanding regime of modernization gradually overtaking a reliance on "tradition" as a salve to alienation.

The particular relevance of Beckett's portrayal of Worm as a hopelessly flawed model of resistance would seem to be indicated by his wry suggestion that "I" will see through the false option of Worm to recognize itself as "a kind of tenth-rate Toussaint L'Ouverture" (349). The invocation of L'Ouverture as an island anticolonial hero reminds

us that the novel's exploration of subjectivity and its limits takes the colonial paradigm as one of its key points of departure.

Underscoring the lack of agency involved in a retreat into primitivism or "tradition," Worm's movement is dictated indirectly by "they" as he instinctively retreats in the opposite direction from "the voice . . . coming from the quarter they want him to retreat from" (357). Interestingly, it is not simply "noise" or "sound" that prompts Worm's flight but "voice." Even if Worm is incapable of comprehending its significance, power still continues to constitute itself in terms of a discourse of representation and "voice." Worm's response can thus be seen to enact the representational double bind of primitivist discourses as the move away from the voice of authority reinstalls a discourse of representation at the very moment it would seem to be most determinedly rejected. The "enraged" (356) flight from representation into an ostensibly deeper "darkness" (358)—whether of "tradition" or "the neolithic," as Forster describes it—is entirely predictable in its exact reversal of the course seemingly prescribed by the voices of imperial authority and postcolonial modernization. The perfection of this inversion produces a singular primitive entity that can be readily defined and directed.

Beckett underscores the final impotence of such an antithetical response by means of the speaker's observation that Worm "cannot set himself in motion, though he often desires to" (358). Indeed, the situation reveals itself to be worse still in that we are quickly told that one may not rightly speak of desire in relation to Worm as it "serves no purpose" (358). Worm's antithetical drive achieves no progress and, indeed, does not even show itself to be possessed of a thwarted volition.

The ostensibly liberated anti-subject of Revivalist fantasy thus finds itself reduced to an inert physicality. We see this rendered quite explicitly in the image of "their arms" hauling Worm "from darkness to light" and the speaker's observation of "How physical this all is!" (357–58). Though the dull somnolence of Worm's physicality may at first seem to distinguish it from the "iridescence" of the Yeatsian circumference that Beckett finds so troubling in "Recent Irish Poetry," it is perhaps more accurately perceived as Beckett's attempt to strip away the illuminations of the Twilight scribes to reveal the homeliness of the reified colonized object they so artfully cover over and distort.

Having thus considered the significant limitations of both the subject and the anti-subject as a means of realizing agency or a connection to self, Beckett then begins to explore an approach more definitively outside the bounds of representation and subjectivity. Though we see Mahood, Worm, and others occasionally surface as part of a renewed effort to ensnare self in traps of "voice" or representation, *The Unnamable* increasingly pursues a course incompatible with reification as Beckett plunges deeper into the maelstrom that churns the wreckage of language and the subject.

Rather than proceeding to another figure such as Mahood or Worm, then, Beckett effectively abandons figuration as a means of presenting the problem and instead approaches the matter of "the breakdown" of object and subject head-on. We see growing efforts to articulate a solution in more truly negative terms that cannot so easily resolve themselves into objective solidity once again. Thus, we find an aspiration to settle "between" speech and thought, a place "where you suffer, rejoice, at being bereft of speech, bereft of thought, and feel nothing, hear nothing, know nothing, say nothing, are nothing" (374). Though this state may at first seem to resemble that initially ascribed to Worm, it differs crucially in its emphasis on the condition of being "bereft" and by virtue of its not being contained by a singular figure. Being "bereft" not only allows for a consciousness of which Worm is incapable but suggests one deeply marked by absence and dispossession. To be "bereft" in this sense is to live in alterity rather than oblivion as Worm does.

Being simultaneously "bereft of speech, bereft of thought" enables a move outside of representation and subjectivity that pushes beyond the simple refusal of antithesis to disclose a dwelling in difference. Speech is neither withheld nor forgotten; it is simply inadequate. The connotations of dispossession and absence carried by "bereft" obviously bear especial weight and significance in the postcolonial context. Rather than reconstituting the object by seeking a return to a premodern wholeness through primitive antithesis, however, the "bereft" consciousness keeps alive a memory of loss.

In that way, Beckett begins to render in *The Unnamable* a poetic and a politics that is as insatiable as it is unquiet. This vision builds upon the power of "regretting" posited a few pages earlier as "what helps you on . . . towards the end of the world, regretting what is, regretting what was, . . . that's what transports you, towards the end of regretting" (371). As Beckett's observation helps clarify, regret infuses a critical postcolonial consciousness that is neither triumphant nor defeated, neither consoled nor disconsolate.

It should come as no surprise that this movement outside of representation and the fatally compromised agency of subject and anti-subject coincides with a stirring of self in *The Unnamable* that has been
long-sought and long-denied. The abandonment of Mahood, Worm,
and the like combined with the shift toward the irreducible absence
of regret enables "me" to begin finally to displace "I" and the authority of "they." Therefore, after speculating about the end of Worm and
"Mahood being abandoned," the speaker boldly claims, "I too have
the right to be shown impossible" (375). With a discourse of rights
attaching inevitably to the subjective "I," Beckett ironically turns that
discourse against the ontological nullity of "I" as a mere placeholder
in the disciplinary regime of modern subjectivity.

Accompanying—and perhaps fueling—all of this disintegration,
we find a stirring of self expressed via the shorthand of "me." The
change wrought by "me" appears to validate the legitimacy and the
desirability of the move beyond representation that emerges from
regret:

> Then it will be over, thanks to me all will be over, and they'll depart,
> one by one, or they'll drop, they'll let themselves drop, where they
> stand, and never move again, thanks to me, who could understand
> nothing, of all they deemed it their duty to tell me, do nothing, of all
> they deemed it their duty to tell me to do, and upon us all the silence
> will fall again, and settle, like dust of sand, on the arena, after the
> massacres. (376)

Perhaps more striking than the repeated claim of "thanks to me"
here is the complete absence of "I."[14] Definitively locating agency outside of the subjective form, Beckett suggests that the abandonment of
the subject for the whirling maelstrom of self has an instantaneous
effect in depriving modern authority of its power. The embodiments
of "they's" authority simply "drop, where they stand." Rather than a
resistance that will almost inevitably reinvigorate the regime of power
by way of subjectivity or anti-subjectivity, we see a resort to a shifting
self concerned neither with "understanding" nor "doing." The silence
that descends and settles "again" is the silence of loss and "regret" as
much as it is also the last resounding echo of that earlier silence shattered by representation.

In likening its descent to the settling of "dust of sand, on the arena,
after the massacres," Beckett compacts violence and quietude into
the same moment. The simile encodes both the lingering trauma of
the invasive violence of Basil, Mahood, and "they" and the jarring

abruptness of the shift from clamoring, baying voices to their quiet "drop[ping] where they stand." As such, the silence is one marked deeply by "regret"; it is not in any sense "innocent." The result is that the vision of self we see unfolding in *The Unnamable* is one that is likewise impure. Beckett does not propose a completely quiescent self lost in its own vicissitudes of being. To do so might come dangerously close to paralleling the anti-subjective course of Worm, if by a slightly different path. As Beckett puts it a short time later, "there is no name for me, no pronoun for me, all the trouble comes from that" (404). To "all the trouble," one might add "all the hope." For it is in that crucial aporia that the possibility and necessity of a critique of the subject emerge most brilliantly.

"Me's" unnamable status obviously resonates with Beckett's earlier interest expressed in "Recent Irish Poetry" and the "German Letter" in a shifting "centre" and a seeping rupture that lurks behind the objective solidity of words. Importantly, however, "me" functions only as a placeholder for that manifestation of self residing there; "me" does not and cannot *name* self even on a provisional basis. As Beckett's earlier critical prose suggests, the nothingness or silence beyond representation is quite substantive.

As a result, Beckett presents two distinct aspects of silence that sustain and distinguish each other. We see the outline of these two mutually important aspects rendered most clearly in one of the late accounts of "the voice" in the novel: "I want it to go silent, it wants to go silent, it can't, it does for a second, then it starts again, that's not the real silence, it says that's not the real silence, what can be said of the real silence, I don't know, that I don't know what it is, that there is no such thing, that perhaps there is such a thing, yes, that perhaps there is, somewhere, I'll never know" (408). The first silence is that of the pause or the absence of noise. It is simply that which occurs when the voice is not speaking. The second or "real" silence is the noise of absence. Though this latter silence remains completely inaccessible to "I," we are nonetheless left with the sense "that perhaps there is such a thing" even if "I" stands incapable of knowing or representing it.

This "real silence" is, of course, not new to us; it is the same as that which we saw previously likened to the sand of the arena after the massacres or sought after so longingly in the "German Letter." At this point in the novel, we can begin to comprehend the "real silence" as the domain of the unnamable. The distinction of the "real silence" from the more mundane version of silence as a brief pause in speech serves a crucial role in preventing "real silence" from being conflated with passivity or unintelligibility.

Far from being unintelligible, however, the notion of "real silence" and a life beyond representation vigorously insists itself upon our imaginations as the novel moves toward its close. The account of the unnamable on the penultimate page strongly suggests that we have come to find ourselves in a place where the subject increasingly gives way to a dynamic new dispensation:

> [T]here I am far again, there I am the absentee again, it's his turn again now, he who neither speaks nor listens, who has neither body nor soul, it's something else he has, he must have something, he must be somewhere, he is made of silence, there's a pretty analysis, he's in the silence, he's the one to be sought, the one to be, the one to be spoken of, the one to speak, but he can't speak, then I could stop, I'd be he, I'd be the silence, I'd be back in the silence, we'd be reunited, his story the story to be told, but he has no story, he hasn't been in story, it's not certain, he's in his own story, unimaginable, unspeakable. (413)

The initial expression of "I's" distance bleeding into "the absentee" brings together a fascinating array of threads that have been running through *The Unnamable* and, indeed, Beckett's work more generally. Most immediately, we have the alienation of the subject. In this regard, "absentee" suggests an alienation or a "being absent" from "there," the unnamable's broad sphere of substantive or "real" silence, in a way that reiterates the earlier accounts of "I's" alienation from self. At the same time, "absentee" conveys the subject's own inner void and alienation from representation in the sense of an "absent presence" or empty shell.

This idea takes on a discernible image in the figure of the absentee landlord and that of the eerily vacant—or uncertainly vacant—Big House linked to the landlord by way of synecdoche and serving as a sort of broken-down panopticon. Such an image obviously reverberates deeply in an Irish context and within the Irish novel tradition in particular, especially when coming from a writer emerging from a background of Protestant privilege such as Beckett. As the Big House novel narrates over the course of more than a century, a culture of Anglo-Irish "absentees" has been successively marginalized by a modernizing "professional" class more akin to Beckett's own background and, after 1922, by succeeding iterations of a new regime of institutional nationalism also bent on modernization in ways often not initially acknowledged. Bringing this full-circle by the midcentury period that Beckett is writing in, the elaboration of a postcolonial subjectivity that would propose to offer the means of a more authentic representation is itself being rapidly outstripped by a new order of absentee capitalism.

Opposing this, the sense of an alternative vitality and agency coursing through the nonalienated zone of the unnamable is conveyed by the understated remark, "it's his turn again now." Neither speaking nor listening and possessed of neither body nor soul, we find the unnamable standing completely outside of the economy of representation and relying instead on "something else." This "something else" combining with the observation that "he is made of silence" further locates—or dislocates—the unnamable self in a state of radical alterity.

Though these accounts of "me" suggest a position of growing strength, it becomes clear that this position of alterity and silence also continues to be under immense pressure. Thus, the succession of "he's the one to be sought, the one to be, the one to be spoken of, the one to speak" communicates at once the unnamable's importance and a sense of being pursued or targeted. Such pursuit obviously drives the novel and the various attempts to enclose "me" within representation.

Arresting the threat of representation, however, is the series of assertions, "but he can't speak, then I could stop, I'd be he, I'd be the silence, I'd be back in the silence, we'd be reunited, his story the story to be told." The unnamable's entry into speech would entail merging with the subject and the shattering of the "real silence" of alterity. In its place, we would be left with the descent of the far more frightening "mundane" silence marking the death of agency and self amid the triumph of a regime of subjectivity and objectification.

Although this merging of the unnamable and the subject is only a nightmare and Beckett offers us elegant assurances that the unnamable remains "unspeakable" and not "in story," we are nonetheless made conscious of the fact that a lapse into representation and subjectivity continues to constitute a very real peril. As we have found so often over the course of *The Unnamable*, however, the disruption of purity and threat of imminent collapse may also play salutary roles in clarifying and maintaining the terms of struggle.

The well-known ending of *The Unnamable* certainly fulfills such a conflicted desire even if a postcolonial reading may cast it in a somewhat different light than that in which it is typically perceived:

> I can't go on, you must go on, I'll go on, you must say words, as long as there are any, until they find me, until they say me, strange pain, strange sin, you must go on, perhaps it's done already, perhaps they

have said me already, perhaps they have carried me to the threshold
of my story, before the door that opens on my story, that would surprise me, if it opens, it will be I, it will be the silence, where I am, I
don't know, I'll never know, in the silence you don't know, you must
go on, I can't go on, I'll go on. (414)

"I's" famous persistence here constitutes less a cause for hope than a
goad to renewed struggle. We hear strange echoes of the letter to Axel
Kaun and the adamant demand that the game must stop. "I," as subject, embodies and perpetuates the game of representation. "I can't go
on" and "I'll go on" thus read as a condemnation of the subject and
an observation of its endurance.

The value of this endurance nonetheless emerges in the contrapuntal opposition of "I" and "you" in the first four segments of the
passage. Rather than following the more typical reading of "you"
as being addressed to the same reluctant subject as "I" in a mode
of command or stern encouragement, we might more profitably read
"I" and "you" as distinct and opposed. Understood in this way, "you
must" at once exhorts the unnamable and the reader(s) to conspire
against the subject and its reifying effects. The urgency of "you's"
obligation in this case does not stem from a need to encourage "I" in
the face of the possibility of "I's" energy giving out but from the need
to vigorously resist "I's" "going on."

In this manner, Beckett not only maintains a consistent use of "I"
as alienated subject but does so in a way that syntactically fractures
the smooth presentation of the subject as a reassuring and desired
presence. In other words, this oppositional or contrapuntal arrangement of "I" and "you" consciously plays against and disrupts the
more conventional reading of the "you" exhortations as expressions
of solidarity with "I."

Just as the question of subjectivity has intertwined with that of
representation throughout *The Unnamable*, we find the two brought
together again in this final passage of the novel. As is apparent as
far back as "Recent Irish Poetry," Beckett needs to combine both to
advance his project of moving from "the circumference" to "the centre." In a fashion similar to the contrapuntal scheme we saw above,
then, the exhortation to "say words, as long as there are any, until
they find me, until they say me" begins to open up in light of *The
Unnamable*'s overarching critique of representation.

Setting the words in search of "me" and specifically the "say[ing]"
of "me" simply restates the dynamic of the novel and reminds us that

it has not come to an end just because we have reached a point where we can more easily appreciate "real silence" and the unnamable that abides there. Mindful of Beckett's stated goals in the "German Letter," the urging to say words "as long as there are any" thus stands at once as an acknowledgment of representation's seeming indefatigability and an imperative to push it to the limits of its exhaustion.

Placing representation itself under pressure, such an effort injects some oppositional force into its transactions of power and illustrates that it is not solely "me" that must contend with a sense of strain. Even more importantly perhaps, such cognizance and engagement with representation maintains the negative quality of these oppositional energies so that they do not lapse into the purity of complete antithesis that would mean the ironic triumph of the regime of representation "on the rebound" as we saw with Worm. This strategic need to effect a sort of striating of representation across the surface of the "real silence" springs from a strange compulsion and results in a strange mixture of damaging and salutary effects.[15] For this impulse toward a curiously beneficial self-laceration, "strange pain, strange sin" would seem an apt response. As we have seen earlier, however, it is precisely such "strange sin" on which critique relies.

While engaging with representation in order to effect this striation, however, the possibility must always remain of a "true" engagement such that the subject and the self—"I" and "me"—do actually meet and the subject can speak. Beckett expresses this in terms of "me" being "said" and being brought into "story." Though it would certainly "surprise" and, indeed, quite literally petrify "me," it would, of course, be the realization of a possibility that was long known to exist. This collision of worlds would essentially be the nightmare come to life, the "unspeakable" being spoken and, indeed, set down "in story." This, effectively, is the function of "tradition" and, indeed, an earlier iteration of modernism in the anthropological mode of the Revival.

We see the same outcome outlined again with "I" at once encountering and conveying "the silence." Whether we read "I" as entering into the domain of "real silence" or inaugurating a regime where "the "mundane" silence that attaches to "I" simply becomes ascendant and "will be," no future for alterity or agency would seem possible. Yet, as this possibility of "me" effectively opening the door on subjectivity must necessarily form a part of the maintenance of negativity, it is a peril that must be hazarded. "You" must risk subjectivity and enter the realm of "I's" mundane and alienated silence, "the silence you don't know," so that the viability of the unnamable might be sustained. The only other options are surrender or "complete" anti-subjective opposition that would in the end amount to the same thing.

Thus, as the novel closes, we see repeated the exhortation, "you must go on." The order of the phrases is reversed from earlier in the passage, however, with "you must go on" now preceding "I can't go on" in a way that suggests that the focus of agency is split or undercut from its earlier iteration. Though "you" and "I" are not identical in these last phrases of the novel, they are perhaps best read simultaneously in two divergent ways: at once in terms of the earlier oppositional reading—where "you" must endeavor to check the power of the subject, "I"—and in terms of the more conventional reading where "I can't go on, I'll go on" expresses the despair and resolve of both "I" and "you," that of the subject and the unnamable that would call it to account.

Overlaying this earlier "disruptive" reading of "you" with the greater assurance of the "conventional" reading ensures that neither is allowed to settle. This contradictory pair of readings not only goes some way in expressing the complicated economy of "sin" operating between the unnamable and the subject but it keeps alive both the need and means of critique. The hope that obtains at the end of *The Unnamable* is thus not that the fight has been won or regret been assuaged but rather that the fight is yet in "me" and the silence not forgotten.

That such modest measures of hope or resolve are necessarily haunted by an equal measure of skepticism and weary resignation is at once a factor of Beckett's precise understanding of the nature of critique and is expressive of the transitional nature of the postwar era for Irish postcoloniality and for late-modernist aesthetics more generally. *The Unnamable*'s stark reflection on the proliferation of objectifying discourses registers the means by which late-modernist aesthetics are being overtaken by an emphasis on surface and a sense that access to an "authentic" or "original" sense of self must be abandoned as naïve. These emphases would, of course, become the signature features of postmodernism and, in Irish writing, of a particular sort of midcentury naturalism wherein the earlier objectifying mode of "tradition" persists to produce an ongoing ironic tension within Irish postmodern narrative.

In charting an alternative narrative form, however, Beckett reveals the potential of a waning variety of a more self-aware late modernism that helps cast this moment of postmodernism's emergence in relief. The ironic coincidence of the publication in 1958 of Beckett's English translation of *The Unnamable* and and T. K. Whitaker's *Economic Development* White Paper underscores the richly divergent responses this moment produced even as the succeeding years leave little doubt as to which response came to narrate a course for late twentieth-century Irish politics and culture that by now has come to seem inevitable for Ireland and for a "globalized" late postcoloniality alike.

CHAPTER FOUR

Postmodern Blaguardry

Frank McCourt, the Celtic Tiger, and the Ashes of History

In a country so devoted to preserving—and marketing—its literary heritage, it was a rather curious sign of the times that one of the most notable additions to the Irish literary tourist circuit in the late 1990s was a tour of a past that had quite literally been razed. To the chagrin of many, the book that unquestionably had the greatest impact on global impressions of Ireland in the era of the Celtic Tiger was Frank McCourt's memoir *Angela's Ashes*. Translated into some twenty languages and selling more than 4 million copies worldwide, McCourt's 1996 catalogue of 1930s and 1940s Limerick poverty met with stunning popular and critical success, garnering an array of awards that included a Pulitzer. This success led to a virtual "McCourt industry" in the late 1990s and early years of the twenty-first century with a feature film, two documentaries, two touring stage-shows, and three more volumes of memoir from McCourt and his brother, Malachy, being put into circulation in little more than five years.

Though *Angela's Ashes* met with some notable success within Ireland, it perhaps goes without saying that the book's most enthusiastic responses came from outside of Ireland itself.[1] But this international reception—especially by American readers—ensured that *Angela's Ashes* remained prominent—or at least unavoidable—in Ireland itself through the late 1990s. McCourt's influence was least avoidable anywhere one might find tourists, which, at least during the summer, is almost everywhere in Ireland. Passing through departure lounges, guest houses, or any other space where tourists might congregate in Ireland, it was remarkable in the late 1990s if one did not see at least one copy of *Angela's Ashes* being pored over by an eager reader. And thus it was perhaps inevitable that McCourt might be made to follow the path of other more hallowed Irish writers and have his book transformed into that old reliable stand-by of literary tourism known as the walking tour.

Ostensibly a "reality tour" of sites featured in McCourt's memoir, the *Angela's Ashes* tour of the late 1990s and early years of the next decade ultimately disclosed a reality of a different sort than what was advertised. Opening a window onto the shifting physical and economic landscape of Ireland in the waning years of the twentieth century, the tour yields an important object lesson on the place of history and mimeticism in the boom era of the Celtic Tiger. With a striking fidelity to McCourt's text ironically underwritten by the very *dissimi-larity* of the late twentieth-century cityscape of Limerick to that presented by McCourt's exceedingly detailed account in *Angela's Ashes*, the tour provided a stark illustration of the ways in which the slow synchronization of Irish postcoloniality with global capitalism had finally yielded the means by which the material traces of empire could seemingly be transcended by an immersion in a postmodern regime of consumption.

Describing his first foray into the Limerick tourist information center, the travel writer Mike Meyer writes in early 2000 of his attempt to push for a more authentic experience of Limerick than that which might be afforded by the more saccharine tourist fare initially presented to him: "I approached the agent again. 'I sort of had more of a walking tour in mind,' I told her. 'Something about true Limerick past, like King John's Castle over there and the Treaty Stone.' 'Yes, you can do that,' she said, 'or take the "Angela's Ashes" tour'" (20). This opposition between McCourt's text and a "true" past is one that recurs continually in discussions of the *Angela's Ashes* phenomenon. Though such discussions usually end up degenerating into questions of the accuracy of McCourt's account, the underlying issue of the status of the past and its representation turns out to be of central importance for Celtic Tiger Ireland and Irish postcoloniality more broadly. *Angela's Ashes* not only provides an occasion to illuminate how much had changed for Ireland as Lemassian modernization came to its fruition under the sign of the Celtic Tiger; it illustrates, more significantly, how fully Ireland's past had entered the realm of commodification as "tradition" was definitively superseded by "globalization" as the operative watchword within late Irish postcoloniality.

The profundity of the shift and the strange historical discordances that underlie it become more apparent as Meyer recounts how the sites of destitution supposedly constituting the destination of the tour have given way to an itinerary of "development" overlaid by the Celtic Tiger: "O'Donnell led us past the old Dock Road, formerly the setting for picking up stray bits of coal, now the home of a luxury hotel. Mill Lane, where [McCourt's father,] Malachy [,] begged for work, now hosts an office block. Limerick is a clanging, booming town and Dell computers have covered the city's billboards with messages like, 'Bored with your job? Join us! No experience necessary'" (21). Although a past of Irish privation remained the impetus of the tour and its route, the eager tourists of the late 1990s and early twenty-first century found themselves repeatedly overtaken by a more pressing—if less colorful—reality of commerce and computers. With its cheery assurance of "No experience necessary," the Dell billboard succinctly expresses the insouciant amnesia celebrated by the Celtic Tiger and offered as a decisive rebuke to any who would want to take the past too seriously.[2]

Though this disposition of history is perhaps most readily apparent in the more immediate context of the walking tour, it is important to realize the extent to which it marks McCourt's text itself. For the discrepancy between history and immediate material reality does not simply arise as a result of the passage of time between the era McCourt depicts and the era in which he writes and publishes his account; it is rather a constitutive aspect of his text. *Angela's Ashes* does not merely offer a recollection of McCourt's life and milieu in 1930s and 1940s Limerick but ultimately stages the historicizing of history itself in the 1990s. McCourt presents an exquisite counterfeit of the past that revels in its own artificiality and that of the past that forms its subject. His text functions to make the past over into myth in such a way that it is now not simply a matter of "forgetting" the past but rather realizing that it never *really* existed. The "Angela's Ashes" tour might thus be understood as offering a surprisingly faithful encounter with the substance—or insubstantiality—of McCourt's text. Though the tour might likely disappoint some of his admirers in its failure to provide sufficient opportunity to indulge the sentimental voyeurism to which the book caters so readily, its evocation of an opulent Irish present at odds with the spectral traces of past penury renders it at once consistent with *Angela's Ashes* and the Celtic Tiger iteration of Irishness that frames it.

In this regard, the postmodern character of McCourt's narrative contrasts significantly with the critique of a descriptive anthropological modernism pursued in different ways by the antimimetic approaches of the late-modernist writers discussed earlier. At the same time, McCourt's approach might be understood in a certain way as antimimetic in that it consistently underscores the artificiality and directedness of its own literary representation by way of obvious exaggerations and repetitions, an ongoing recourse to dramatic irony and shifts in perspective, and striking portrayals of markets wherein narrative functions explicitly as a commodity. Rather than challenging the capacity of a literary representation to present a full or accurate account of either materiality or selfhood as the late-modernist writers do, however, McCourt instead privileges representation itself. Representation, for McCourt, even in its most extensively detailed accounts, only draws upon materiality to supersede it and show it to be always already constituted by an accumulation of representational frameworks.

McCourt's approach can be understood as the postmodern apotheosis of naturalism. This is true most immediately in the sense of McCourt's reliance on naturalism as a narrative technique that seeks to overwhelm the reader with an immersion in detail. More profoundly, however, we can understand *Angela's Ashes* as representing the apotheosis of naturalism in the Lukácsian sense in that McCourt detaches the individual from a larger historical context and emphasizes surfaces and objects at the expense of attending to any underlying essences that might disrupt objects' solidity or position them as part of a dynamic ongoing process.

Given McCourt's use of an exaggerated naturalist mode that revels in the extremity of its detail, it is perhaps not entirely surprising that *Angela's Ashes* has attracted a good deal of commentary challenging the factual accuracy of many of its accounts. Most notably, perhaps, R. F. Foster repeatedly takes McCourt to task for numerous lapses in the believability of *Angela's Ashes* from the details of IRA pension claims to the likely behavior of cows (*Story* 169). Many in Limerick have similarly asserted that the book's portrait bears little resemblance to the life that they knew and, indeed, shared with McCourt. One literary entrepreneur, Gerard Hannan, even went so far as to pen two parallel texts responding to McCourt's memoirs, *Ashes* and *'Tis in Me Ass*.[3] Others have pointed to the stock Irish characters that people the book and in many ways determine its development.

While such concerns generally form a less than useful—though common—response to autobiography or memoir, they seem especially misplaced for a work that found its earliest enunciation in a barroom drama entitled *A Couple of Blaguards*. McCourt's intimate drama written for and about himself and his brother, Malachy, was his first successful effort at turning his skill as pub raconteur to some commercial success. Though the stories of Limerick and the lanes may take on a more sobering cast as he expands upon them for *Angela's Ashes*, one should nonetheless remain mindful of their provenance and of McCourt's primary vocation as storyteller. Such an orientation allows for a more sustained analysis of *Angela's Ashes* as postmodern narrative rather than unmediated chronicle.

If we begin to move beyond the severe limitations imposed by discussions of factual accuracy and consider what *Angela's Ashes* might tell us about the status of representation in late twentieth-century Irish culture, our efforts may bear more fruit. Not only does *Angela's Ashes* provide an especially useful site to reflect upon the fate of earlier postcolonial narrative modes, it offers surprising insight into the Celtic Tiger society with which its appearance coincides. Such claims may prompt the reasonable objection that *Angela's Ashes* should rightly be seen as an American rather than an Irish text. To discuss the text in terms of its Irishness might seem to be taken in by McCourt's bogus sentimentalism and stage Irishry. But it is precisely its ersatz Irishness that makes the book so emblematic of late postcolonial culture and the Celtic Tiger phenomenon in particular. In that regard, it should be neither surprising nor especially scandalous that the text comes from a diasporic writer, especially one based in the United States. One might wish that American inflection to be more scandalous than it is, but to do so is to wish that late twentieth-century Ireland were less fully in the thrall of American capital than was actually the case.

Such underlying "structural" aspects might ultimately prove insufficient to framing our reading of *Angela's Ashes*, however, unless considered in terms of the specific historical context of the Celtic Tiger and the remarkable shift it signals in Ireland's material and cultural histories. Most fundamentally, we can understand the Celtic Tiger as the product of an intense modernization drive beginning with the Lemassian initiative of the late 1950s, continuing with Ireland's 1973 entry into the European Economic Community—precursor to the European Union—and culminating in the late 1990s with Ireland posting GDP growth that outpaced most of Europe. Low corporate tax rates, a strong governmental role in negotiating the broad cooperation of labor unions under the umbrella of "social partnership" agreements, and the massive infusion of EEC/EU funds for transportation and infrastructure improvement all worked to make Ireland an attractive site for the late twentieth-century initiatives of multinational capital in peripheral and semi-peripheral spaces typically referenced by the upbeat term of "globalization." Thus, Ireland followed in the wake of the Asian "tiger" economies of the early 1990s such as Singapore, Taiwan, and South Korea to become—at least briefly—an important site for high-tech and pharmaceutical design and manufacturing and customer-service "call centers." Not surprisingly, this brought huge social and cultural change as conspicuous consumption became more normalized and the large-scale emigration of those looking for work that had marked the 1980s and early 1990s gave way to an unprecedented flow of *immigrants* now coming to Ireland in search of work.

The overwhelming emphasis of the Celtic Tiger era was not simply on Ireland's "modernness" but on its effective interchangeability with any other "globalized" space. This interchangeability was suggested as much by the growing ethnic diversity of its population as by the increasingly harsh regimes of immigration and citizenship law instituted to "manage" the immigrant population and signal Ireland's arrival as a "developed" and prosperous nation.[4] The rather incongruous "Celtic Tiger" term, derived as it is from the term for surging East Asian economies, only underscores this sense of interchangeability.

A shift from a sense of originality or discrete difference to a reveling in interchangeability and endless substitution constitutes, of course, one of the hallmarks of postmodernity. Considered in relation to the trajectory of Irish postcoloniality we have been tracing since the 1920s, we can see how the rise of a postmodern sensibility effectively transposes the dominant grammar of Irish politics and narrative so that both are defined by an excess of representation rather than the sense of lack or incompleteness that had previously been their signature. With the lingering issues of Northern partition and "the Troubles" seemingly put to rest by the Northern Ireland peace process and an aura of prosperity surrounding the Republic, the notion of the historical transcendence of empire was more readily advanced, and nationalism—even in its most institutional guise—was increasingly seen as an embarrassing relic.[5]

Reflecting this shift within *Angela's Ashes*, we see "tradition" and naturalism entirely mediated through the filters of irony and kitsch as the spectacles of primitivism or privation they present are detached from their material referents. The objects of Revivalist fantasy and midcentury nightmare alike disintegrate. As globalization increasingly comes to define late postcoloniality in Ireland, these objects retain coherence only within representation itself and, as such, are quintessentially naturalist in a Lukácsian sense.

The importance of the postmodern frame of "late" postcoloniality becomes apparent on the very first page of *Angela's Ashes*. After remarking on the foolishness of his parents' decision to leave New York and the particular misery of an Irish Catholic childhood, McCourt lays out the crucial elements of Irish misery that he will proceed to elaborate: "People everywhere brag and whimper about the woes of their early years, but nothing can compare with the Irish version: the poverty; the shiftless loquacious alcoholic father; the pious defeated mother moaning by the fire; pompous priests; bullying schoolmasters; the English and the terrible things they did to us for eight hundred long years" (11). McCourt thus begins his account by anatomizing the Irish narrative he is about to present as his own. This foregrounding of the narrative elements and, indeed, the very possibility of such an anatomy obviously signal McCourt's divergence from a direct relationship with materiality in his text. The neat catalogue of misery and the ease with which he rattles it off make it immediately clear that the content and meaning of his sad story are borrowed from a storehouse of stock Irish images that predetermine his account. McCourt does not at all claim originality in his memoir; he readily proclaims himself a trafficker in Irish simulacra from the outset.

The notion of "incomparable" Irish woe and the hackneyed phrase about the English that marks the culmination of McCourt's inventory only underscore his disengagement from the miseries he lists. As becomes increasingly clear over the course of the book, McCourt presents such trite formulae of nationalist grievance quite sardonically. The lack of specificity in the complaint about the English and its seeming applicability to anything bad that happens in Ireland either during or after the colonial era render it extremely suspect, especially as we begin to see the degree of McCourt's antipathy toward Irish fatalism and his repeated emphasis on the efficacy of sustained individual action. Inserting such a platitude here amplifies the artificiality of his litany of misery and introduces the element of humor that pushes it toward parody. For it is not simply that McCourt's experience sadly proves the legitimacy of Irish stereotypes. Even as McCourt presents the reality of such stereotypes in harrowing detail, he also seeks to highlight their status *as* stereotype in order to emphasize the especially pathetic case of a people who would come to be overtaken by their own clichés.

This jocose relationship to cliché and simulacrum constitutes a key affective feature of *Angela's Ashes*. At some level, everything is a joke in McCourt's text; nothing can really be taken at face value. Even McCourt's waggish air shows itself to be marked by affectation in his ongoing recourse to the staging of dramatic irony and his tendency to shift mood abruptly so that the contrast might exaggerate the pathos of some episode in the life of his family. Such pathos then comes, in turn, to yield entry into yet another field of simulacra, another tragic script that one must see through in order to transcend. This constant alternation between facetiousness and fact is what makes *Angela's Ashes* so slippery and prompts so much of the focus on questions of authenticity.

Approaching the text from the perspective of postmodernism allows one to avoid being drawn into such sterile debate over authenticity and "the facts", however, so as to attend more directly to the function of these unsettling moves into and out of the domain of the real. In different ways, the antimimeticism of the late-modernist practices of the Blasket writers, O'Faoláin, and Beckett underscores the inadequacy of mimeticism as a means of pointing to aspects of materiality and consciousness exceeding the bounds of representation or figuration. For McCourt, however, nothing exceeds the bounds of representation. The artificiality of "the real" and the reality of "the artificial" are crucial aspects of this new postmodern dispensation; "authenticity" no longer obtains as a valid category.[6] The laughter and play of McCourt's text must thus be seen as bases for consolidating a more far-reaching order rather than providing the means of a critique.

Fredric Jameson's concept of pastiche helps clarify this point. Parody both illuminates the features of the dominant form and reveals its failure as representation by revealing a space of critique beyond its borders. Pastiche, on the other hand, lacks this outside space of critique and can thus merely point to the form's continuity with other representations. The imitation we see in pastiche is therefore "blank parody"—what Jameson describes as "a neutral practice

of . . . mimicry without any of parody's ulterior motives, [and] ampu-
tated of the satiric impulse" (17). The effect of pastiche, then, is to
naturalize artifice in such a way that dominant regimes and forms
might be immune to a critique that would question their legitimacy
or inevitability. In this sense, pastiche might be seen as antiparodic or
metaparodic, a turning of parody against itself.

The comic tilt of McCourt's text must thus be primarily understood as a performance of wry Irish wit for its own sake; it is a pastiche of Irish drollery rather than comedy with a particular critical
intent.[7] McCourt's general purpose is to expose the pretense of the
real—most especially in cases where elements of the symbolic or
sacred realm come to operate in the domain of the real as if they were
themselves real. Thus, his unflattering accounts of his father's fervor
for Ireland mock the figure of the rebel rather than comment directly
on the nationalist cause itself. Though his father's claim of having
"done his bit" echoes throughout the book, McCourt undermines the
power of that assertion from the very beginning: "My father, Malachy McCourt, was born on a farm in Toome, County Antrim. Like
his father before, he grew up wild, in trouble with the English, or the
Irish, or both. He fought with the Old IRA and for some desperate act
he wound up a fugitive with a price on his head" (12). McCourt does
not challenge the substance of his father's claim but rather its significance. He renders rebellion a genetic trait that Malachy inherits from
his father and directs at whatever authorities happen to be about, "the
English, or the Irish, or both."

As such, McCourt encloses action within prefigured representation. He reduces whatever his father may have done to "some desperate act" for which "he *wound up* a fugitive." The details of Malachy's
action are irrelevant and may even be nonexistent; the important thing
for McCourt's purposes is to shift the register from the real to the
representational. Malachy is bound to fulfill the terms of the stereotype of the Irish rebel by committing a desperate act that will render
him a fugitive. Emphasizing his father's lack of agency in the matter,
McCourt insists on the overwhelming importance of the role that is
scripted for him. Malachy's pathetic descent into barroom brawls and
seemingly constant drunken singing of rebel songs (25, 28, 39–40, 75,
77, 110, 145, 170, 185) serves as McCourt's commentary on the hol-
lowness of the rebel figure and the emptiness of his inevitably tragic
end. Malachy's own tragic decline comes close to parodying that of
the rebel but ultimately serves to highlight the rebel's continuity with

another romanticized Irish figure marked by defiance and doom—
that of the grandiloquent drunk. In this way, McCourt's account of
his father registers the rebel's cause as ultimately unimportant and
points instead to the extent to which rebellion itself has been subsumed by representation to become a caricature. History and agency
are rendered obsolete or effectively displaced. Change or action can
occur only within the domain of representation.

This shadow-play of representation and materiality in *Angela's
Ashes* becomes increasingly complicated as McCourt abandons the
perspective of mature narrator presenting stories of his infancy and
the details of his and his parents' origins. About twenty pages into the
book, the narrator abruptly takes on the viewpoint of his naïve four-
year-old self and proceeds through the rest of the text to narrate the
events of his life from the ostensible perspective of whatever age he
happens to be at that point in the narrative. Obviously a conceit, the
adoption of an "immediate" childhood perspective initiates a much
more intricate narrative array than it may first appear.

Considered out of context of the book's opening section, the effect
of the gradually maturing outlook might seem a straightforward and
well-established means for conveying a greater sense of sincerity or
authenticity to an autobiographical text. However, when considered
alongside the immediate confession of a lack of originality and a reveling in the play of simulacra that marks the opening of the text and,
indeed, precedes the rather belated adoption of the child's perspective,
it becomes clear that the device is ironically deployed to highlight the
artificiality of such an effect of authenticity. From the deployment
of pastiche to the detailed account of events to which he could not
possibly be privy,[8] McCourt thus repeatedly highlights the postmodern frame of the text. The appearance of the inauthentic does not
result from an inadvertent slipping of the mask but is something glee-
fully proclaimed as a constitutive element of the text. We are thus
a long way from the "inauthenticity" that Gregory Castle identifies
as the signature feature of Joyce's anthropological modernism (176)
and further still from the late-modernist practices of the early postcolonial period that consistently eat away at the very possibility of
representation.

As the book continues and McCourt enters into the "immediate"
narration more fully, it is perhaps easy to forget the initial foregrounding of artificiality, especially given McCourt's propensity for lurid
detail. Indeed, McCourt himself seems anxious to disavow artifice

and sentimentalism so as to invoke the searing reality of his child-hood and the honesty of his reassembled perspective.[9] That he meets with some real success in this regard cannot be gainsaid. A few crit-ics take *Angela's Ashes* at face value as an inspired and deeply hon-est portrayal of the travails of 1930s Ireland and the courage of those who sought a better life through emigration.[10] While conceding vary-ing degrees of artifice in *Angela's Ashes*, these critics tend to dismiss concerns about "factual" veracity as irrelevant distractions from the underlying emotional honesty of the book. Indeed, Darlene Erickson surprisingly goes so far as to praise *Angela's Ashes* for its lack of sen-timentalism (69).

Such critical responses fail to contend with the tensions between the interweaving personae of the narrator, however. Whether inten-tional or not, the opening section of *Angela's Ashes* must be seen as a confession of the book's project of pastiche and its immersion within postmodern narrative. A careful reading shows that these aspects only become more and more evident over the course of the text. Thus, it is not that the introductory pages prescribe a certain reading of *Ange-la's Ashes* that would not otherwise be tenable. The text's compatibil-ity with the broader currents of globalization and the emergence of the Celtic Tiger perhaps inclines us toward a postmodern perspective. McCourt's opening simply makes it too compelling to overlook.

Despite that, readers of *Angela's Ashes* might not initially appreciate the postmodern aspect of the text. Indeed, much in the text conspires to occlude it. McCourt's heavy reliance on an immediate, present-tense narration style proves one of his most effective techniques in conveying an air of guilelessness and frustrating attempts at critique. As George O'Brien observes: "Because this speech is the idiom of the moment, of unmediated experience, rather than the language of reflection or argu-ment or evaluation, the reader is powerless before it. To interrogate the moment risks denying the improvisatory, restless, insecure, unstruc-tured nature that typifies McCourt family life" (238–39). McCourt thus attempts to undercut the very possibility of a critical reading by insisting on the artlessness of his prose and posing it as a "pure" repre-sentation of the chaos of the McCourts' world. As O'Brien notes, this tilts the textual field decidedly to McCourt's advantage and makes the reader almost "powerless." To approach the text critically is thus per-haps to risk being perceived as an academic humbug.

The combination of such "innocent" narration with the conven-tions of naturalism makes it even more difficult to appreciate the postmodern inflection of *Angela's Ashes*. A postmodernist text might perhaps be expected to wear its postmodernism on its sleeve and frolic conspicuously in its metafictions or artificiality. It would not, seemingly, take the form of a relatively straightforward autobiographical text that dwells in excruciating detail on the perceived inescapability of slum life and family disintegration even if, in that portrait, he is not particularly original, as he readily acknowledges from the outset.[11]

The postmodern aspect of McCourt's naturalism begins to become more apparent, however, as we consider how it involves a conscious reassembling of preceding representations. As with nationalism, McCourt does not seek to critique naturalist technique or demonstrate its "falseness." Rather, he presents the naturalist narrative as the new ground of reality for a postmodern regime of representation. McCourt's naturalism is thus quite "real." Indeed, its acknowledgment of its fictiveness makes his naturalism more "real" than its precursors by resolving the tension between the domains of fiction and materiality. In that wholeness, postmodern naturalism may constitute a "purer" naturalism. At the same time, naturalism's fatalism and sense of an overarching and inescapable order produces a "purer" postmodernism that is potentially more grounded and far-reaching than the more "difficult" arabesques upon which a more playful or theoretical postmodernism sometimes embarks. The sense of disenchanted inevitability attaching to both postmodernism and naturalism is thus reinforced and amplified.

This binding of postmodernism and naturalism proves consistent with a late postcoloniality whose effect is to make of the past an assemblage of myths and representations that haunt the imagination of the present but have no real purchase on it. Like late postcoloniality, postmodern naturalism does not seek to suppress the traumatic details of the past but rather to question their ongoing effect and contest their status as traces of a more enduring order of material inequality. As we see in *Angela's Ashes*, even the most painful and materially urgent fact immediately enters the realm of fiction and can only be apprehended in terms of representation; indeed, it has most likely already been anticipated by representation. The fact is never "real" outside of representation. Or if it is, it remains unknowable.

For McCourt, the naturalist portrait of *Angela's Ashes* coheres around his father's alcoholism. He hints quite broadly at the shadow Malachy's drinking will cast over the family in his opening textual anatomy and such early accounts as his father's drunken accosting of the priest at his baptism (18). These early references only establish the stereotyped figuration of Malachy's alcoholism, however. The initial description of "the shiftless loquacious alcoholic father" (11) as an essential aspect of the difficult Irish childhood foregrounds its status as an overdetermined Irish type. McCourt then animates this type as one among other Irish types in order to manufacture the humor of the baptismal scene. It is not until the onset of the child's perspective that such types begin gradually to shift from farcical character to imprisoning force in some larger tragic drama.

McCourt increases the tension from Frankie's first mention of Malachy sometimes coming home "with the smell of whiskey" (22) to his not showing up on the evening of payday when the rest of the family awaits him so they can go buy food (24–25). The situation continues to deteriorate to the point that McCourt describes his mother, Angela, wandering the streets of Brooklyn with four children scouring the bars for a sign of Malachy and having to rely on a kindly barman for milk for the infant twins (26–28). This rather pathetic sequence culminates in a rather curious domestic scene arranged around the twins: "The twins fall asleep after eating and Mam lays them on the bed to change their diapers. She sends me down the hall to rinse the dirty diapers in the lavatory so that they can be hung up to dry and used the next day. Malachy [Junior] helps her wash the twins' bottoms though he's ready to fall asleep himself" (28). At its most basic level, the passage seems aimed at highlighting the ways in which the father's neglect causes a breakdown of family structure. Malachy's irresponsibility seems greater when contrasted with the other family members' care of each other, especially with Frankie and the younger Malachy being forced to shoulder parental roles so prematurely at the age of four and two respectively.

It is curious, however, that McCourt would use this particular detail to illustrate this point. Its significance looms larger as the book continues. In true naturalist style, McCourt turns repeatedly to scatological detail as a means of marking the family's descent. Control of feces comes to function as a strange index of civility in *Angela's Ashes*. At this early point, things have just begun to unravel. Thus, we have the mild disturbance of slight scatological detail intrude into the narrative somewhat unexpectedly. The disturbance simply stems from the fact that such detail is not typically included in autobiography, and its presence here is neither dictated by the narrative flow nor really sustained by it. Its inclusion, therefore, seems more a naturalist *interruption* than a predictable aspect of a more smoothly executed naturalist narrative. As a result, it leaves some sense of the artificiality of McCourt's naturalism, providing some indication of its status as pastiche.

This impression grows stronger as the intensity of the text's naturalism increases. Angela gives birth to another child, Margaret, who dies before reaching two months. With her dies much of the family's remaining sense of hope. So enchanted by his daughter had Malachy been that he had stopped drinking. When she dies, however, he plunges into drinking with a renewed fervor. The sense of impotence that McCourt conveys as the parents desperately try to revive the sick child only deepens as Malachy abandons the family and begins drinking again. We thus have a typically naturalist pattern of a slight glimmer of hope giving way to an even greater despair as the unyielding cruelty of a brutal world seems to expand to enclose the family more definitively. McCourt records this in the subtle but sure decay of domesticity that follows Margaret's death: "Mam stays in bed all day, hardly moving. Malachy and I fill the twins' bottles with water and sugar. In the kitchen we find a half loaf of stale bread and two cold sausages. We can't have tea because the milk is sour in the icebox where the ice is melted again and everyone knows you can't drink tea without milk unless your father gives it to you out of his mug while he's telling you about Cuchulain" (36).

The artificiality and instrumentality of McCourt's naturalism are quite apparent here. On the one hand, we have the collapse of domestic civility with an incapacitated mother, an absent father, raw or rotten foodstuffs, and affairs being handled by a four-year-old. On the other, we have the memory of domestic bliss with the invocation of a doting father telling stories and offering sips of his tea. McCourt sets these opposite each other in a somewhat weak attempt to highlight the poignancy of the family's decline as he documents its disheartening material circumstances.

This mix of the sentimental and the documentary modes underlines the bad faith of McCourt's naturalist portrait and exposes its postmodern inflection. The passage presents a pastiche of naturalism that rejects the "scientific" or "documentary" aspirations of standard naturalism in favor of eliciting sympathy and signaling the veiled presence of the mature narrator contriving the scene. Instead of attempting to "brush out" the authorial presence as one would typically expect with naturalism, McCourt's assertion that "everyone

knows you can't drink tea without milk unless your father gives it
to you out of his mug while he's telling you tales about Cuchulain"
reminds us of the author's lingering behind the façade. His ongoing
use of the present tense does not minimize the presence of the adult
narrator's perspective, as Fred Miller Robinson suggests (22). The
"adult retrospection" (22) that Robinson sees being largely effaced
by Frankie's present-tense narration emerges quite clearly here and is
indeed projected onto four year-old Frankie in his precocious nostalgia for better days with his father.

As he does so often in *Angela's Ashes*, McCourt relies here on dramatic irony to intensify the emotion of the scene. The pathos evoked
by Frankie's naiveté only really comes through if the reader consciously
shares the inside-knowledge with McCourt about the real dimensions
of the situation and the sad folly of looking to Malachy for any care or
succor. The impotence of the child and his inability to grasp it stands in
for the more totalizing impotence of naturalism. Frankie and the others
do really stand impotent in the face of a harsh world arrayed against
them. But as a result of McCourt's continual resort to dramatic irony,
it is a situation that we always perceive as being first fixed by representation and standing apart from material reality.

McCourt marks the accelerating dissolution of the domestic sphere
through a rapid accumulation of squalid naturalist detail. Inter-
spersed with numerous accounts of the neighbors' kindness needed
to sustain them in the wake of the complete abdication of responsibility by Angela and Malachy, McCourt treats us to comments about
how difficult it is for Frankie and young Malachy to keep the twins
and their diapers clean as they constantly get everything "all shitty"
(42). He further illustrates the inversion of the parent-child roles by
describing Frankie's new duty of having to dump and wash the bucket
of his mother's vomit that she is constantly filling (41). All of this
comes to a head when the neighbors alert Angela's relatives that the
kids are "runnin' wild" and her two sanctimonious cousins come to
survey the scene (43). They are mortified to find Angela catatonic
in bed, the apartment in shambles, and the twins running around
naked. Asked if the twins have any clothes, young Malachy cheerily
responds, "They're all shitty" to the horror of the cousins (43). The
profusion of feces serves as a reliable indicator of the unraveling of the
family and its civility.

The result of the cousins' intervention is that they deem the
McCourts incapable of making it in America, and the family soon

finds itself thrust from the bosom of American civility back into the
poverty and squalor of Ireland. As a final commentary on the family's
wretchedness and incompatibility with American civility, he describes
the family's last glimpse of New York in a way that brings the earlier
naturalist detail to an almost absurd crescendo:

> The ship pulled away from the dock. Mam said, That's the Statue
> of Liberty and that's Ellis Island where all the immigrants came in.
> Then she leaned over the side and vomited and the wind from the
> Atlantic blew it all over us and other happy people admiring the view.
> Passengers cursed and ran, seagulls came from all over the harbor
> and Mam hung limp and pale on the ship's rail. (46)

The sudden eruption of the corporeal into the visual field forces a
jarring shift in focus from the majestic panorama surveyed from a
privileged distance to the tiny bits of vomit now perceived from a disgusting propinquity. Though McCourt makes use of the contrast to
emphasize the inescapable quality of physicality and filth in the narrative, he nonetheless frames it in such a way that the reader is still able
to maintain a more distant perspective as they view Angela draped
over the rail.

McCourt's introduction of a comedic element through a sarcastic
reference to "other happy people enjoying the view" followed by his
rapid slide into the sentimental with "Mam hung limp and pale on the
ship's rail" serves as a reminder of the representational quality of the
details and the extent to which naturalism is being consciously and
openly staged for effect. Though McCourt does not plunge into the
more unrelenting enumeration of detail that might be more standard
naturalist fare, the earthiness of the passage does serve as an important marker of Angela's "un-Americanness" and confirmation of the
narrative sense of her return to Ireland. Angela does not vomit "on"
just any view; it is, of course, the storied prospect of the "successful" immigrant who has finally reached the precincts of civility and
prosperity. Her revolting and pathetic retching in the face of it thus
affirms the legitimacy of her voyage back into the netherworld of the
poor, the tired, and the huddled mass.

The return to Ireland in *Angela's Ashes* must then be viewed in
terms of a quantum leap in the process of naturalist devolution. The
hallmarks of McCourt's vision of Ireland are provincialism, cruelty,
filth, damp, disease, and grinding poverty. Whatever depths the family may have sunk to in New York, their denigrated condition was
always presented as anomalous. In Ireland, however, their situation

is not at all unusual. While McCourt does depict some wealthy families, most of those he portrays either live in similar circumstances to the McCourts or remain perilously close to doing so. Significantly, McCourt repeatedly presents this impoverishment and nasty backbiting as a function of Ireland and Irishness. He never offers the slightest hint that this sense of Ireland may be affected by the perspective afforded by life in the lanes nor does he ever suggest that the Depression or the recent emergence from imperial rule really play any significant role.[12]

Indeed, poverty and squalor are such essential features of Irishness for McCourt that the ironic intensity of his postmodern naturalism completely overtakes his account. In the American section of the book, the postmodern aspect of McCourt's naturalism generally can be detected only in small details around the edges of his narrative. In the account of Ireland, however, it becomes so overwhelming as to constitute much of the basis of reality. On the family's first night on their own in Limerick, then, we see them awakened by a plague of fleas. Malachy and Frankie drag the family's single mattress outside and exert themselves in a largely ineffectual attempt to beat the fleas out of the mattress and drown them. Describing this, the child-narrator, Frankie, waxes lyrically about how he would like to try scooping up bits of the moon that he sees shimmering in the water but is unable to because he is so afflicted by the fleas (60). The lyrical and the naturalist elements can thus be seen to intertwine; poverty becomes beautiful, and representation envelops materiality down to its finest and ugliest detail.

As they are engaged in this effort, a man approaches on a bicycle and proceeds to offer his disquisition on fleas. After making a suggestion about the best method of dealing with them, he continues with his observations about fleas' place in Irish history:

> They're a right bloody torment an' I should know for didn't I grow
> up in Limerick, down in the Irishtown, an' the fleas there were so
> plentiful an' forward they'd sit on the toe of your boot an' discuss
> Ireland's woeful history with you. It is said there were no fleas in
> ancient Ireland, that they were brought in be the English to drive us
> out of our wits entirely, an' I wouldn't put it past the English. An'
> isn't it a very curious thing that St. Patrick drove the snakes out of
> Ireland an' the English brought in the fleas. For centuries Ireland was
> a lovely peaceful place, snakes gone, not a flea to be found. You could
> stroll the four green fields of Ireland without fear of snakes an' have
> a good night's sleep with no fleas to bother you. Them snakes were

doin' no harm, they wouldn't bother you unless you cornered them
an' they lived off other creatures that move under bushes an' such
places, whereas the flea sucks the blood from you mornin' noon an'
night for that's his nature an' he can't help himself. . . . I have to be
careful standin' here for if one of them gets on my clothes I might as
well invite his whole family home. They multiply faster than Hindus.
(60–61)

Considered in the context of the surrounding narrative, it seems quite
clear that McCourt does not present this scene ironically. Such long
discussions about fleas and their part in colonial conspiracy would
seem to be a quite normal, if somewhat amusing, event in Irish life.
Indeed, the speaker turns out to be Frankie's uncle, brother-in-law to
Angela, and one of Frankie's wisest counselors as he is growing up.
His account of the fleas mixes complaints about poverty and colonial
rule rendering both absurdly quaint. He effectively becomes the flea
he imagines discussing "Ireland's woeful history" as he rambles on
about the English and St. Patrick.

The effect is to realize in a small way the naturalist transformation
of human into beast. Of course, the transformation is only hinted at
here and not fully effected. With material concerns being progressively overtaken by the "real representation" of postmodern narrative, McCourt has no interest in the disruptive effect of such a radical transformation. He contents himself instead with transforming
the Irish poor into charming caricatures who good-naturedly come
to terms with their material hardships by apostrophizing them and
framing them within a simplistic and inevitable narrative of "Ireland's woeful history." McCourt completes this circuit of similitude
with the closing comment about Hindus. The comparison between
fleas and "Hindus" repeats the metonymic link between the poor and
the vermin that afflict them. The ethnocentrism of the comment only
enhances the colorfulness of the commentator and facilitates a guilt-
less indulgence of ethnocentrism or classism on the part of the reader
as the comic value of the comment emerges from the reader's sense of
the "ignorance" of the speaker and his ironic failure to appreciate the
resemblance of the stereotype of his own people to the "Hindus" he
describes.

The real consequences of such living conditions become painfully
clear in very short time as both of the McCourt twins die within
six months of each other. McCourt's Limerick is so rife with disease and death, however, that it is nearly impossible to apprehend the

twins' deaths as anything but moments of extreme sentimentalism
within a broader pastiche of economic and social devastation. With
each child's death, we have Malachy beating his thighs with his fists
(36, 74, 82), saying "Och," and heading off to drink while Angela
collapses and the other children look on confusedly and wait to have
it poignantly explained to them what it means that their sibling is
dead. Whatever real trauma this rapid succession of deaths must have
constituted within McCourt's family—and it must indeed have been
immense—his overwrought portrait of the deaths and tedious repetition of language and textual detail render them an escalating series
of incidents of pastiche such that each successive death amplifies the
maudlin artificiality of the preceding depictions.

Perhaps the only reliable indication that the deaths drag the family progressively lower rather than simply reiterate each other is the
renewed profusion of feces. In the wake of the second twin's, Eugene's,
death, the family moves house to a set of rooms adjacent to a toilet
serving eleven families, and Angela is told to expect that she will want
a gas mask by the time the warm weather arrives and it gets "very
powerful altogether" (92). Though that development does seem to
mark a new low for the McCourts, the reality of the living conditions
and the deaths ultimately seems completely subordinate to their presence and function as representations within a mode of postmodern
naturalism.

The absurdity of McCourt's naturalist staging perhaps reaches its
height with his sketch of the family of one of Frankie's classmates,
Paddy Clohessy. The Clohessys live in an especially godforsaken slum,
an area of tenements down by the river where Frankie is warned not to
go because "the people down there are wild and ye could get robbed
and killed" (163). Despite this, Frankie accompanies Paddy home one
evening in an attempt to evade the wrath of his parents for what he
has done at school that day. In his nightmarish portrait of the Clohessys, McCourt brings together all of the book's most striking naturalist elements and lays them out in the space of a few pages. Thus,
upon climbing to the fourth floor of the tenement after being careful
to watch for the missing stairs and avoid slipping on the human excre-
ment that litters the steps, Frankie reaches the Clohessys' flat:

> Paddy's family live in one big room with a high ceiling and a small
> fireplace. There are two tall windows and you can see out to the
> Shannon. His father is in a bed in the corner, groaning and spitting
> into a bucket. Paddy's brothers and sisters are on mattresses on the

floor, sleeping, talking, looking at the ceiling. There's a baby with no
clothes crawling over to Paddy's father's bucket and Paddy pulls him
away. . . .

Paddy lies down on a mattress by the window and I lie beside him.
I keep my clothes on like everybody else and I even forget to take
off my other shoe, which is wet and squishy and stinks. Paddy falls
asleep right away and I look at his mother sitting by the bit of a fire
smoking another cigarette. Paddy's father groans and coughs and
spits into the bucket. He says, Feckin' blood, and she says, You'll have
to go into the sanatorium sooner or later.

I will not. The day they put you in there is the end of you.

You could be givin' the consumption to the children. I could get
the guards to take you away you're that much of a danger to the
children.

If they were to get it they'd have it be now.

The fire dies and Mrs. Clohessy climbs over him into the bed.
(164–65)

The Clohessys seem to embody what the McCourts stand in danger of
becoming; they have abandoned—or been stripped of—almost all the
conventions of civility, and any notion of domesticity has largely given
way to a mode of life scarcely distinguishable from that of animals. In
addition to presenting the requisite profusion of bodily fluids—in this
case phlegm and blood—McCourt seems at pains to emphasize the
almost complete absence of a filial bond. The various family members
seem to have almost nothing to say to each other. Indeed, we do not
even know how many of them there are. McCourt just refers to them
as "Paddy's brothers and sisters" and describes them as engaged in a
variety of activities that emphasize their individuality and undermine
any sense of a collective identity. They resemble occupants of a flop-
house more than members of a family.

The lack of filial connection emerges most tellingly, of course, in
Mr. Clohessy's callous dismissal of concern about the threat his illness poses to the health of the rest of the family. McCourt makes the
threat disturbingly real in his detailed descriptions of Mr. Clohessy's
"ropes of green and yellow stuff" (165) and his mention of the naked
baby heading for the bucket. Given that, the parental disregard crucially reinforces the sense of the Clohessys' dehumanization so that
they move beyond mere poverty and any accompanying claim of vic-
timhood to enter the domain of savagery. As such, they forfeit pity in
favor of opprobrium.

Given the extremity of McCourt's depiction of the Clohessys and
its near-perfect expression of the text's larger naturalist thrust, it is

worth considering the account of breakfast at the Clohessys'. The very normality of the family meal and its totemic status as occasion of familial unity and health make it especially useful for McCourt as a moment for illustrating the Clohessys' gross deformation of domestic ritual. Thus, he depicts Mrs. Clohessy as a slattern only *just* capable of fulfilling the barest outline of a maternal role:

> Mrs. Clohessy is spooning porridge into mugs and jam jars and one bowl and telling us to eat up and go to school. She sits at the table eating her porridge. Her hair is gray black and dirty. It dangles in the bowl and picks up bits of porridge and drops of milk. The children slurp the porridge and complain they didn't get enough, they're starving with the hunger. They have snotty noses and sore eyes and scabby knees. Mr. Clohessy coughs and squirms on the bed and brings up the great gobs of blood and I run out of the room and puke on the stairs where there's a step missing and there's a shower of porridge and bits of apple to the floor below where people go back and forth to the lavatory in the yard. Paddy comes down and says, Sure that's all right. Everywan gets sick and shits on them stairs an' the whole feckin' place is falling down anyway. (166)

Ironically, it is the Clohessys' remaining shreds of domesticity and humanity that most strikingly illuminate their degradation. Mrs. Clohessy's sad maternal effort represented by her providing breakfast and encouraging the children "to eat up and go to school" makes her slovenly ways and her failure to provide enough food all the more apparent. McCourt's description of her appearance and her less-than-hygienic eating render her a pathetic parody of the efficient, scrubbed, and solicitous stereotype of maternal virtue. Rather than the source of domestic order and health, she is a source of filth and disease at its center. The dangling of her hair in the porridge conveys the notion that she contaminates the domestic sphere at the very point where it should be nourished and made healthy. McCourt expresses this in short order with a brief catalogue of the children's unhealthiness— snotty noses, sore eyes, and scabby knees—and yet another mention of Mr. Clohessy's consumptive phlegm. In keeping with his emphasis on pure representation, McCourt displays no sympathy for Mrs. Clohessy but simply uses her as an example of how the most celebrated repositories of human dignity and love—mother and family—have been degraded.

McCourt's return to bodily effluvia as a means of illustrating the depravity of the Clohessys and their poverty makes the account almost a parody of his own writing elsewhere in the text. Though he

faithfully renders Mr. Clohessy's expectoration and Frankie's vomit-
ing in pure naturalist detail, it has become such an overused effect
that it cannot be taken seriously. McCourt actually undermines the
sense of reality of such details the more that he emphasizes the gritty
detail of scenes as contrived as those featuring the Clohessys.

This does not mean, however, that he dispenses with the "real"
entirely. It involves, rather, a postmodern processing of the real, a
new grounding of the real in a matrix of representation. With the
representational structures and recycled naturalist narrative modes
the only enduring and cohesive substance holding "reality" together,
the grim actualities evaporate or are rendered inaccessible. Coming
to terms with the past is thus no longer a question of determining
facts or sifting through myths but developing a sense of the present ends to which representations of the past can be deployed in any
given moment. McCourt's work can thus be seen as coinciding with
the globalized cosmopolitanism of the Celtic Tiger in that it relies on
this sense that the past has ceased to really matter and can and should
only be recovered indirectly through a pastiche of "tradition" and
naturalist excess.

Confirming the artificiality of the naturalist depiction of the Clohessys, then, McCourt executes a rapid shift to the sentimental with
the arrival of Angela. By wonderful coincidence, she turns out to
have been a favorite dancing partner of Mr. Clohessy in their youth.
McCourt thus humanizes Mr. Clohessy for the briefest moment only
to exchange naturalist cliché for that of the sentimental mode. Rather
than the uncaring and disgusting consumptive coughing up "ropes"
of green and red in the corner, he becomes the pitiful figure lying on
his sickbed regretting the loss of youth and the cure that remains out
of reach: "Mam goes to the bed to take Mr. Clohessy's hand. His face
is caved in all around his eyes and his hair is shiny black with the
sweat running from the top of his head. His children stand around
the bed looking at him and looking at Mam. . . . Mr. Clohessy gasps,
I'd be all right if I could live in a dry place. Angela, is America a dry
place?" (167–68).

The shift in tone parallels a shift in perspective such that we now
see Mr. Clohessy from above and at much closer range as we look
down on him in the bed. In this way, McCourt separates him from
his disease in a way that the harshness of the earlier naturalism did
not allow. With the new focus on his caved-in face and head bathed in
sweat, we see the toll the illness has taken on his body and the sense of

Mr. Clohessy as an agent of disease gives way to a sense of his being its victim.

Though this shift admits of a much greater dose of sympathy on McCourt's part, it ultimately only serves to make more evident the condescension that underlies his naturalism. Indeed, it is perhaps a "softer" naturalism that continues to cast the Clohessys as irredeemably bound for doom but less brutally merged with the forces that will prove their undoing. The trite tableau of the children ranged around the sickbed listening to the poor invalid naively inquire about a cure that can never come reinforces both the sentimentalism of the scene and the sense of the Clohessys' inferiority and intrinsic vulnerability. Though the "soft" and "hard" modes of naturalism may in the end be seen to buttress each other, the tonal dissonance of their coinciding intensifies the apparent artificiality of both.

McCourt brings all of this to its appropriately bathetic conclusion by having it dissolve into that most stereotyped expression of Irish emotion: the singing of a ballad. Though the notion of breaking into a ballad early in the morning amid the disease and decrepitude of the Clohessys' flat would seem to strain credibility, it is of a piece with McCourt's account of the Clohessys and with the larger project of *Angela's Ashes* to transform representational cliché into reality. It should therefore not be at all surprising that the disgusting naturalist detail that begins his account of the encounter with the Clohessys should culminate in the excessive sentiment of Angela's song. McCourt's framing of the scene even lends it the air of a dying man's last request:

Before you go, Angela, will you do one thing for me?
    I will, Dennis, if 'tis in my power.
    Would you ever give us a verse of that song you sang the night before you went to America?
    That's a hard song, Dennis. I wouldn't have the wind for it.
    Ah, come on, Angela. I never hear a song anymore. There isn't a song in this house. The wife there doesn't have a note in her head an' no step in her foot.
    Mam says, All right. I'll try.

> *Oh, the nights of the Kerry dancing, Oh the ring of the piper's tune,*
>   *Oh, for one of those hours of gladness, gone, alas like our youth too soon.*
>   *When the boys began to gather in the glen of a Summer night,*
>   *And the Kerry piper's tuning made us long with wild delight.*

> She stops and presses her hand to her chest, Oh, God, my wind is
> gone. Help me, Frank, with the song, and I sing along,
>
>> *Oh, to think of it, Oh, to dream of it, fills my heart with tears.*
>> *Oh, the nights of the Kerry dancing, Oh, the ring of the piper's*
>> *tune*
>> *Oh, for one of those hours of gladness, gone, alas like our*
>> *youth too soon.*
>
> Mr. Clohessy tries to sing with us, gone, alas, like our youth too
> soon, but it brings on the cough. He shakes his head and cries, I
> wouldn't doubt you, Angela. It takes me back. God bless you. (168)

McCourt strives to intensify the pathos of the scene by rapidly inflat-
ing the tension surrounding the song and bringing it to a quick
catharsis. He heightens the initial drama of Mr. Clohessy's "one last
request" with the grandiloquence of Angela's response of "if 'tis in
my power." Having the song be the one she sang the night before
she went to America injects the emotion surrounding emigration and
leave-taking and reinforces Mr. Clohessy's position as the innocent
left behind by the more worldly Angela.

Angela's initial refusal and protestation of the song's difficulty
only build the dramatic tension further and provide the opportunity for Mr. Clohessy to cut an even more mournful figure as one
confined to a house without song. As Angela finally embarks on
the singing, the scene reaches its mawkish pinnacle—or nadir—with
her being overcome by the emotional and physical strain of the song
and calling on Frank to assist her. In this way, McCourt attempts to
lay particular stress on the song's doleful refrain and its lamenting
of a youth and a music gone too soon. All of this, of course, only
serves to emphasize Mr. Clohessy's tragic condition as one bereft of
music and painfully conscious of his body's wasting. McCourt then
brings this all to catharsis by transmuting Mr. Clohessy's physical
infirmity into emotional release as his cough gives way to tears and
shouts of blessing.

In terms of condensing and discharging emotion, McCourt's technique in this passage displays a remarkable efficacy and economy.
But the degree of the technique's success only serves to illuminate the
contrived quality of the scene and the extent to which reality is overtaken by its own "non-satiric parody" in *Angela's Ashes*. For while
the account of the Clohessys may be absurd in many separate respects
and most strikingly in its swing from cold naturalism to cloying sentiment, McCourt does not present it as overtly absurd. On the contrary,

he presents it quite straightforwardly and realistically even as he does not hide the signs of its counterfeit.

This irreducible pretense of *Angela's Ashes* is not simply the result of McCourt's clumsiness as a writer. Indeed, he shows himself to be quite adept at managing complex narrative structures throughout the book. This reprocessing of materiality in its grossest detail is instead a quite complicated narrative effect expressive of the dematerialized vision of the real we see coming into bloom in the electronic sunshine of the Celtic Tiger. Indeed, to such a postmodern sensibility, it would seem that the more real something appears, the more *un*real it actually is.

One important result of this ascendance of representation over materiality is that representations of materiality increasingly come to take on the status of commodities. In a stunningly perfect inversion— or redemption—of a late-modernist emphasis on open-endedness, absence, and subtraction that reaches its zenith in Beckett's realm of "real silence," McCourt's postmodern naturalism transmutes lack into a commodity to be traded both within and through the text. Indeed, *Angela's Ashes* repeatedly demonstrates that the more profound the loss or lack, the greater is its potential value.

We see this economy of abjection operating throughout the text. From Malachy's efforts to trade on the story of his child's death for pints (76) to the crass materialism of the various workers in the funeral "industry" the family encounters (86–89), McCourt records how this ultimate loss constitutes an important nexus of exchange within an otherwise devastated economy. Perhaps the most interesting elaboration of the commodification of death in the text is to be found in McCourt's account of Mickey Spellacy: "I'm nine years old and I have a pal, Mickey Spellacy, whose relations are dropping one by one of the galloping consumption. I envy Mickey because every time someone dies in his family he gets a week off from school and his mother stitches a black diamond patch on his sleeve so that he can wander from lane to lane and street to street and people will know he has the grief and pat his head and give him money and sweets for his sorrow" (171). In this case, grieving has become a sort of cottage industry. Significantly, the economy of abjection operates on the basis of a *signifier* of death and grief—the black diamond patch—rather than on the specificity of any particular death. The patch functions as a "strong" currency that enables entry into a wider market of sympathy beyond that arising from the immediate context of those intimate enough to know the details of the individual loss. Mickey's patch functions as a far more sophisticated version of Malachy's barroom tale of woe. Standing at another representational remove from the "real" event of loss, it operates much more efficiently and can be seen as almost a monetization of death.

The extent to which Mickey views death in market terms becomes clear when we come to see how concerned he is about the timing of his sister Brenda's imminent demise. If she dies during the summer when school is out of session, the market will not yet be fully ripe, and her death will be worth far less; he may be able to parlay the death into money and sweets but will lose the additional benefit of a week's freedom from school. In an attempt to stave off this devaluing of his prematurely ripening commodity, he invests resources in the parallel economy of prayer. To maximize the impact of such investment, he enlists the help of his friends Billy Campbell and young Frankie McCourt to go to the local church and pray with him "for Brenda to hang on till September" (171).

A shrewd businessman, Mickey effectively takes on the role of a subcontractor who doles out a tiny portion of his potential death profits to those who can help him realize them in full: "Well, if Brenda hangs on and I get me week off ye can come to the wake and have ham and cheese and cake and sherry and lemonade and everything and ye can listen to the songs and stories all night" (171). The sophistication of Mickey's dealings in the wages of death can be seen in his arrangement that Frankie's and Billy's payment only comes if their prayers prove completely successful and, even then, their "cut" will come solely from the general profusion of goods surrounding the death rituals and not out of his individual profits.

Even so, when the prayers turn out to be successful and Brenda dies on the second day of school, Mickey reneges on his subcontractors and turns them away when they show up for the wake. In retaliation, they return to the church to pray that all of Mickey's family will thenceforth die in the summer and he will never again get a day off from school. Reporting the result of this second round of prayers, McCourt impishly observes, "One of our prayers is surely powerful because next summer Mickey himself is carried off by the galloping consumption and he doesn't get a day off from school and that will surely teach him a lesson" (172). In this ironic twist, we see the logic of the market reveal itself even as the market implodes. Mickey is himself consumed as the market turns to feed upon itself.

The "galloping consumption" that carries him off may thus be read in more than its epidemiological sense.

The appropriateness of such a reading is underwritten by the way in which *Angela's Ashes*, as a whole, operates within a larger economy of abjection. McCourt seeks to incorporate the fullness of material and emotional losses within his text so as to commodify them and turn them to as complete a profit as possible. By repeatedly representing this economy in more miniature form throughout the text, however, McCourt discloses the outlines and terms of such an economy in such fine detail that he likewise draws himself and his text within it. Trying to recoup the losses of those such as Mickey or his own father, Malachy, McCourt transforms them into facets of his own "black diamond" in order to trade on them as commodities within a market of a higher order.

More than just underscoring the artificiality of his accounts, this layering of economies of abjection drives the postmodern "leap" of McCourt's naturalist aesthetic. His naturalism is not simply overwrought but, rather, discursively overdetermined. McCourt does not repeatedly render the commodification of lack in order to parody it. It is, more simply, an inscribing of the postmodern implosion of economy brought on by commodification's own outstripping of itself. Jameson's description of the fate of the market in postmodern culture is one that resonates significantly with what we see in *Angela's Ashes*: "[T]he market has become a substitute for itself and fully as much a commodity as any of the items it includes within itself: modernism was still minimally and tendentially the critique of the commodity and the effort to make it transcend itself. Postmodernism is the consumption of sheer commodification as a process" (x). For McCourt, this consumption simply revolves around an inverted market; it is the "galloping consumption" of commodified want and disease.

McCourt makes this understanding of the market quite explicit in his portrayal of the way England's wartime labor market plays out on the streets of Limerick. Given Britain's pressing need for factory labor to sustain the war effort while much of its normal workforce has been pressed into military service, Irish laborers find themselves very much in demand by British labor recruiters. McCourt's portrait of the situation suggests, however, that the Irish are not really capable of smoothly integrating themselves into the market and that the market and its mechanisms remain readily distinguishable as a result. Depicting the scene as the men depart for their new jobs, then, McCourt paints a scene of bedlam:

> Some men are already too drunk to walk and the English agents are paying sober men to drag them out of the pubs and throw them on a great horse-drawn float to be hauled to the station and dumped into the train. The agents are desperate to get everyone out of the pubs. Come on, men. Miss the train and you'll miss a good job. Come on, men, we have the Guinness in England. We have the Jameson. Now, men, please, men. You're drinking your food money and you'll get no more.
>
> The men tell the agents to kiss their Irish arses, that the agents are lucky they're alive, lucky they're not hanging from the nearest lamp-post after what they did to Ireland. And the men sing,
>
>> *On Mountjoy one Monday morning*
>> *High upon the gallows tree,*
>> *Kevin Barry gave his young life*
>> *For the cause of liberty.*
>
> The train wails in the station and the agents beg the women to get their men out of the pubs and the men stumble out singing and crying and hugging their wives and children and promising to send so much money Limerick will be turned into another New York. The men climb the station steps and the women and children call after them. (220)

McCourt again presents an almost parodic vision of the market. Here we have some of the most trite and odious elements of Irish stereotype trotted out and combined to absurd effect. The drunken, unruly, and undifferentiated mass of Irishmen lurches from hedonistic indulgence to rage to lachrymose nationalism while demonstrating its complete incapacity for discipline by means of outrageously reckless spending and wild threats to the forces of order and civility. All the while, this mass of fiends is attended by a pathetic coterie of anxious wives and ragged children desperately dependent on the men for material survival but finding themselves to be little more than another excuse for the men to vent their excess of sentiment.

These representations stand in stark contrast to the savvy, disciplined workers and sleekly contoured market institutions of the Celtic Tiger that would seem to signal Irish accession to globalization. McCourt's chaotic scene thus seems designed to show early Irish postcoloniality to be in need of further historical development and civilizing. The reference to New York makes it clear what model such "civilizing" or "development" should follow; Ireland needs to be

Americanized. The particular context of the labor recruitment is significant, however, as it recalls a distinctly imperial narrative of political economy linking the market with the civilizing project. McCourt's portrait presents a slightly updated and exaggerated version of this nexus with the twentieth-century urban factory laborer replacing the nineteenth-century rural cottier.

In keeping with the tone of the book, the immediacy and detail of the passage draw the reader in even as the rapid accumulation of stereotype and the carnivalesque air make it seem larger than life. From the horse-drawn float of drunks to the by now ridiculous burst into ballad to the absurdly omnipresent invocation of sentimental nationalism, McCourt appears eager to invest his account with the colorful extravagance that most of his readers will have come to expect. As a result, he offers what amounts to a parody of the Irish inability to come to terms with the market. The lineaments of parody can be seen in both the exaggeration of Irish incivility and the explicit outlining of the market and its mechanisms. We are not left to infer the relations of labor and capital, supply and demand, or immigration and national markets nor are we left to wonder about the market's mechanisms of discipline and inducement. All of these are made quite apparent and interwoven with the underlying cultural bases of economic inequality and proclivity toward consumption that produce the primary actors of the market—laborer and capitalist—and drive its unrelenting growth.

More than simply repeating the same tired clichés of Irish fecklessness and volatility, however, the scene presents a pastiche of the market that undergirds and mediates them. This pastiche not only provides an important elaboration on the reasons for Irish poverty that McCourt hints at broadly elsewhere; it also offers a means for their transcendence. It is only when the Irish are sufficiently cognizant of the market to see it, parody it, and, indeed, commodify it as McCourt does that they can hope to begin moving beyond their subordinate state. Such is the sort of insight that the globalized postcoloniality of the Celtic Tiger era would purport to bestow.

McCourt extends this pastiche of the market as both index and tool of civility through his portrayal of the Limerick beneficiaries of the wartime labor boom. Those receiving the telegram money orders from England quite literally make a spectacle of themselves in their attempts to mimic bourgeois manners and lifestyle. McCourt savages this nouveau riche of the lanes that is so conspicuous in its consumption and so cruelly ostentatious in the face of the neighbors who still have less than nothing. He mocks their pretension in seeking the expensive seats in the fancy Savoy Cinema, "where you'll meet a better class of people than the lower classes who fill up the tuppenny seats in the gods at the Lyric Cinema" (216) and avoiding the fish-and-chip shops where you see "nothing . . . but drunken soldiers and night girls and men that drank their dole and their wives screeching at them to come home" (217).

McCourt's point, of course, is that those exhibiting such priggishness are looking down their noses at those in a position they themselves had occupied until very recently and to which they are likely to return in a short time. Addressing this even more directly, he excoriates the newly flush lane dwellers for publicly wallowing in delicacies while drawing upon the surrounding poverty and envy for extra savor: "Sean, Josie, Peggy, come in for yeer tea, come in at wanst for the fresh bread and butter and the gorgeous blue duck egg what no one else in the lane have. Brendan, Annie, Patsy, come in for the fried black puddin', the sizzlin' sausages and the lovely trifle soaked in the best of Spanish sherry" (217). The opulence of these tables is, of course, at odds with the heavily accented speech that McCourt puts in the mouths of those who preside over them. The discordance offers a cheap means of calling the legitimacy of these families' prosperity into question. Beneath the sumptuous trappings, they remain destitute, uncivilized, and undisciplined, McCourt implies.

Though McCourt is bitterly sarcastic here at a number of points, he does not ultimately slide into satire or "true" parody. He remains very focused on factual description and states his point quite explicitly: "The families with fathers in England are able to lord it over the families that don't" (217). Rather than resorting to overt exaggeration, he instead seeks to have the people of the lanes indict themselves through direct depiction of their cruelty and their pathetic caricature of bourgeois respectability.

McCourt's hammering at the hypocrisy of the classist pretensions of those lucky enough to get a piece of the war's windfall falls flat, however, and must itself be seen as the greater hypocrisy. For McCourt's critique of their classism rests entirely on their unworthiness to wield it rather than a more general attack on such elitism and class bias. His slightly cartoonish account once again tends toward pastiche by confirming the imperial notion of Irish savagery and insisting that mere cash is insufficient to civilize the Irish poor. They remain a base commodity within the market, ignorant of its dimensions and structures and unable to act *upon* it. McCourt's capacity to render this portrait of Irish ignorance and incivility, by contrast, effectively positions him as one more fully aware of the market and capable of manipulating the representations that constitute the substance of its matrices and its traffic.

One of the few figures in *Angela's Ashes* who does have some sense of the market is the moneylender Mrs. Finucane. People in need of a suit or dress for a child come to her for a voucher that they redeem at the clothing shop. Mrs. Finucane receives a discount from the shop and then charges the full price plus interest, which her customers pay weekly over an extended period. In a limited fashion, she thus demonstrates an understanding of the market and a capacity for acting upon it. This understanding and careful marshaling of a relatively small amount of capital sets her apart in an important way from the improvident and ignorant figures that otherwise populate the book and appear in such stark relief in McCourt's account of the war-industry workers and their families.

More importantly, however, Mrs. Finucane provides a crucial means for McCourt to articulate his own relationship to the market through his youthful narrating persona, Frankie. For Frankie quite literally represents the market for Mrs. Finucane and turns those representations into commodities. Mrs. Finucane hires him to write threatening letters to the clients who have fallen behind in their payments:

> In a large ledger she gives me the names and addresses of six customers behind in their payments. Threaten 'em, by. Frighten the life out of 'em.
>
>   My first letter,
>   Dear Mrs. O'Brien,
>   Inasmuch as you have not seen fit to pay me what you owe me I may be forced to resort to legal action. There's your son, Michael, parading around the world in his new suit which I paid for while I myself have barely a crust to keep body and soul together. I am sure you don't want to languish in the dungeons of Limerick jail far from friends and family.
>   I remain, yours in litigious anticipation,
>   Mrs. Brigid Finucane
>
> She tells me, That's a powerful letter, by, better than anything you'd read in the *Limerick Leader*. That word, inasmuch, that's a holy terror of a word. What does it mean?
> I think it means this is your last chance. (332–33)

Significantly, McCourt shows Frankie to have an observable intellectual advantage over Mrs. Finucane even as he is economically subordinate to her. When asked what "inasmuch" means, he replies patronizingly, "I think it means this is your last chance." Whether the condescension is more precisely attributed to Frankie or the mature authorial persona, its function is to mark the difference in power by means of an assertion of the overarching importance of representation. Actual meaning ultimately proves far less important than the impression of representational agency and authority.

The inaccuracy of Frankie's gloss of "inasmuch" underlines this both because it effectively *does* mean "this is your last chance" in this instance and because its "actual" denotative meaning has ceased to matter. The point is not representation but the representation of representation. Through Frankie's dealings with Mrs. Finucane, McCourt emphasizes the insatiability of the market as expressed through a limitless proliferation of untethered representation. With money little more than the meanest of representations, he shows civility—and power—to reside not in the accumulation of capital but rather in the understanding and manipulation of the regime of representation and infinite substitution upon which the market establishes itself.

The contrast between the language of Mrs. Finucane and Frankie not only marks a difference between those two but a difference between Mrs. Finucane and the collectivity constituted by McCourt's dramatic irony. McCourt comically combines and contrasts linguistic registers in the scene as a means of inscribing the relative primitiveness of Mrs. Finucane and the concomitant superiority of the mature author and his readers more capable of perceiving the nuance and irony of the language being used. Rather than being enthralled by the mystery of uncommon words such as "inasmuch" or "litigious," they are in on the joke and able to appreciate the delicate interplay of language executed by combining such an elite register with phrases such as "parading around the world."

McCourt's skillful blending of linguistic registers encodes a layering of representation for Mrs. O'Brien, Mrs. Finucane, and the narrative of *Angela's Ashes*. Ultimately, the purpose of Frankie's language for Mrs. Finucane, as much as for Mrs. O'Brien, is more to confound and intimidate than to represent. Depicting the success of this effect, in turn, McCourt marks both as subordinate objects to himself and his readers and inscribes his status as one who is able to turn the market inside-out to offer a shifting series of representations of representation itself. Frankie earns his pay from Mrs. Finucane by creating a "meta-market" of sorts for himself and representing the market to her debtors. McCourt profits still more through recourse to an even higher order of representation and a depiction of the complexities of this transaction for his readers. In the process, he shows the market to comprise a series of infinitely regressing representations familiar to any student of postmodernism.

The power accorded representation becomes still more evident in McCourt's account of the ultimate disposition of Mrs. Finucane and her affairs. After a well-paid tenure as Mrs. Finucane's epistolary henchman and general errand boy supplemented by frequent pilfering of cash from her house and funds entrusted for various errands, Frankie comes to her house to find her dead in her chair. Having long abandoned any sense of compunction about the source of the funds he is accumulating for his "escape" to America, Frankie rifles through the house for money and leaves the house with forty pounds, her ledger of debtors, and the bottle of sherry Mrs. Finucane had sent him to buy.[13]

McCourt then treats us to a scene of contemplation for Frankie that functions as both coda for his career with Mrs. Finucane and an opening to the representation of Irish poverty for a broader market:

> I sit by the River Shannon near the dry docks sipping Mrs. Finucane's sherry. Aunt Aggie's name is on the ledger. She owes nine pounds. It might have been the money she spent on my clothes a long time ago but now she'll never have to pay because I heave the ledger into the river. I'm sorry I'll never be able to tell Aunt Aggie I saved her nine pounds. I'm sorry I wrote threatening letters to the poor people in the lanes of Limerick, my own people, but the ledger is gone, no one will ever know what they owe and they won't have to pay their balances. I wish I could tell them, I'm your Robin Hood.
>
> Another sip of the sherry. I'll spare a pound or two for a Mass for Mrs. Finucane's soul. Her ledger is well on its way down the Shannon and out to the Atlantic and I know I'll follow it someday soon. (356)

The ledger affords entry into the intimate details of his neighbors' lives and offers a more concrete inscription of the poverty and economic subjugation than McCourt has otherwise recorded through fetishistic lingering on the more sensational elements of Limerick's squalor. Despite this, McCourt once again rejects such a focus on the "concrete" or structural dimensions of poverty in favor of a more free-floating realm of representation. McCourt casts Frankie as a sort of judge—forgiving debts and his own culpability in harassing his neighbors and airily deciding to spare "a pound or two" for a mass for Mrs. Finucane—who secretly knows all and magnanimously sets things right.

Frankie quite literally tosses away the more pressingly material inscription of poverty and economic hierarchy in favor of a regime of representation that will allow him to recast himself as "Robin Hood." Such is the power of postmodern representation that Frankie can present himself as Robin Hood when he is the only one getting rich from his thievery.

Such a pose might be able to be dismissed as the naïve grandiosity of a nineteen-year-old having a first taste of power and freedom were it not for the fact that McCourt strikes a similar pose as one driven to write *Angela's Ashes* by a deep identification with the travails of poverty. The disingenuousness of his position may be seen quite clearly in this passage. Whatever Frankie may say about how "no one will ever know what they owe," we *do* know of the debts in the ledger, most especially Aggie's, because McCourt stands to profit from their representation. In this sense, McCourt's image of following the ledger out to the Atlantic might be read as more than a reference to Frankie's imminent emigration. He effectively retrieves the ledger on the other side of the Atlantic and lays it open for all to see in the more elaborated form of *Angela's Ashes*.

The "actual" record of Limerick penury becomes just one more neat detail for McCourt to draw upon for a pinch of "authentic" flavor. Mrs. Finucane's carefully arranged ledger columns of pounds and pence give way to an even more meticulous accounting of Irish poverty rendered in the more easily convertible "meta-currency" of postmodern representation. McCourt's superseding of the actual monetary debt through Frankie's drowning of the ledger and his own postmodern transmutation underscores the market's representational substance and builds upon the logic of the earlier representation of the market in Frankie's dunning letters. Here we see further proof of the market's capacity to enfold itself and find an assertion of the inevitable subordination of any "material" notion of economy to one more consumed with successive orders of commodification.

The move to America that swiftly follows signals the text's ultimate affirmation of this perspective. Having treated us to a seemingly endless series of pronouncements on America's endless opportunity and limitless possibility throughout the text, it is to be expected that McCourt should provide some means for their fulfillment and round off his book with Frankie's return to New York. *Angela's Ashes'* American conclusion is perhaps most completely understood, however, as both guarantor and balance for the naturalist portrait of Ireland that precedes it. The sense of American openness and propensity for ongoing reinvention underwrites the postmodern energies of the text's account of Irish poverty and provides a model for the Celtic Tiger's re-visioning of Ireland and its history.

McCourt's narration of the ship's entry into the New York harbor almost perfectly inverts the earlier vision he presents as the family sets off for Ireland and hapless Angela vomits on the other "happy" passengers:

> I'm on deck the dawn we sail into New York. I'm sure I'm in a film,
> that it will end and lights will come up in the Lyric Cinema. The
> priest wants to point out things but he doesn't have to. I can pick
> out the Statue of Liberty, Ellis Island, the Empire State Building, the
> Chrysler Building, the Brooklyn Bridge. There are thousands of cars
> speeding along the roads and the sun turns everything to gold. Rich
> Americans in top hats white ties and tails must be going home to
> bed with the gorgeous women with white teeth. The rest are going to
> work in warm comfortable offices and no one has a care in the world.
> (360)

Though obviously absurd in its stock images of a comfortable and industrious America quite literally gilded by the dawn's early light, this is, of course, the point. Frankie has found himself back in the land of representation's greatest ascendance, where everything seems cinematic and "no one has a care in the world."

Unlike Ireland with its oppressively materialist minutiae, McCourt suggests that even the most monumental items in America transcend materiality's shimmering edge to enter the domain of the symbolic. The buildings and sites are rendered a collection of surreal set-pieces. This vision of New York frames Ireland and its poverty both in terms of providing a "normative" contrast and in suggesting that all material reality is ultimately saturated by the fluidity of representation. The absurdity of McCourt's earlier depictions of Irish wretchedness now resolves itself definitively into the cinematic realm of postmodern naturalism. Frankie's triumphant arrival in New York composes a postcard from the Celtic Tiger telling us that Irish late postcoloniality has reached its destination of globalized cosmopolitanism.

It is, of course, quite possible to read these last few pages of the book as signs of the absolute "Americanness" of the text wherein

Ireland serves as a convenient backdrop for a tale of immigrant success or a contemporary update of the American captivity narrative tradition. But such a reading is ultimately most compelling and comprehensive when it takes the text's Irish dimension more fully into account and considers how this celebration of America and the richness of representation resonates with the narratives of late postcoloniality characterizing the Celtic Tiger era. An "American" reading of *Angela's Ashes* is bound to be severely lacking unless it consider the text's inscription of American presence within the broader global contexts of the rise of postmodernity and late capitalism's ongoing commodification of the market. As a space that constitutes the "object" of such globalizing fantasy and transformation under both the classic imperial mode and its more oblique contemporary counterpart of "globalization," Ireland is arguably the better site for considering the signs and implications of this process than the United States itself.

To such a view, McCourt's American ending reads most immediately as an endorsement of the regime of postmodern representation and a refracted vision of the slickly efficient prosperity of Celtic Tiger Ireland. From a destination for emigrants, we see "America" become a destination for postcoloniality itself—at least for postcoloniality of a certain "developmental" variety. McCourt significantly does not offer much detail of this new world beyond an extremely brief sample of its leisurely ways and greater sexual freedom (361–63). In this, he maintains the postmodern thrust of the narrative and avoids falling into an approach that would pose America as a "factual" or material counterexample to Ireland.

McCourt captures this with a striking succinctness in the single word of his last chapter: "'Tis" (364). The pithy rejoinder comes on the heels of a question from the ship's Irish wireless officer to Frankie that concludes the penultimate chapter: "Isn't this a great country altogether?" (363). McCourt's unusual rendering of the response in a separate chapter comprising a single word compacts a huge array of possible meanings into one syllable. Equally attributable to Frankie and to the mature authorial presence looming in the background, the response enables McCourt to telescope time and character so as to encompass American "greatness" then and since without need for elaboration.

As such, "'Tis" functions as a particularly apt expression of an Irish-inflected vision of American boundlessness and the infinity of postmodern presence. Intriguingly, the Irish inflection of the contraction signifies more than just "the bit of ethnic color" that McCourt no doubt intends to achieve by it. Considered in the context of the text as a whole, "'Tis" encodes the limitless presence of postmodernity and late postcoloniality finally brought to fruition by the Americanization we see realized most fully in the era of the Celtic Tiger. In *Angela's Ashes*, as in the Celtic Tiger, commodification has completely overtaken history and "the real" has itself become a quaint anachronism. Rather than the critique of primitivism, "tradition," and subjectivity that we see in the late-modernist aesthetics of the early postcolonial era, the "backwardness" of the Ireland McCourt portrays would seem to reside most fundamentally in its unsophisticated belief in its own reality.

Conclusion

Dispatches from the Modernist Frontier: "European and Asiatic papers please copy"

The extent to which the Celtic Tiger fantasy of a sleek decollateralized global cosmopolitanism has proven the real chimera has, of course, been tragically confirmed by the spectacular collapse of the Irish economy. The boarded-up shop fronts and jagged rebar of thousands of abandoned building sites and "ghost estates" that scar the blasted landscape of post–Celtic Tiger Ireland offer a bleakly ironic testimony to the persistent materiality underlying the patina of seamless consumption and endlessly repeating postmodern play. International press dispatches chronicling debt "contagion" and the implosion of global finance now inscribe Ireland at the frontier of a new regime of "bailouts," mass unemployment, and a program of public austerity that brooks no questioning.

As we survey globalization's baneful historical wreckage, we might do well, however, to recall an international dispatch from another frontier:

> *April 14.* John Alphonsus Mulrennan has just returned from the west of Ireland. European and Asiatic papers please copy. He told us he met an old man there in a mountain cabin. Old man had red eyes and short pipe. Old man spoke Irish. Mulrennan spoke Irish. Then old man and Mulrennan spoke English. Mulrennan spoke to him about universe and stars. Old man sat, listened, smoked, spat. Then said:
>
> —Ah, there must be terrible queer creatures at the latter end of the world.—
>
> I fear him. I fear his red-rimmed horny eyes. It is with him I must struggle all through this night till day come, till he or I lie dead,

gripping him by the sinewy throat till . . . Till what? Till he yield to
me? No. I mean him no harm. (251–52)

Perhaps the most resonant element of this curious vignette from the
last pages of Joyce's *Portrait* is its far-reaching skepticism. The target of Joyce's skepticism has often been mistaken to be the old man
himself or, at least, the old man as a figuration of a sentimental Irish
nationalism that Joyce repudiates. An overinvestment in a "cosmopolitan Joyce" can even lead some to read here a rejection of Ireland
and Irishness altogether.

A more subtle analysis of tone and the shifting voices in the entry
reveals the more precise target of Joyce's satire to be not the old man
or Irishness, however, but the ethnographic discourse of the Revival
and its primitivist framing of the west of Ireland. As Gregory Castle insightfully observes, "The clipped telegraphic style of the entry
parodies not Synge's style so much as the sovereign position of the
participant-observer who uses his knowledge of Irish to establish a
rapport with his native informant" (206). A key implication of this
critique of the ethnographer, as Castle elaborates, is that Stephen—
and ultimately Joyce—must come to terms with a sense of connection and perhaps even filiation with the old man: "The figure of the
peasant, no longer trapped in Manichean opposition to him, reminds
him of the inescapable fact of his hybridized identity, one that has
incurred powerful and half-repudiated debts to Revivalism and its
ethnographic imagination" (207).

Though Castle rightly underscores the importance of shattering
the primitivist binary, an emphasis on Joyce's debts to an "ethnographic imagination" may give the Revival too much credit in this
instance and underestimates the immensely productive value of the
diary entry's more far-reaching skepticism. Far-reaching most immediately in a geographic sense, Joyce's parody of wire-service instructions rendered via "European and Asiatic papers please copy" mocks
the Revival's commodification of the people, places, and practices
of the west of Ireland as very much an *international* enterprise.
As reflected elsewhere in his fiction, such as in Chandler's fantasy
in *Dubliners* of being recognized in London critics' reviews for the
"Celtic note" of a poetry he does not even seem capable of compos-
ing and his notable resolution to alter his name to be "more Irish-
looking" so he can more easily market his works on the international
circuit (74), Joyce shows himself to be acutely aware of the commodity status of Irish literary and cultural phenomena and of the tactics

shaping the international prominence of the Revival. Indeed, in that regard Joyce anticipates many of the recent postcolonial critiques of cultural commodification and the marketing of colonial exoticism—a phenomenon that reaches a curious postmodern zenith (or nadir) in a work like *Angela's Ashes*.[1]

The importance of the international context for Joyce's satirical treatment of the Revival in Stephen's famous diary entry emerges more clearly when we compare the portrayal of the old man in *Portrait of the Artist* with an earlier version in *Stephen Hero*. Rather than framing the old man through the stark telegraphic account of Mulrennan and Stephen's subsequent reflection, Joyce, in *Stephen Hero*, introduces the old man as a figure in a tale "intended to poke fun at countrified ideas" told by a Captain Starkie whom Stephen encounters in Mullingar (242). Starkie's more extended account differs from what we find in *Portrait* in that he clearly presents the old man himself as the object of mockery—albeit a gentle mockery. We encounter little emphasis on the ethnographic discourse itself except perhaps in the slightly awkward rendering of the old man's female interlocutor being "much amused" by his quaint responses and in the rather vague sense of detachment and coercion that Joyce evokes by emphasizing the story's more abstract status as a performance to be assessed as being "told . . . very well" and to be appropriately responded to by "the laugh that followed it" (243).

Most importantly, however, the encounter with the old man is presented orally for an immediate local consumption in *Stephen Hero*. By contrast, as the old man shifts from an embedded oral account to a more complicated narrative realm in *Portrait* that Castle succinctly labels as "textual" (206), Joyce's engagement with the exoticism of Revivalist ethnographic discourse is no longer such a local affair as the instructions to the international papers and the ironic Orientalism of "Asiatic papers" help to reveal.

The import of shifting the story from a local to a global scale in *Portrait* only becomes fully clear, however, when considered in relation to the details of the conversation between the old man and Mulrennan. For rather than being prompted by tales of "the animals of prehistoric times" before he delivers his famous line about "quare craythurs at the latther end of the world" as in *Stephen Hero* (243), the old man in *Portrait* must listen to Mulrennan speak to him "about universe and stars" (251). The change is of great significance because, as Marjorie Howes perceptively remarks, the old man's response in

Portrait connects him with "an alternative, and problematic, conception of scale to match Stephen's ambivalent alternative to conventional nationalism. . . . Mulrennan's remarks . . . give the old man a chance to repeat Stephen's earlier trip up-scale from his own individual being, through the nation to the universe. But the old man refuses, and his reply figures space in terms of immense, mythic geographical distance and utter alienation, rather than in terms of linkage and commensurability" (78). Thus, the skepticism of this entry that helps usher *Portrait* to its close is not simply a skepticism of sentimental nationalism or Revivalist ethnography or even of the international marketing of colonial exoticism but, more profoundly, of the investments in commensurability upon which each of these, to varying degrees, relies.

Equally important is the fact that the source of this more fundamental skepticism is the old man himself rather than the knowing Revivalist ethnographer interested in "countrified ideas" or even the discerning reader who can appreciate the parody of that perspective so as to see its exoticist condescension more plainly. The challenge posed by the old man with which Stephen must "struggle" so intensely is therefore not simply that posed by the need to acknowledge a degree of affiliation or a "hybridized identity" that might shatter the segregated vision of Revivalist elitism by recognizing one's country cousins as one's own. As the intense physicality of the struggle helps to reinforce, the old man must be reckoned with on his own terms and not just as the mere figure of the Revival that most critical responses tend to suggest.

The challenge the old man poses for Stephen—and, ultimately, for modernism—is a challenge to the intellectual and ethical legitimacy of an inevitable orientation toward universality. When he spits—which he notably does not in his tamer *Stephen Hero* incarnation—and declares to Mulrennan, "Ah, there must be terrible queer creatures at the latter end of the world," his insistence on incommensurable difference is at once a rebuke to Mulrennan for his overly confident pronouncements on the universe and a curt dismissal of the topic as one even worth discussing. Rather than the wide-eyed wonder and colorful phrasing that make him a figure of mockery for his "countrified" naiveté in *Stephen Hero*, a withering skepticism and an air of equanimity help to define the old man in *Portrait* as a worthy challenger for Stephen and more than a match for Mulrennan and his fatuous philosophizing.

That this skepticism is eminently productive is indicated by the fact that Stephen—and Joycean modernism—ultimately must come to terms with the old man in all his complexity rather than following through on an initial impulse to kill him or force him to yield. One is reminded once again of Said's insistence on modernism's need—and general failure—"to take the Other seriously" (223). Reading *Portrait* now in the context of the broader sweep of Irish modernism, it seems almost impossible not to see its account of the old man as an uncanny premonition of the challenge posed by the Blasket writers, especially Tomás Ó Criomhthain. We thus encounter glimpses of a late-modernist vision that will come into sharper focus with the next generation of postcolonial Irish writers and the more far-reaching critiques of subjectivity offered by Ó Criomhthain and Beckett that are effectively seeded by Joyce in moments such as this.

In the wake of the Celtic Tiger and a barren postmodern irony that revels in endless figuration and caricature, the more materially grounded skepticism of Joyce and of late modernism may once again provide a model for a critical engagement with overconfident discourses of a global modernity. By attending to the "perverse modernity" that Howes identifies as characteristic of an early twentieth-century Irish countryside transformed by an ongoing procession of emigrants whose spectral traces nonetheless linger in families and communities and which enable Joyce's "alternative narratives of the nation," we can gain a new appreciation for more localized modernist practices and what Howes describes as "the complex materialities of spatial scales" (71–72). We might likewise find reason to reconsider the bases and the implications of parallel investments in more globalized discourses and perspectives within modernist studies. As we begin to move beyond the familiar "cosmopolitan" frameworks to discover new vistas of modernist thought that would otherwise be occluded, we may yet find that for his part, the old man, too, means us no harm.

NOTES

INTRODUCTION. REROUTING IRISH MODERNISM:
POSTCOLONIAL AESTHETICS AND THE IMPERATIVE OF
COSMOPOLITANISM

1. Indeed, Anne Saddlemyer asserts in her edition of Synge's letters that Synge ultimately considered his experience staying on the Blaskets "even more valuable than that of [visiting] Aran" and notes that Synge discussed with Yeats the prospect of gathering an acting troupe of Blasket Islanders which Yeats seemed to take seriously enough to note in a letter: "[W]e will have to consider it presently. Synge would stage manage it himself" (1: 102–3). References to the Blaskets recur in Synge's letters after his visit there, including a July 1906 letter noting that he hoped to return there after finishing *Playboy* (1: 177) and an August 1907 letter expressing a desire to write a book on the Blaskets that might complement his famous volume on the Aran Islands (2: 22). Synge's interest in the Blaskets remained strong to the end of his short life as evidenced by his report to his fiancée on a doctor's visit eight months before his death noting that his physician advised him against a trip there (2: 171). Despite their ongoing presence in his thoughts, however, Synge never returned to the Blaskets after his initial 1905 visit.

2. For some of the key discussions of primitivism and modernism, see Torgovnik's *Gone Primitive* (1990); Manganaro's collection *Modernist Anthropology* (1990); Barkan and Bush's collection *Prehistories of the Future* (1995); and Mattar's *Primitivism, Science, and the Irish Revival* (2004).

3. This is not to say, however, that late-modernist aesthetics are necessarily incompatible with a more radical nationalist politics as O'Faoláin's republican critiques amply illustrate.

4. See, for example, Ellmann's *Eminent Domain: Yeats among Wilde, Joyce, Pound, Eliot and Auden* (1967); or Kenner's *Dublin's Joyce* (1962) or *A Homemade World* (1974).

5. The same caution should apply, of course, to modernist criticism that emphasizes local dimensions and *is* informed by an Irish studies perspective or that of a similar national or regional studies scholarship. Manganaro's work just makes this point more unavoidable.

6. For considerations of the Irish and colonial dimensions of Irish modernism, see, for example, Lloyd's *Anomalous States* (1993); Nolan's *James*

Joyce and Nationalism (1995); Cheng's *Joyce, Race, and Empire* (1995); Attridge and Howes's collection *Semicolonial Joyce* (2000); and Lloyd's *Irish Times* (2008).

7. Other relevant treatments of modernist form and postcoloniality in different contexts include Gikandi's *Writing in Limbo: Modernism and Caribbean Literature* (1992); Hedrick's *Mestizo Modernism* (2003); and Pollard's *New World Modernisms* (2004).

8. This adds to the burgeoning body of scholarship exploring Beckett's Irish and postcolonial dimensions as exemplified by Bixby's *Samuel Beckett and the Postcolonial Novel* (2009); Morin's *Samuel Beckett and the Problem of Irishness* (2009); Kennedy's edited volume *Beckett and Ireland* (2010); and David Lloyd's ongoing work.

9. See, for example, David Lloyd's "Republics of Difference: Yeats, Mac-Greevy, Beckett"; and Patricia Coughlan and Alex Davis, eds., *Modernism and Ireland: The Poetry of the 1930s.*

10. See Terence Brown's "Ireland, Modernism, and the 1930s," esp. 37–38.

11. In the Irish case, the most interesting recent discussions of these early postcolonial magazines are those offered by Shovlin in *The Irish Literary Periodical, 1923–1958;* and Allen in *Modernism, Ireland, and Civil War.*

12. See Beckett's 1934 essay "Recent Irish Poetry" (75), collected in *Disjecta.* Strikingly, Beckett includes O'Faoláin among the avant-garde poets now being "re-discovered" by scholars of 1930s Irish modernism even though O'Faoláin never had a profile as a poet. At the very least, this "error" may suggest an awareness on Beckett's part of a shared late-modernist sensibility between this more typically modernist poetry and the ostensibly more conventional prose being developed by O'Faoláin and his coterie.

13. See Cleary's *Outrageous Fortune,* esp. 111–79.

14. As Whelan observes, the outbreak of "the Troubles" in Northern Ireland only serves to accelerate this redefinition of terms as "tradition" increasingly comes to be dissevered from modernity and defined as "atavistic" and "savage" or, at best, "dangerous"and "benighted" (190–92).

I. MODERNITY'S EDGE: SPEAKING SILENCE ON THE BLASKETS

1. Peig Sayers's slightly later autobiography, *Peig* (1936), was actually dictated to her son Micheál Ó Gaoithín rather than being written by her directly. As *Peig* is from a slightly later moment more associated with de Valera's Ireland and is more fully embedded in the oral tradition of storytelling rather than the transition to literature and the mediated autobiographical subject, however, it lies just outside of the historical and formal scope of what I discuss here.

2. Philip O'Leary (*Gaelic Prose* 98) notes how the interpretation of the Blasket texts in anthropological terms framed much of the initial critical response in the 1920s and 1930s, and Irene Lucchitti observes how dominant this perspective continues to be in the contemporary era (14).

3. For purposes of clarity, my use of "the Revival" and "Revivalist" refers to the movement in English-language Irish literature most readily associated with Yeats and Synge. This movement, of course, borrows from, conflicts with, and is inspired by a series of parallel revivals in sport, music, dance, and Gaelic language and literature, and I discuss some of their points of overlap below. Given the importance of the English-language Irish literary movement to the history of modernism, however, that remains my primary point of reference and is distinguished from the other revivals by its capitalization.

4. O'Leary distills the impact this has on the reception of the Blasket texts and other writers from the Gaelic periphery when he notes how the lack of attention to their literary style and technique coincided with a broader apprehension of the Gaeltacht in the early postcolonial era as a space "rife with undifferentiated literary geniuses all sharing in some sort of collective Gaelic consciousness for the edification of the rest of the nation" (*Gaelic Prose* 140).

5. Brian Ó Nualláin (Flann O'Brien/Myles na gCopaleen) insightfully analyzes this reproducibility and its implications in his brilliant satire, perhaps most notably in *An Béal Bocht* (*The Poor Mouth*).

6. As Diarmuid Ó Giolláin notes, reports of famine in the West persisted into the 1920s and were met at turns with aid programs and claims of exaggeration by the new Free State government (143). In the context of such famine and poverty, emigration hit particularly hard in the Irish-speaking regions such that the popularity of the prevailing depictions of "simple living" in the Gaeltacht seems savagely ironic. As Ó Giolláin eloquently observes: "[E]migration from the Gaeltacht, like that from the West in general, was particularly high, and its implications for the country which had rested its claim to independent nationhood on its Gaelic culture were particularly grave. Little wonder that folkloristic paeans to illiteracy, the Middle Ages, and traditional rural life seemed to some in particularly bad taste" (144).

7. Though *An Gúm*'s project was marked by much controversy and complaint about its bureaucratic approach to literature and its inefficiency and delays in putting books into circulation, its overall impact on the publication of Irish-language texts is quite impressive. O'Leary notes that government reports show that over its first decade (1926–36), An Gúm published 305 titles with total sales of 250,000 (*Gaelic Prose* 506–10).

8. That the Ardnacrusha project ironically functioned to underscore a separation between a rural Irish periphery and more modernized towns and cities despite the promises of the Cosgrave government is indicated by the fact that, as Michael Rubenstein notes, "the scheme ended up supplying only the larger cities and towns [with electricity] until well after 1945" (125). Commenting on its iconic status, Rubenstein succinctly sums up the importance of the Ardncrusha project to the modernizing initiative of the early Free State: "Certainly now its cultural significance has surpassed its utility, though this was arguably true even at the time [of its construction], when few people—especially the rural agricultural workers to whom the promise of Ardnacrusha's electricity-generating potential was explicitly directed—felt that electricity would make much difference in their lives one way or the other. The dam was born a symbol; became in the 1930s, '40s, and '50s a

center of electrical power production; and receded again . . . into a sleepy monumentality" (130–31).

9. Though Ó Súillebháin's autobiography was not published until after the beginning of the Fianna Fáil era following the 1932 election, it arguably belongs more fully to the transitional period of the early 1930s. Publication of the Gaelic version of the text was delayed considerably due to protracted debate with *An Gúm* over the material to be included, with the result that it was eventually published by the Talbot Press in 1933. The era that Ó Súillebháin recounts and his experience as a recruit to the newly established police force, however, is that of the Free State under the Cumann na nGaedhael government. For an account of the negotiations with *An Gúm* over publication of *Fiche Blian ag Fás*, see Mac Conghaill (151).

10. Though, as noted, Ó Súillebháin's text belongs most fully to the transitional period of the early 1930s, this function of "tradition" remains largely operative under the subsequent Fianna Fáil regime, as the discussion of Sean O'Faoláin in the next chapter explores.

11. For the definitive statement of this understanding of autobiography, see James Olney's *Metaphors of Self*. Indeed, Olney's analysis proves so formidable that it tends to encompass most of Anglo-American autobiography theory, even that which explicitly seeks to repudiate him. For a refreshing exception, see Sidonie Smith's wonderful essay "Performativity, Autobiographical Practice, Resistance." For a more explicit application of autobiography theory to the colonial situation, see Georges Gusdorf's chillingly prescient "Conditions and Limits of Autobiography."

12. Giving some sense of the terms of the arrangement and Ó Criomhthain's perception of them, Tomás's son Seán Ó Criomhthain writes of *An tOileánach* in a letter to George Chambers, "The manuscript was given to the Government for £60 and that was all the money my father got for it" (Ní Shúilleabháin 24).

13. Flower does not even grant much agency to Ó Criomhthain as a recorder. Describing Ó Criomhthain's suitability for the role, Flower asserts that "[f]or the purposes of such a record Tomás was admirably fitted by a *long and unconscious preparation*" (vii, emphasis mine). Flower seems to suggest that Ó Criomhthain's lack of consciousness makes his account all the more authentic and valuable.

14. For an account of this process and Ó Criomhthain's response to the request for a different ending, see Lucchitti (126–30) and O'Leary's *Gaelic Prose* (138–42).

15. This rather limited understanding of "literature" and Flower's insistence on *The Islandman*'s departure from it is reinforced a few pages later in the preface by Flower's observation about Ó Criomhthain's style: "For the narrative runs easily in the ordinary language of the island, with only an occasional literary allusion of a straightforward kind" (ix). The notion of a "straightforward" allusion suggests a real anxiety on Flower's part that everything in the book be confined within the terms of unmediated representation. Though he has previously denied pretensions to any "literary effect" on Ó Criomhthain's part, Flower here acknowledges

literary aspects of the text only to neutralize them by rendering them "straightforward."

16. This account of a Gaelic poetic tradition also coincides with the arguments made by Daniel Corkery in *The Hidden Ireland* (1924) and a range of Irish-Ireland polemicists in the 1930s. Though the Irish-Ireland commentators aggressively seek to position themselves in opposition to a Revivalist position they see as irredeemably tainted by its Anglo-Irish associations, the two positions are remarkably close, as Sean O'Faoláin convincingly argues in *King of the Beggars* and his *Bell* editorials.

17. This view of Ó Siochfhrada would seem to be sustained by O'Leary's account of a December 1909 contribution he wrote for *An Claidheamh Soluis*, the leading newspaper of the Gaelic League: "He faulted efforts to Europeanize Gaelic literature and urged his fellow authors to turn again for inspiration to 'the old stories . . . all stories the Gaels created out of their own spirit when they had no knowledge of or contact with any storytelling but their own'" (*Prose Literature* 103).

18. Declan Kiberd suggests that Ó Criomhthain's restrained language and decision to eschew a more straightforward narrative may be driven by a desire to divide the text into condensed thematic units. Such a model would, of course, be somewhat at odds with a chronicle that records the events of his life and offers his reflections on them. The result instead, Kiberd suggests, is that of "an anthropological textbook" for secondary students who might read a chapter each week in school (526). The reasons for this stance and for Ó Criomhthain's general caution and reticence are quite complex, however, and may ultimately point to an evasiveness that is quite calculated.

19. This is not to say that Marstrander completely removes himself from the wider rhythms of work on the island, however. As Mac Conghaill (136) and Lucchitti (139) note, both Marstrander and Flower worked alongside the islanders on various tasks of farming, fishing, and the construction of roads and piers.

20. Further emphasizing the relationship between the writing of the autobiography and a broader experience of commodification, we might note Ó Criomhthain's correspondence with Ó Ceallaigh, which Lucchitti notes often effectively boils down to, "I have sent you my pages, I was hoping you would send me some tobacco" (75).

21. For a discussion of the self-consciousness of the commodity, see Lukács's *History and Class Consciousness* (168).

22. Myles na gCopaleen's (Flann O'Brien's/Brian Ó Nualláin's) parody captures this wonderfully. His account of Sitric O'Sanassa in his 1941 novel *An Béal Bocht* (translated as *The Poor Mouth* in 1973) is particularly brilliant in this regard: "The gentlemen from Dublin who came in motors to inspect the paupers praised him for his Gaelic poverty and stated that they never saw anyone who appeared so truly Gaelic. One of the gentlemen broke a little bottle of water which Sitric had, because, said he, it spoiled the effect. There was no one in Ireland comparable to O'Sanassa in the excellence of his poverty; the amount of famine which was delineated in his person" (88–89). See also the account of the *feis* in chapter 4 (53–61), where the residents of

Corkadoragha literally dance and talk themselves to death in their attempts
to please the metropolitan *Gaeligorí* whom they hope to make their patrons.

23. See de Man's "Autobiography as De-Facement." De Man essentially
argues that autobiography necessarily fails as representation because it relies
on a linguistic trick of closure/referentiality that can never be fully effected:
"The interest of autobiography, then, is not that it reveals reliable self-knowl-
edge—it does not—but that it demonstrates in a striking way the impossibility of closure and totalization (that is the impossibility of coming into being)
of all textual systems made up of tropological substitutions" (922). Having
made the point about the evident counterfeit of autobiographical representation, de Man continues with his argument to imply that autobiography
should be understood as a mode of power rather than just another example
of linguistic play. He suggests that autobiography functions more as a "figure
of reading" (921) than a mode of writing. As a result, the autobiographical
project may have a coercive effect with the autobiography "itself produc[ing]
and determin[ing] the life" in such a way that the figure of autobiography
"acquires a degree of referential productivity" (920). Thus, the autobiographical portrait is not simply a falsification but a "de-facement," with all
of the violence such a term implies.

24. The description of Thomson and the fraught tone of the passage are
also significant in terms of the level of intimacy they suggest. Indeed, the intensity of Ó Súilleabháin's and Thomson's attachment makes Ó Háinle reluctant
to even comment very extensively on *Fiche Blian ag Fás*: "George Thomson's
influence on Muiris's life and on the production of his autobiography was so
pervasive as to render an analysis of the book too complex a matter to be conducted here" (138). This observation provides an intriguing backdrop as one
considers the descriptions of their encounters in the book. Indeed, many of the
passages dealing with their parting and reunion (231, 235, 238, 239, 240, 241)
would seem to portray the predicament of separated lovers.

25. For Benedict Anderson's application of Benjamin's notion of secular
temporality and his argument about administrative pilgrimages, see, respectively, chapters 2 and 4 of *Imagined Communities*.

26. Indeed, Mac Conghaill notes that Ó Súilleabháin joins the force under a
program specifically aimed at recruiting young men from the *Gaeltacht* (150).

27. This is not to say, of course, that the clothing, houses, or dialect of
the Connemara *gaeltacht* are the same as those of the Blaskets. The point is
not that these are identical in their specifics but rather that Ó Súilleabháin
constructs them as particularly "Gaelic" and as elements of "the old ways"
of "tradition."

2. SEAN O'FAOLÁIN AND THE END OF REPUBLICAN REALISM

1. For key accounts of O'Faoláin's IRA activity and roles played in the
Civil War, see Harmon's biography (50–62); O'Faoláin's autobiography,
Vive Moi! (137–71); and his *Bell* essay "Principles and Propaganda" (200).

2. See O'Faoláin's "One World" editorial in the March 1944 *Bell* (469–72).

3. Indeed, scholars as diametrically opposed in the revisionism debate as Kevin Whelan and R. F. Foster both see the founding of the *Bell* in 1940 as key to laying the early intellectual and cultural foundations for revisionism (see Whelan's "The Revisionist Debate in Ireland" [186–87]; and Foster's *Paddy and Mr. Punch* [111]). As I explore, however, a revisionist reading of the *Bell* stands at odds with the content of many of O'Faoláin's contributions to the magazine and the fact that it is the leftist republican Peadar O'Donnell who actually founds the *Bell* and recruits O'Faoláin to serve as editor.

4. See Arndt's *Critical Study of Sean O'Faolain's Life and Work* (30, 69–73, 90–91, 239); and Foster's *Paddy and Mr. Punch* (111) and *The Irish Story* (41–42). Arndt surprisingly attributes almost no significance to O'Faoláin's involvement with nationalism or leftist politics, whereas Foster more carefully suggests that by at least 1940 O'Faoláin had distanced himself from republican "purists." As O'Faoláin continues to call himself a republican in a number of *Bell* editorials running until almost the end of his editorship in 1946 and, indeed, criticizes de Valera and Fianna Fáil for their inadequate republicanism, however, the nature of republican "purism" would not seem to be as straightforward as Foster suggests.

5. O'Donovan would a few years later be a key architect of the "S-Plan" bombing campaign in England in 1939 and 1940. For an overview of O'Donovan's involvement, see David O'Donoghue's *The Devil's Deal*.

6. O'Faoláin's recollections of the War of Independence and Civil War and the stark realities of the era's violence can be traced in his first story collection, *Midsummer Night's Madness*, and his subsequent autobiography, *Vive Moi!* (139–71). For an account of the disillusionment he felt over his sense of a lack of a political program, see his *Bell* essay "Principles and Propaganda."

7. In "Narrate or Describe?," Lukács distinguishes as "narration" the work of Scott, Balzac, and Tolstoy, where "we experience events which are inherently significant because of the direct involvement of the characters in the events and because of the general social significance emerging in the unfolding of the characters' lives" (116). By contrast, in the descriptive method of Flaubert and Zola, "the characters are merely spectators, more or less interested in the events. As a result, the events themselves become only a tableau for the reader, or, at best, a series of tableaux" (116). Presenting the implications of the two narrative modes, he writes, "The decisive ideological weakness of the writers of the descriptive method is in their passive capitulation to . . . these phenomena of fully-developed capitalism, and in their seeing the result but not the struggles of the opposing forces" (146).

8. His description of French naturalism in a later essay helps clarify O'Faoláin's sense of the naturalist method and its roots in a late nineteenth-century materialism: "The so-called Naturalistic novel and its ironical, skeptical, materialist, rationalist influence dominated world-fiction up to the opening of the present War [World War II]. . . . Gradually these descriptions became an end in themselves. It became wholly admirable if the naked illusion of physical reality was produced with taste and skill" ("Two Kinds" 70).

9. Though published in 1948, Lukács's preface to *Studies in European Realism* refers to essays written some ten years earlier, which suggests that many of the ideas of the book emerge from Lukács's work in the 1930s.

10. Interestingly, O'Faoláin partly revises his view of Joyce a few years later, perhaps in the light of his more extensive experience of being unable to realize the late-modernist vision of his own novels in an entirely satisfactory way. He proposes in a 1941 essay that the "virtue" of *Ulysses* as "the greatest Irish novel" is the way that it signals "something inexpressible by the very naturalistic tools it employs" ("Ah, Wisha" 273). In a 1942 essay, O'Faoláin similarly argues for the greatness of *Ulysses* as "the only masterpiece of Naturalism written by an Irish author" but nonetheless argues that its greatness lies in its defiance of naturalist tendencies and the ways it "is shot through with intellectual fantasy and bitter idealism" ("Two Kinds" 70). Both of these latter accounts, however, frame Joyce in ways that parallel O'Faoláin's own vision of an engaged realist mode that undercuts naturalism's solidity from within.

11. O'Faoláin writes two years later in a *London Mercury* essay titled "The Proletarian Novel" that the communist novel must nevertheless also guard against being reduced to mere descriptive naturalism by failing to contend with the mysterious elements of life (587).

12. O'Faoláin's complex relationship to Catholicism and the ways it unsettles his relationship to the institutions of an emergent Irish postcoloniality are illuminated by Julia O'Faoláin's association of her father with "a brand of Left-Wing Catholicism which was never widespread in Ireland" and her recollection that in this period "he used to take French Left-Catholic magazines such as *L'Esprit*" (22).

13. O'Faoláin's subsequent account of the writing process of *A Nest of Simple Folk* in his autobiography, *Vive Moi!*, reinforces the sense that he saw the novel very much in terms of the classical realism sketched as an alternative to naturalism in his and Lukács's essays: "While I was working at it . . . I felt less disjunction between myself at my table and the countryman passing along the road outside, or the girl in the kitchen humming over her work, or the old tramp we called Forty Coats pausing at the gate to talk to my small daughter Julie playing inside it on the lawn. . . . Yes, that novel made me feel less separated from life than some other things I have written. . . . That novel gave me the greatest pleasure I have had in writing fiction . . . because the jolt between fact and fiction was so slight" (286–87).

14. O'Faoláin's second biography of de Valera, *De Valera*, provides an almost identical account of the landscape of the Deel plain as that which nurtured de Valera's boyhood consciousness on his uncle's farm in rural Limerick (7–9). Though published five years after *A Nest of Simple Folk*, the strikingly similar rendering of the Deel plain in the 1939 de Valera biography reinforces the sense of a connection for O'Faoláin between sentimental nationalism and an anesthetizing lyrical aesthetic.

15. In the hands of Flann O'Brien, this notion of infinite recurrence becomes the basis for comic brilliance and insightful analysis of the strictures of naturalist form in novels such as *An Béal Bocht* and *The Third Policeman*.

16. See, for example, Luke Gibbons's insightful analysis of the hazards of a Celticist discourse "playing into the hands of the colonial régime" (563) in "Challenging the Canon." Though Gibbons reads O'Faoláin's "attack on the Gaelic mystique" (568) in terms of an early revisionist strategy to disrupt the continuity of a nationalist historical narrative, Gibbons's analyses of Celticism coincide in many ways with O'Faoláin's own early objections to "the Gaelic cult" and the disingenuous invocations of tradition by a postcolonial bourgeois elite.

17. In an oft-quoted passage from *Vive Moi!*, O'Faoláin describes his childhood in terms that clearly parallel the Hussey household: "We were shabby-genteels at the lowest possible social level, always living on the edge of false shames and stupid affections, caught between painful strugglings and gallant strivings, never either where we were or where we hoped to be, Janus-faced, throwing glances of desire and admiration upwards and ahead, glances of hatred or contempt downwards and behind" (61). Interestingly, however, O'Faoláin inverts the names of himself and his father, Denis, in the novel. Johnny Hussey is thus the striving policeman and Denis is his son. This may be O'Faoláin's gesture of sympathy or solidarity toward his father and an admission that things could have been different if their generational positions had been reversed.

18. This vision of historical dynamism coincides with Lukács's claim in *History and Class Consciousness* that "the nature of history is precisely that every definition degenerates into an illusion: *history is the history of the unceasing overthrow of the objective forms that shape the life of man*" (186, emphasis in original).

19. O'Faoláin insists even more strongly on the parallels between Corkery's vision of Irish literature and Nazi thought in an April 1937 essay in the *Irish Press*, where he asserts that "Goebbels and Hitler are laying down precisely the same excluding law for Germany that de Blacam and Corkery want to lay down for Ireland" ("Let Ireland Pride" 8).

20. Cleary's argument lends more theoretical precision to the observation Harmon makes about O'Faoláin's lack of success as a novelist: "The fact that O'Faoláin has been very successful as a historical biographer makes his relative lack of success as a novelist easier to explain. The two forms are so similar in the demands that they make upon a writer that there is good ground for believing that his inability to produce more than one really good novel is not altogether due to a personal weakness but rather to some external disadvantages inherent in the society in which he lives" (*Critical Introduction* 28).

21. For an account of *King of the Beggars* as an antinationalist argument, see Whelan (186–87).

22. The self-serving aspect of O'Connell's parliamentary maneuverings and the shortcomings of constitutional nationalism are topics to which O'Faoláin returns repeatedly in *King of the Beggars* (235–43, 257, 267–68, 275, 282).

23. This grounding of a dynamic new anticolonial political consciousness in the very reduction of the colonized to object status parallels Lukács's account of the disruption of reification from within by the proletarian.

According to Lukács's analysis in *History and Class Consciousness*, the consciousness of the proletarian "is the *self-consciousness of the commodity.*" In similar fashion, the colonized "object" reveals and disrupts the logic of colonial power. As Lukács notes, "since consciousness . . . is not the knowledge of an opposed object but is the self-consciousness of the object *the act of consciousness overthrows the objective form of its object*" (168, 178, emphasis in original).

24. Terence Brown ("After" 587) and Frank Shovlin (102) both argue that O'Faoláin's turn to the *Bell* in 1940 stems in significant part from his sense that the narrative possibilities of realist fiction had been exhausted or shown to be impossible in 1930s Ireland. I want to pursue a slightly different but parallel argument that O'Faoláin attempts to develop the *Bell* as an alternative realist form.

25. O'Donnell's founding role with the *Bell* is documented in Maurice Harmon's biography *Sean O'Faolain* (126, 128) and Donal Ó Drisceoil's biography *Peadar O'Donnell* (110, 114–15), as well as the *Irish Times* letters from O'Faoláin and O'Donnell in February and March 1970.

26. For an account of the campaign leading to the demise of *Ireland To-Day*, see Shovlin's chapter on *Ireland To-Day*, esp. 78–83 and 93–95.

27. Harmon describes O'Faoláin's approach as he launches the *Bell* as "tactically . . . subtle, and long-ranged" and intriguingly compares his techniques to those of the sixteenth-century Earl of Tyrone, Hugh O'Neill ("Man of Ideas" 41). O'Neill is, of course, famous for tactical avowals of loyalty that he would repeatedly break as he mounted assaults strategically timed for maximum effectiveness. A keen admirer of O'Neill's, O'Faoláin published his biography of him, *The Great O'Neill*, in 1942.

28. O'Faoláin cleverly builds on this approach in subsequent editorials such as when he rejects calls for more "fight" and "controversy" in the *Bell* by insisting that it will only traffic in "facts" and "Life" and proposing: "[I]s not everything that is alive controversial? Every time life walks into this magazine it must stir up argument" ("Answer" 6). O'Faoláin's critique of "tradition" and his alternative of republican realism are thus naturalized as "Life."

29. The most succinct statement of the standard view of O'Faoláin's relationship to modernization is probably Kevin Whelan's suggestion that the *Bell* "operated within a comforting set of binaries—modernization and tradition, the city and the country, the archive and tradition, text and orality, east and west, secular and religious, fact and myth" (187). An editorial such as "Beginnings and Blind Alleys," however, shows how O'Faoláin actually works against those binaries and, indeed, has more in common with Whelan's own critique of the construction of tradition by "the ossifying orthodoxy of the new state" (183–84).

30. The extent to which these arguments of O'Faoláin's clearly draw from an established left-republican analysis is apparent if one compares them to the assertions of George Gilmore, one of Peadar O'Donnell's most important allies in the 1934 Republican Congress initiative. See, for example, Gilmore's letter entitled "Fianna Fail and the Republic" in the October 1937 issue of *Ireland To-Day*.

31. This vision essentially marks the consolidation of what O'Faoláin describes in a 1942 *Bell* editorial as a "censorship-consciousness . . . that sentimentalise[s] everything into a pretty fable which is no less a lie for being pretty and is far more insidious" ("Fifty Years" 333).

32. See Cleary's *Outrageous Fortune* (144–50) and his "Distress Signals: Sean O'Faoláin and the Fate of Twentieth-Century Irish Literature."

3. UNNAMING THE SUBJECT: SAMUEL BECKETT AND POSTCOLONIAL ABSENCE

1. See, for example, Mercier's *Beckett/Beckett* or his more celebrated *The Irish Comic Tradition*; Deane's *Celtic Revivals*; Kenner's *Samuel Beckett*; Kiberd's *Irish Classics*; and Lloyd's *Anomalous States*. Mercier is a particularly interesting figure in this regard. Though by his own account he publicly emphasizes Beckett's importance to Irish letters as early as 1943 (*Beckett* x), Mercier nonetheless remarks in *Beckett/Beckett* that while Beckett may be "an Irishman," "to call him an Irish writer involves some semantic sleight of hand" (21). This seems especially surprising given that Mercier includes his stress on Beckett's "Irishness and his comic techniques" in 1955 and 1957 reviews as the first example of critical attitudes toward Beckett that he helped popularize (*Beckett* xii). Indeed, Mercier does offer brilliant and innovative analyses of Beckett's relationship to Gaelic tradition in his classic work *The Irish Comic Tradition*, published fifteen years before *Beckett/Beckett*, where he again curiously describes Beckett as being "*in* the Gaelic tradition but not *of* it" (76).

2. A welcome development in this regard has been the recent work produced by Patrick Bixby, Emilie Morin, and Seán Kennedy, which has linked analyses of Beckett's broader philosophical and aesthetic orientations with considerations of his place within specific Irish, postcolonial, and postwar historical contexts. See Bixby's *Samuel Beckett and the Postcolonial Novel*; Morin's *Samuel Beckett and the Problem of Irishness*; and Kennedy's edited volumes *Samuel Beckett: History, Memory, Archive* and *Beckett and Ireland*.

3. Bixby suggests, however, that the underlying experience of dislocation and "being between cultures, between nations" may be one that is quite common to a large number of Irish exiles in the early to mid-twentieth century and is thus potentially as much expressive of Irishness as of a sophisticated cosmopolitan detachment (34).

4. For an account of naturalism along these lines, see Cleary's remarkably illuminating discussion of naturalism in *Outrageous Fortune*, esp. 123.

5. Seán Kennedy argues along similar lines for the importance of grounding Beckett in history as he addresses the need to "explore the extent to which Beckett's relentless deconstruction of 'subjectivity' and 'identity-in-language' might have occurred as an ethical response to history and not some aesthetic negation of it" ("Beckett in History" 2). Highlighting the material stakes of Beckett's work, Kennedy adds, "While there can be no doubt that Beckett's assault on representation was informed by his readings in philosophy, . . . it was also impelled by a realization of the complicity of concepts

like 'Identity' and 'History' in the production of authoritarian master narratives and patterns of domination" ("Beckett in History" 2).

6. "Reason not to" might present itself quite suddenly, however, if one were to travel to England. As J. C. C. Mays notes, Beckett was quite angrily conscious of the condescension he would encounter in England when he would be perceived to "talk like a Paddy" (28).

7. Perhaps most striking in this regard is Beckett's firsthand experience of the border of partition being established in the precincts of his boarding school in Enniskillen. As W. J. McCormack notes, Beckett's attendance at Portora Royal School in a period spanning the 1920 Government of Ireland Act, the 1921 Treaty, and the Irish Civil War would have afforded him an amazingly intimate outlook on the tectonic clashes surrounding the shift from the imperial era to the postcolonial era: "The altering relations between territory and power, between division and authority, the violent ambiguity of Black-and-Tan terrorism, the emergence of a uniformed southern army where previously had been an unknown number of 'mufti' volunteers, border warfare and fratricidal civil conflict—these tangible features of Beckett's late childhood and adolescence are not wholly remote from the intimate dislocations of his writing" (380).

8. Beckett punctuates this idea most famously with his celebrated outburst: "They have buggered us into glory!" (Bair 493). That he should offer this observation in 1965 indicates that his analysis is not simply attributable to any immediate antipathy attending his initial exile or to a reaction against the more extreme actions of the early postcolonial governments in power at the time of the writing of his now well-known (but long unpublished) attack on Free State censorship, "Censorship in the Saorstat," in 1934–35.

9. Beckett offers a more explicit comment on allegory in a review of Jack B. Yeats's novel *The Amaranthers*, also included in *Disjecta*, wherein he refers to allegory as "that glorious double-entry, with every credit in the said account a debit in the meant, and inversely" (90). Praising *The Amaranthers* for not trafficking in allegory, Beckett asserts that Jack Yeats instead offers "a single series of imaginative transactions" (90). Though Beckett does not directly present his argument in "Recent Irish Poetry" in terms of allegory, his points about representation in the essay seem to parallel this critique.

10. Interestingly, he also names Seán O'Faoláin among this group of poets he favors and describes him as someone he is "sure" writes verse (75). This is all the more intriguing given that Beckett clearly has not read any actual poetry written by O'Faoláin and it is generally not a genre in which O'Faoláin was known to work. Two years later, in 1936, the famously sardonic Beckett scathingly refers to O'Faoláin in private correspondence to Thomas McGreevy as "All Forlorn" (Letters 1: 299, 334). Whether Beckett's perspective on O'Faoláin changed in the intervening years or he was liable to make such private jokes at O'Faoláin's expense in 1934, however, it arguably only underscores the significance of the connection he draws in "Recent Irish Poetry" between O'Faoláin and the modernist poets for whom Beckett had such admiration and to whom he had such a close personal connection if despite any potential personal distaste he includes O'Faoláin among the young modernist writers throwing off the dead hand of the Yeatsian Revival.

11. For analysis of Beckett's parodic reworking of Revivalist ethnography, see Patrick Bixby's insightful readings of *Watt* (135–50) and the trilogy (185–97).

12. For an account of this revelation and Beckett's comments on it, see James Knowlson's *Damned to Fame* (318–20).

13. Alysia E. Garrison has recently argued for reading *The Unnamable*'s plunge into aporia as "an *effect* of [the] atrocities" of the Holocaust and, following Dominick LaCapra, an effort to sketch the relationship between the "absences" of transhistorical trauma and the "losses" of historical or individual trauma (93–94, emphasis in original). While obviously differing from a postcolonial reading, Garrison's work on situating Beckett's work in history and reflecting on the subtle differences in his narration of loss and trauma provides a useful complement to postcolonial analyses that seek to complicate the "purely aesthetic" readings of Beckett.

14. Compare this account of "me" to a resurgent account of "I" a few pages later: "I'm in words, made of words, others' words, what others, the place too, the air, the walls, the floor, the ceiling, all words, the world is here with me, I'm the air, the walls, the walled-in one, everything yields, opens, ebbs, flows, like flakes, I'm all these flakes, meeting, mingling, falling asunder, wherever I go I find me, leave me, go towards me, come from me, nothing ever but me, a particle of me, retrieved, lost, gone astray, I'm all these words, all these strangers, this dust of words, with no ground for their settling" (386). "I" is not only caught up in words' realm of representation but finds itself rendered inextricably material as a result. Even as "I" encounters "me" in the flow and the "falling asunder" of the object, "I" remains unable to escape its material prison and can only be a "flake" or a "particle of me"; "I" must content itself with an alienated existence amongst "strangers" in "this dust of words." In many ways, this portrayal of an alienating materiality and all-consuming rise of representation can be seen as offering an early glimpse of the more troubling aspects of postmodern commodification we see coming into full-bloom under the auspices of globalization.

15. This same kind of striation is of course evident in the contradictory articulation of "the Unnamable." To say "the Unnamable" is at once to name and to express the impossibility of naming.

4. POSTMODERN BLAGUARDRY: FRANK MCCOURT, THE CELTIC TIGER, AND THE ASHES OF HISTORY

1. Remarking on the book's reception in Ireland, R. F. Foster observes, "McCourt's success in Ireland says something important about where we now are. *Angela's Ashes* may have aroused some local annoyance, and provoked an exciting exchange on the Late Late Show; but these are comparatively minor tremors. In general, it has been overpraised by the quality press and adored by the popular market; on the promotional tour for *'Tis* [the sequel memoir to *Angela's Ashes*], five hundred copies a day of that lacklustre volume were shifting in Limerick alone [where McCourt is most reviled], along with a hundred paperbacks of its predecessor. And it has meant a tourism bonanza in Limerick: 'a city', according to the *Irish Times*, 'which has

traditionally found it a challenge to attract visitors.' It is now attracting them
by revelling in misery tourism" (*Story* 173). This would seem to suggest that
McCourt was not entirely without admirers in Ireland whether as readers
inclined toward a Celtic Tiger vision of historical detachment or those profit-
ing from the ensuing tourist boom.

2. The recent implosion of the Irish economy lends this portrayal yet
another ironic twist as Limerick has become one of the most tragic sites of
globalization's blasted aftermath. With one of the country's highest unemployment rates and a devastated and largely abandoned urban core caught
between urban renewal schemes mounted under the ambitious "Regenera-
tion" project and now left to molder, the specter of McCourt's Limerick
has returned with a vengeance since 2007. Unlike McCourt's account of the
vitality of 1930s Limerick that persisted amid the difficult conditions and
was sustained by the local practices and culture that had developed over
generations, however, the blighted areas in contemporary Limerick stand
strangely silent and dissevered from history in ways that offer stark testimony to the blank superficiality of Irish postmodernity.

3. Given that Hannan explicitly states his motivation for writing the
book is to respond to McCourt and present the story of "another side to
life in Limerick" (3), one might expect a brighter picture of 1930s and
1940s Limerick. Surprisingly, though, *Ashes* offers an even bleaker portrait
with its accounts of poverty, rape by priests, and IRA genital mutilation.
If anything, Hannan's book would seem to confirm the general accuracy
of *Angela's Ashes* or even suggest that McCourt makes things seem better
than they actually were. The only significant difference would seem to be
Hannan's rejection of the solution of emigration and his insistence on the
importance of staying and enduring all of the difficulties Limerick or Ireland might have to offer.

4. For analysis of the relationship between Irish immigration and citizenship policy and the ideological structures of Celtic Tiger prosperity, see Ronit
Lentin's insightful essay "Illegals in Ireland, Irish Illegals: Diaspora Nation
as Racial State."

5. One intriguing indication of this shift was the installation in 2002 and
2003 of the Millennium Spire sculpture in the middle of Dublin's O'Connell
Street as part of a larger government project of "re-branding" the city center
as more up-market. The enormous stainless-steel "spike" is most notable for
its lack of distinguishing Irish characteristics and commemorative purpose.
Though monumental, it is not a monument to anything or any place in particular; it could literally be set anywhere. Standing in front of and dwarfing
the General Post Office building that has historically functioned as a shrine
to Irish nationalism and the martyrdom of 1916, it seems designed to signal
a movement away from nationalist—or even national—commemoration and
entry into a postmodern cultural amnesia where an ever-recurring present is
the only temporal referent.

6. George O'Brien usefully suggests that this may be attributed, in part,
to the theatrical origins of McCourt's tale as told in fragments through *A
Couple of Blaguards*: "Such authority as it possesses derives less from any

interest the author might have in total recall, much less in ethnographic authenticity, than from the performative dimension of *Angela's Ashes*" (239).

7. McCourt's account of his own baptism with his father challenging the priest to a fight and young Frankie being dropped into the baptismal font amid all of the confusion would seem to be a striking example of this (18). Though McCourt is certainly offering an unflattering account of his father's pugnacity and alcoholism, the baptismal vignette mainly functions as absurd slapstick bringing together the Irish stereotypes of priest, drunkard, henpecked husband, and sanctimonious scold. Reminiscent of the antics of *Tristram Shandy*, the tone of the passage is far too light to convey any deep anger or rebuke.

8. Most notable in this regard is, of course, McCourt's account of his mother's birth (14).

9. In his interview with Carolyn T. Hughes for *Poets & Writers*, for example, McCourt is especially keen to emphasize truth-telling as the only way to write (29).

10. See, for example, Darlene Erickson's "With Skill, Endurance, and Generosity of Heart: Frank McCourt's *Angela's Ashes*"; Edward A. Hagan's "Really an Alley Cat? *Angela's Ashes* and Critical Orthodoxy"; and Fred Miller Robinson's "'The One Way Out': Limerick and *Angela's Ashes*."

11. In addition to the broad stereotypes he invokes, specific elements of McCourt's portrait bear strong resemblance to other Irish autobiographies. The similarities between *Angela's Ashes* and Sean O'Casey's account of life in the Dublin tenements are particularly striking, as Roy Foster and others have suggested. Foster also notes correspondences with Mícheál Mac Liammóir's autobiography and Joyce's *Portrait of the Artist* (*Story* 169–70).

12. Given the strong presence of the adult author hanging over the text and his very explicit objectives, this cannot simply be explained by young Frankie's lack of sophistication.

13. The presentation of America as a salvation that can justify any action offers a disturbing parallel to the ruthless logic of "efficiency" and deregulation in Celtic Tiger Ireland. This is rendered with a particular starkness in Frankie's reflection on his savings and his misgivings about writing threatening letters to his neighbors: "I have a post office savings account and if I keep writing successful threatening letters, helping myself to the odd few shillings from her purse and keeping the stamp money, I'll have my escape money to America. If my whole family dropped from the hunger I wouldn't touch this money in the post office. Often I have to write threatening letters to neighbors and friends of my mother and I worry they might discover me. . . . I'm sorry for their troubles but there's no other way for me to save the money for America. I know someday I'll be a rich Yank and send home hundreds of dollars and my family will never have to worry about threatening letters again" (333–34).

CONCLUSION. DISPATCHES FROM THE MODERNIST FRONTIER: "EUROPEAN AND ASIATIC PAPERS PLEASE COPY"

1. For extended analyses of the commodification of postcoloniality, see Huggan's *The Postcolonial Exotic* (2001); and Brouillette's *Postcolonial Writers in the Global Literary Marketplace* (2007).

Abbott, H. Porter. *Beckett Writing Beckett: The Author in the Autograph.* Ithaca: Cornell University Press, 1996.

Allen, Nicholas. *Modernism, Ireland, and Civil War.* Cambridge: Cambridge UP, 2009.

Anderson, Benedict. *Imagined Communities.* Rev. ed. New York: Verso, 1991.

Arndt, Marie. *A Critical Study of Sean O'Faolain's Life and Work.* Lewiston, N.Y.: Edwin Mellen Press, 2001.

Attridge, Derek, and Marjorie Howes, eds. *Semicolonial Joyce.* Cambridge: Cambridge UP, 2000.

Bair, Deirdre. *Samuel Beckett: A Biography.* New York: Harcourt Brace Jovanovich, 1978.

Barkan, Elazar, and Ronald Bush, eds. *Prehistories of the Future: The Primitivist Project and the Culture of Modernism.* Stanford: Stanford UP, 1995.

Battersby, Eileen. "The Great Anger." *Irish Times* 31 October 1996: 15.

Beckett, Samuel. *Disjecta: Miscellaneous Writings and a Dramatic Fragment.* Ed. Ruby Cohn. New York: Grove Press, 1984.

———. *The Letters of Samuel Beckett.* Ed. Martha Dow Fehsenfeld and Lois More Overbeck. Cambridge: Cambridge UP, 2009.

———. *Proust.* New York: Grove Press, 1970.

———. *Three Novels.* New York: Grove Press, 1965.

Benjamin, Walter. *Illuminations: Essays and Reflections.* Ed. Hannah Arendt. Trans. Harry Zohn. New York: Schocken, 1969.

Bixby, Patrick. *Samuel Beckett and the Postcolonial Novel.* Cambridge: Cambridge UP, 2009.

Brown, Terence. "After the Revival: The Problem of Adequacy and Genre." *Genre* 12.4 (Winter 1979): 565–89.

———. "The Counter Revival: Provincialism and Censorship, 1930–65."

Field Day Anthology of Irish Writing. Vol. 3. Ed. Seamus Deane. Derry:
    Field Day, 1991. 89–93.

———. *Ireland: A Social and Cultural History, 1922–2002.* London: Harper
    Perennial, 2004.

———. "Ireland, Modernism, and the 1930s." *Modernism and Ireland: The
    Poetry of the 1930s.* Ed. Patricia Coughlan and Alex Davis. Cork: Cork
    UP, 1995. 24–42.

Brouillette, Sarah. *Postcolonial Writers in the Global Literary Marketplace.*
    New York: Palgrave, 2007.

Castle, Gregory. *Modernism and the Celtic Revival.* Cambridge: Cambridge
    UP, 2001.

Cheng, Vincent. *Joyce, Race, and Empire.* Cambridge: Cambridge UP, 1995.

Cleary, Joe. "Distress Signals: Sean O'Faoláin and the Fate of Twentieth-
    Century Irish Literature." *Field Day Review* 5 (2009): 49–73.

———. *Outrageous Fortune: Capital and Culture in Modern Ireland.* Dub-
    lin: Field Day, 2007.

Coughlan, Patricia, and Alex Davis, eds. *Modernism and Ireland: The
    Poetry of the 1930s.* Cork: Cork UP, 1995.

Crawford, Robert. *Devolving English Literature.* Edinburgh: Edinburgh UP,
    2000.

Deane, Seamus. *Celtic Revivals: Essays in Modern Irish Literature, 1880–
    1980.* London: Faber and Faber, 1985.

De Man, Paul. "Autobiography as De-Facement." *MLN* 94.5 (1979):
    919–30.

Doyle, Laura, and Laura Winkiel. "The Global Horizons of Modernism."
    Geomodernisms: Race, Modernism, Modernity. Ed. Doyle and Winkiel.
    Bloomington: Indiana UP, 2005. 1–14.

Eagleton, Terry. *Exiles and Émigrés: Studies in Modern Literature.* London:
    Chatto and Windus, 1970.

Ellmann, Richard. *Eminent Domain: Yeats among Wilde, Joyce, Pound,
    Eliot and Auden.* New York: Oxford UP, 1967.

Erickson, Darlene. "With Skill, Endurance, and Generosity of Heart: Frank
    McCourt's *Angela's Ashes.*" *Ireland: Towards New Identities.* Ed. Karl-
    Heinz Westarp and Michael Boss. Aarhus, Denmark: Aarhus University
    Press, 1998. 68–79.

Esty, Jed. *A Shrinking Island: Modernism and National Culture in England.*
    Princeton: Princeton UP, 2004.

Fanon, Frantz. *The Wretched of the Earth.* Trans. Constance Farrington.
    New York: Grove Weidenfeld, 1963.

Forster, E. M. "Introductory Note." *Twenty Years A-Growing.* By Muiris

Ó Súilleabháin. Trans. Moya Llewelyn Davies and George Thomson. Oxford: Oxford UP, 1953.

Foster, R. F. *The Irish Story: Telling Lies and Making It Up in Ireland.* London: Penguin, 2001.

———. *Modern Ireland: 1600–1972.* London: Penguin, 1989.

———. *Paddy and Mr. Punch: Connections in Irish and English History.* London: Allen Lane, 1991.

Garrison, Alysia. "'Faintly Struggling Things': Trauma, Testimony, and Inscrutable Life in Beckett's *The Unnamable.*" *Samuel Beckett: History, Memory, Archive.* Ed. Seán Kennedy and Katherine Weiss. London: Palgrave, 2009. 89–109.

Gibbons, Luke. "Challenging the Canon: Revisionism and Cultural Criticism." *Field Day Anthology of Irish Writing.* Vol. 3. Ed. Seamus Deane. Derry: Field Day, 1991. 561–68.

Gikandi, Simon. *Writing in Limbo: Modernism and Caribbean Literature.* Ithaca: Cornell UP, 1992.

Gilmore, George. "Fianna Fáil and the Republic." *Ireland To-Day* 2.4 (October 1937): 74–75.

Gusdorf, Georges. "Conditions and Limits of Autobiography." Trans. James Olney. *Autobiography: Essays Theoretical and Critical.* Ed. James Olney. Princeton: Princeton UP, 1980. 28–48.

Hagan, Edward A. "Really an Alley Cat? *Angela's Ashes* and Critical Orthodoxy." *New Hibernia Review* 4.4 (2000): 39–52.

Hannan, Gerard. *Ashes.* Limerick: Treaty Stone, 1997.

———. *'Tis in Me Ass.* Limerick: Treaty Stone, 1999.

Harmon, Maurice. "Man of Ideas." *Sean O'Faolain: A Centenary Celebration.* Ed. Marie Arndt, Donatella Abbate Badin, Melisa Cataldi, and Valerio Fissure. Turin: Trauben, 2001. 35–46.

———. *Sean O'Faolain.* London: Constable, 1994.

———. *Sean O'Faolain: A Critical Introduction.* Dublin: Wolfhound Press, 1984.

Harrington, John P. *The Irish Beckett.* Syracuse: Syracuse University Press, 1991.

Hedrick, Tace. *Mestizo Modernism: Race, Nation and Identity in Latin American Culture, 1900–1940.* Piscataway, N.J.: Rutgers University Press, 2003.

Hesla, David H. *The Shape of Chaos: An Interpretation of the Art of Samuel Beckett.* Minneapolis: University of Minnesota Press, 1971.

Howes, Marjorie. *Colonial Crossings: Figures in Irish Literary History.* Dublin: Field Day, 2006.

Huggan, Graham. *The Postcolonial Exotic: Marketing the Margins.* London: Routledge, 2001.

Hughes, Carolyn T. "Looking Forward to the Past: A Profile of Frank McCourt." *Poets & Writers* 27.5 (1999): 22–29.

Jameson, Fredric. *Marxism and Form.* Princeton: Princeton UP, 1971.

———. *Postmodernism, or The Cultural Logic of Late Capitalism.* Durham: Duke UP, 1991.

Joyce, James. *Dubliners: Text and Criticism.* Ed. Robert Scholes and A. Walton Litz. New York: Penguin, 1996.

———. *A Portrait of the Artist As a Young Man: Text, Criticism and Notes.* Ed. Chester G. Anderson. New York: Penguin, 1977.

———. *Stephen Hero.* New York: New Directions, 1963.

Katz, Daniel. *Saying I No More: Subjectivity and Consciousness in the Prose of Samuel Beckett.* Evanston: Northwestern UP, 1999.

Kennedy, Seán. "Beckett in History, Memory, Archive." *Samuel Beckett: History, Memory, Archive.* Ed. Kennedy and Katherine Weiss. London: Palgrave, 2009. 1–10.

———. "Ireland/Europe . . . Beckett/Beckett." *Beckett and Ireland.* Ed. Kennedy. Cambridge: Cambridge UP, 2010. 1–15.

Kenner, Hugh. *Dublin's Joyce.* Boston: Beacon Press, 1962.

———. *A Homemade World: The American Modernist Writers.* New York: Knopf, 1974.

———. *Samuel Beckett: A Critical Study.* Berkeley: University of California Press, 1968.

Kiberd, Declan. *Irish Classics.* London: Granta, 2000.

Knowlson, James. *Damned to Fame: The Life of Samuel Beckett.* London: Bloomsbury, 1996.

Lentin, Ronit. "Illegals in Ireland, Irish Illegals: Diaspora Nation as Racial State." *Irish Political Studies* 22.4 (2007): 433–53.

Lloyd, David. *Anomalous States: Irish Writing and the Post-Colonial Moment.* Durham: Duke UP, 1993.

———. *Irish Times: Temporalities of Modernity.* Dublin: Field Day Press, 2008.

———. *Nationalism and Minor Literature: James Clarence Mangan and the Emergence of Irish Cultural Nationalism.* Berkeley: University of California Press, 1987.

———. "Republics of Difference: Yeats, MacGreevy, Beckett." *Field Day Review* 1 (2005): 43–69.

Longley, Edna. *Poetry in the Wars.* Newark: University of Delaware Press, 1987.

Lucchitti, Irene. *The Islandman: The Hidden Life of Tomás O'Crohan.* Bern: Peter Lang, 2009.

Lukács, Georg. *History and Class Consciousness.* Trans. Rodney Livingstone. Cambridge: MIT Press, 1971.

———. "Narrate or Describe?" *Writer and Critic and Other Essays.* Ed. and trans. Arthur Kahn. London: Merlin Press, 1970. 110–48.

———. Preface. *Studies in European Realism.* London: Merlin Press, 1972.1–19.

———. "Realism in the Balance." *Aesthetics and Politics.* Trans. Rodney Livingstone. London: Verso, 1980. 28–59.

———. *The Theory of the Novel.* Trans. Anna Bostock. Cambridge: MIT Press, 1971.

———. "The Zola Centenary." *Studies in European Realism.* London: Merlin Press, 1972. 85–96.

Mac Conghail, Muiris. *The Blaskets: People and Literature.* Dublin: Country House Press, 1994.

Majumdar, Saikat. "'A Pebblehard Soap': Objecthood, Banality, and Refusal in Ulysses." *James Joyce Quarterly* 42/43.1/4 (2006): 219–38.

Manganaro, Marc. *Culture, 1922: The Emergence of a Concept.* Princeton: Princeton UP, 2002.

———. "Textual Play, Power, and Cultural Critique: An Orientation to Modernist Anthropology." *Modernist Anthropology: From Fieldwork to Text.* Ed. Manganaro. Princeton: Princeton UP, 1990. 3–47.

Mao, Douglas, and Rebecca L. Walkowitz. "Modernisms Bad and New." *Bad Modernisms.* Ed. Mao and Walkowitz. Durham: Duke UP, 2006.

———. "The New Modernist Studies." *PMLA* 123.3 (2008): 737–48.

Mattar, Sinéad Garrigan. *Primitivism, Science, and the Irish Revival.* New York: Oxford UP, 2004.

Mays, J. C. C. "Young Beckett's Irish Roots." *Irish University Review* 14.1 (1984): 18–33.

McCarthy, Conor. *Modernisation, Crisis and Culture in Ireland.* Dublin: Four Courts, 2000.

McCartney, Donal. "Seán O'Faoláin: A Nationalist Right Enough." *Irish University Review* 6.1 (1976): 73–86.

McCormack, W.J. *From Burke to Beckett: Ascendancy, Tradition, and Betrayal in Irish Literary History.* Cork: Cork UP, 1994.

McCourt, Frank. *Angela's Ashes: A Memoir.* New York: Scribner, 1996.

McNaughton, James. "The Politics of Aftermath: Beckett, Modernism, and the Irish Free State." *Beckett and Ireland.* Ed. Seán Kennedy. Cambridge: Cambridge UP, 2010: 56–77.

Mercier, Vivian. *Beckett/Beckett*. New York: Oxford UP, 1977.

———. "The Fourth Estate—VI: Verdict on 'The Bell.'" *Bell* 10.2 (1945): 154–64.

———. *The Irish Comic Tradition*. London: Oxford UP, 1962.

Meyer, Mike. "Ashes to Ashes: Limerick Burns over 'Angela.'" *Chicago Tribune* 30 January 2000, sec. 8: 1+.

Miller, Tyrus. *Late Modernism: Politics, Fiction and the Arts between the World Wars*. Berkeley: University of California Press, 1999.

Morin, Emilie. *Samuel Beckett and the Problem of Irishness*. Houndmills, Basingstoke: Palgrave, 2009.

Morrisson, Mark S. *The Public Face of Modernism: Little Magazines, Audiences, and Reception, 1905–1920*. Madison: University of Wisconsin Press, 2001.

Na gCopaleen, Myles. *The Poor Mouth (An Béal Bocht)*. Trans. Patrick C. Power. London: Hart-Davis, MacGibbon, 1973.

Ní Shúilleabháin, Eibhlís. *Letters from the Great Blasket*. Cork: Mercier Press, 1978.

Nolan, Emer. *James Joyce and Nationalism*. London: Routledge, 1995.

O'Brien, George. "The Last Word: Reflections on *Angela's Ashes*." *New Perspectives on the Irish Diaspora*. Ed. Charles Fanning. Carbondale: Southern Illinois UP, 2001. 236–49.

Ó Criomhthain, Tomás. *The Islandman*. Trans. Robin Flower. Oxford: Oxford UP, 1951.

O'Donnell, Peadar. Letter to the editor. *Irish Times* 4 March 1970: 11.

O'Donoghue, David. *The Devil's Deal: The IRA, Nazi Germany and the Double Life of Jim O'Donovan*. Dublin: New Island, 2010.

Ó Drisceoil, Donal. *Peadar O'Donnell*. Cork: Cork UP, 2001.

O'Faoláin, Julia. "The Irishman Who Stayed." *Sean O'Faolain: A Centenary Celebration*. Ed. Marie Arndt, Donatella Abbate Badin, Melisa Cataldi, and Valerio Fissure. Turin: Trauben, 2001. 21–34.

O'Faoláin, Seán. "Ah, Wisha! The Irish Novel." *Virginia Quarterly Review* 17 (1941): 265–74.

———. "Answer to a Criticism." *Bell* 1.3 (December 1940): 5–6.

———. "Attitudes." *Bell* 2.6 (September 1941): 5–12.

———. "Beginnings and Blind Alleys." *Bell* 3.1 (October 1941): 1–5.

———. *Bird Alone*. London: Jonathan Cape, 1936.

———. *Come Back to Erin*. London: Jonathan Cape, 1940.

———. "Commentary on the Foregoing." *Ireland To-Day* 1.5 (October 1936): 32.

———. *Constance Markievicz*. London: Jonathan Cape, 1934.

———. "Daniel Corkery." *Dublin Magazine* April–June 1936: 49–61.

———. *De Valera*. Harmondsworth, U.K.: Penguin, 1939.

———. "The Death of Nationalism." *Bell* 17.2 (May 1951): 44–53.

———. "The Dilemma of Irish Letters." *Month* 2.6 (December 1949): 366–79.

———. "Eamon De Valera." *Bell* 10.1 (April 1945): 1–18.

———. "The Emancipation of Irish Writers." *Yale Review* 23 (1934): 485–503.

———. "Fifty Years of Irish Literature." *Bell* 3.5 (February 1942): 327–34.

———. "Ireland and the Modern World." *Bell* 5.6 (March 1943): 423–28.

———. "It No Longer Matters, or The Death of the English Novel." *Criterion* 15.58 (1935): 49–56.

———. *King of the Beggars: A Life of Daniel O'Connell, the Irish Liberator, in a Study of the Rise of the Modern Irish Democracy (1775–1847)*. New York: Viking, 1938.

———. "Let Ireland Pride—In What She Has." *Irish Press* 2 April 1937: 8.

———. Letter to the Editor. *Commonweal* 6 January 1932: 273.

———. Letter to the Editor. *Irish Times* 25 February 1970: 11.

———. "Literary Provincialism." *Commonweal* 21 December 1932: 214–15.

———. *Midsummer Night's Madness and Other Stories*. London: Jonathan Cape, 1932.

———. "The Modern Novel: A Catholic Point of View." *Virginia Quarterly Review* 11 (1935): 339–51.

———. *A Nest of Simple Folk*. New York: Viking, 1934.

———. "The New Irish Revolutionaries." *Commonweal* 11 November 1931: 39–41.

———. "On State Control." *Bell* 6.1 (April 1943): 1–6.

———. "One World." *Bell* 7.6 (March 1944): 465–74.

———. "One World." *Bell* 9.1 (October 1944): 1–10.

———. "Our Nasty Novelists." *Bell* 2.5 (August 1941): 5–12.

———. "The Plain People of Ireland." *Bell* 7.1 (1943): 1–7.

———. "Plea for a New Type of Novel." *Virginia Quarterly Review* 10.2 (April 1934): 189–99.

———. "Principles and Propaganda." *Bell* 10.3 (June 1945): 189–205.

———. "The Proletarian Novel," *London Mercury* April 1937: 583–89.

———. *A Purse of Coppers: Short Stories*. London: Jonathan Cape, 1937.

———. "Review of Liam O'Flaherty's *Famine*." *Ireland To-Day* February 1937: 81–82.

———. "Romance and Realism." *Bell* 10.5 (August 1945): 373–82.

———."The Senate and Censorship." *Bell* 5.4 (January 1943): 247–52.

———. "Signing Off." *Bell* 12.1 (April 1946): 1–4.

———. "Silent Ireland." *Bell* 6.6 (September 1943): 457–66.

———. "The State and Its Writers." *Bell* 7 (1943): 93–99.

———. "The Stuffed Shirts." *Bell* 6.3 (June 1943): 181–92.

———. "That Typical Irishman." *Bell* 5 (1942): 77–82.

———. "This Is Your Magazine." *Bell* 1.1 (October 1940): 5–9.

———. "Two Kinds of Novel." *Bell* 4.1 (April 1942): 64–70.

———. *Vive Moi! An Autobiography*. London: Rupert Hart-Davis, 1965.

———. "Yeats and the Younger Generation." *Horizon* 5.25 (1942): 43–54.

Ó Giolláin, Diarmuid. *Locating Irish Folklore: Tradition, Modernity, Identity*. Cork: Cork UP, 2000.

Ó Háinle, Cathal G. "Deformation of History in Blasket Autobiographies." *Biography and Autobiography*. Ed. James Noonan. Ottawa: Carleton UP, 1993.

O'Leary, Philip. *Gaelic Prose in the Irish Free State, 1922–1939*. University Park: Pennsylvania State UP, 2004.

———. *The Prose Literature of the Gaelic Revival, 1880–1921: Ideology and Innovation*. University Park: Pennsylvania State UP, 1994.

Olney, James. *Metaphors of Self: The Meaning of Autobiography*. Princeton: Princeton UP, 1972.

Ó Súilleabháin, Muiris. *Twenty Years A-Growing*. Trans. Moya Llewelyn Davies and George Thomson. Oxford: Oxford UP, 1953.

Pollard, Charles. *New World Modernisms: T. S. Eliot, Derek Walcott, and Kamau Brathwaite*. Charlottesville: University of Virginia Press, 2004.

Ramazani, Jahan. "Modernist Bricolage, Postcolonial Hybridity." *Modernism/modernity* 13.3 (2006): 445–63.

Robinson, Fred Miller. "'The One Way Out': Limerick and *Angela's Ashes*." *New Hibernia Review* 4.2 (2000): 9–25.

Rubenstein, Michael. *Public Works: Infrastructure, Irish Modernism and the Postcolonial*. Notre Dame: University of Notre Dame Press, 2010.

Said, Edward. "Representing the Colonized: Anthropology's Interlocutors." *Critical Inquiry* 15.2 (1989): 205–25.

Sayers, Peig. *Peig: The Autobiography of Peig Sayers of the Great Blasket Island*. Trans. Bryan MacMahon. Syracuse: Syracuse UP, 1974.

Schor, Naomi. *Reading in Detail: Aesthetics and the Feminine*. New York: Methuen, 1987.

Shovlin, Frank. *The Irish Literary Periodical, 1923–1958.* Oxford: Oxford UP, 2003.

Smith, Sidonie. "Performativity, Autobiographical Practice, Resistance." *Women, Autobiography, Theory.* Ed. Smith and Julia Watson. Madison: University of Wisconsin Press, 1998. 108–15.

Spivak, Gayatri Chakravorty. "Can the Subaltern Speak?" *Marxism and the Interpretation of Culture.* Ed. Lawrence Grossberg and Cary Nelson. Chicago: University of Illinois Press, 1988. 271–313.

Stanford Friedman, Susan. "Periodizing Modernism: Postcolonial Modernities and the Space/Time Borders of Modernist Studies." *Modernism/ modernity* 12.3 (2006): 425–43.

Stewart, James. "*An tOileánach*—More or Less." *Zeitschrift für Celtische Philologie* 35 (1976): 234–63.

Synge, John Millington. *The Collected Letters of John Millington Synge.* Ed. Ann Saddlemyer. London: Oxford UP, 1983.

Thomas, Dylan. *A Film Script of Twenty Years A-Growing.* London: J. M. Dent and Sons, 1964.

Torgovnik, Marianna. *Gone Primitive: Savage Intellects, Modern Lives.* Chicago: University of Chicago Press, 1990.

Walkowitz, Rebecca. *Cosmopolitan Style: Modernism Beyond the Nation.* New York: Columbia UP, 2006.

Whelan, Kevin. "The Revisionist Debate in Ireland." *boundary 2* 31.1 (2004): 179–205.

Wills, Clair. *That Neutral Island: A Cultural History of Ireland during the Second World War.* New York: Faber and Faber, 2007.

INDEX

Abbott, H. Porter, 139
alienation: in Beckett's works, 138, 142,
    145, 148–49, 151, 153, 155–59,
    164; and modernism, 27, 32, 34–35,
    56; and postcolonial subjectivity,
    27, 33–34, 56, 60–61, 153, 156; and
    tradition, 32, 35, 56, 60–61, 159
Allen, Nicholas, 73, 75, 112, 214n11
The Amaranthers (Jack B. Yeats), 224n9
Anderson, Benedict, 218n25
Angela's Ashes (McCourt): as American
    text, 174, 204–5; comedy in,
    176–78, 182, 185–87, 200–1,
    227n7; death in, 183, 187–88,
    194–96; economy of abjection in,
    194–97; family dysfunction in, 179,
    182–92, 227n7; Irishness of, 23,
    174–76, 197–98, 204–6; market
    formation in, 23, 196–200, 201–3;
    narration in, 179–81, 182–84,
    185–86, 201–3; and naturalism, 23,
    173, 176, 180, 181–89, 190–94,
    196, 204; origins in *A Couple
    of Blaguards* pub drama, 174,
    226–27n6; and pastiche, 177–80,
    182–83, 188, 191, 193, 198–99;
    portrayal of Limerick contrasted
    with post-Celtic-Tiger collapse,
    226n2; and postmodernism, 15,
    23, 171, 173–77, 179–81, 183,
    186–88, 191, 194, 196, 202–6;
    reception of, 170–71, 173, 176–77,
    225n1, 226n3, 227n10, 227n11;
    relationship to Celtic Tiger era,
    15, 17, 22–23, 170–72, 174, 180,
    191, 194, 197–98, 204–6, 225–
    26n1, 227n13; relationship to Irish
    literary tradition, 17, 22–23, 173,
    176, 178–79, 227n7, 227n11;
    sentimentalism in, 183–84, 187–88,
    191–93

Anglo-Irish Big House, 89, 92–93, 96,
    112, 164
anthropological modernism: and
    Beckett, 127, 132, 135–38, 167; and
    the Gaeltacht, 2–3, 27, 33, 138; and
    Joyce, 2, 4, 14, 120, 179, 208–10;
    and late modernism, 1, 4, 6, 7–8,
    13, 33, 137–38, 142, 173, 179; and
    the Revival, 1–2, 4, 8, 33, 127, 132,
    135–36, 138, 167; W.B. Yeats, 2, 4.
    See also Castle, Gregory; Esty, Jed;
    Manganaro, Marc
antimimeticism, 3–6, 8, 19, 21, 23,
    77–78, 98, 124, 131, 133, 138,
    140, 143, 173, 177. *See also* late
    modernism
antiquarianism, 131–38, 153, 224n9
Aran Islands, 2, 33–34, 213n1, 213n2
Ardnacrusha, Shannon hydroelectric
    scheme at, 31, 215–16n8
Arndt, Marie, 219n4
Ashes (Hannan), 173, 226n3
autobiography: and commodification,
    18–19, 44–47, 49, 217n20; and
    cosmopolitanism, 22, 33; as
    de-facement (de Man), 48, 218n23;
    false closure of autobiographical
    portrait, 49–50, 174, 179, 181,
    218n23; and folk culture, 40–42;
    formation of the postcolonial
    subject, 18–19, 31–32, 36–37,
    42–43, 49–51, 53, 54–55, 58, 148;
    and modernism, 19, 27, 33, 37,
    46–47, 52; and official nationalism
    of the Irish Free State, 22, 25,
    31–32, 36–37, 41, 45–46, 53,
    216n9; reifying demands of, 18,
    42–50, 58; speaking subject in,
    36–37, 48–51; tension between
    representation and self-abnegation,
    38–39, 42–43, 47–51, 58; theory